RICHARD G. HINCKLEY • JANA PETERSON STAPLES • VIVIAN MCCONKIE ADAMS
ARCUS H. MARTINS • NEYLAN MCBAINE • ROBERT L. MCKAY • MIKE WINDER
D • JASON CHAFFETZ • MATTHEW GODFREY • ER • DOU
N ROSEMARIE SLOVER MAZZEO • BOB EVANS • KRISTIN
NE PROCTOR • TIFFANY GEE LEWIS • GLENN NE • BRYA
J. W. "BILL" MARRIOTT JR. • ROBERT P. DOTSON • MARK ALLRED • MATTHEW DEA
Y BARKDULL • RICHARD EYRE • SHARLENE W. HAWKES • LAUREN JOHNSON • ST
ARSHA WARD • KATHI ORAM PETERSON • TRISTI PINKSTON • JANETTE RALLISON
D • GRANT HARDY • PATRICK MADDEN • KERRY MUHLESTEIN • GENE A. SESSION
GERILYN BECK MERRILL, • SILVIA H. ALLRED • ROSEMARY M. WIXOM • RICHARD
AN BUSHMAN • SUSAN EASTON BLACK • CAMILLE FRONK OLSON • MARCUS
ERT • MIKE LEE • CHAD B. MCKAY • RONALD C. PACKARD • HARRY REID • JASC
DRA STALLINGS JENKINS • NATALIE CLEMENS • MARK EUBANK • MAREN ROSEM
ERICKSON • JORDAN MARIE GREEN • WENDY HALE MCKAY • MAURINE PROCTO
FREDETTE • PETER VIDMAR • KYLE WHITTINGHAM • STEVE YOUNG • J. W. "BIL
OSH ROMNEY • CLAYTON M. CHRISTENSEN • STEEVUN LEMON • LARRY BARKDU
Y • JULIE BELLON • GREG OLSEN • JEFF SAVAGE • RICK WALTON • MARSHA WAF
• JOHN BENNION • CAROL ANNE CLAYSON • H. WALLACE GODDARD • GRAI
THAYER • HEATHER A. WILLOUGHBY • TWILA WOOD • JULIE B. BECK • GERILY
JANA PETERSON STAPLES • VIVIAN MCCONKIE ADAMS • RICHARD LYMAN BUS
EYLAN MCBAINE • ROBERT L. MCKAY • MIKE WINDER • GARY R. HERBERT • MI
ATTHEW GODFREY • MARK R. VAN WAGONER • DOUG WRIGHT • SANDRA STAL
AZZEO • BOB EVANS • SHAWNI EYRE POTHIER • KRISTINE WARDLE FREDERICKSO
EE LEWIS • GLENN RAWSON • TRENT TOONE • BRYAN MILLER • JIMMER FREDET
• ROBERT P. DOTSON • MARK ALLRED • MATTHEW DEAN BARKDULL • JOSH ROA
EYRE • SHARLENE W. HAWKES • LAUREN JOHNSON • STEVEN KAPP PERRY • JUL
RAM PETERSON • TRISTI PINKSTON • JANETTE RALLISON • PHILIP N. HALE • JOH
TRICK MADDEN • KERRY MUHLESTEIN • GENE A. SESSIONS • DOUGLAS THAYER
• SILVIA H. ALLRED • ROSEMARY M. WIXOM • RICHARD G. HINCKLEY • JANA P
AN EASTON BLACK • CAMILLE FRONK OLSON • MARCUS H. MARTINS • NEYLA
D B. MCKAY • RONALD C. PACKARD • HARRY REID • JASON CHAFFETZ • MATTHE
NS • NATALIE CLEMENS • MARK EUBANK • MAREN ROSEMARIE SLOVER MAZZEO
MARIE GREEN • WENDY HALE MCKAY • MAURINE PROCTOR • TIFFANY GEE LEW
MAR • KYLE WHITTINGHAM • STEVE YOUNG • J. W. "BILL" MARRIOTT JR. • ROBE
TON M. CHRISTENSEN • STEEVUN LEMON • LARRY BARKDULL • RICHARD EYRE
• GREG OLSEN • JEFF SAVAGE • RICK WALTON • MARSHA WARD • KATHI ORA
N • CAROL ANNE CLAYSON • H. WALLACE GODDARD • GRANT HARDY • PATRIC
A. WILLOUGHBY • TWILA WOOD • JULIE B. BECK • GERILYN BECK MERRILL, • SILV
LES • VIVIAN MCCONKIE ADAMS • RICHARD LYMAN BUSHMAN • SUSAN EASTO
RT L. MCKAY • MIKE WINDER • GARY R. HERBERT • MIKE LEE • CHAD B. MCKAY
RK R. VAN WAGONER • DOUG WRIGHT • SANDRA STALLINGS JENKINS • NATAL
AWNI EYRE POTHIER • KRISTINE WARDLE FREDERICKSON • JORDAN MARIE GRE
N • TRENT TOONE • BRYAN MILLER • JIMMER FREDETTE • PETER VIDMAR • MAF
ARK ALLRED • MATTHEW DEAN BARKDULL • JOSH ROMNEY • CLAYTON M. CH

LIE B. BECK • GERILYN BECK MERRILL,• SILVIA H. ALLRED • ROSEMARY M. WIXO
CHARD LYMAN BUSHMAN • SUSAN EASTON BLACK • CAMILLE FRONK OLSON
ARY R. HERBERT • MIKE LEE • CHAD B. MCKAY • RONALD C. PACKARD • HARRY
RIGHT • SANDRA STALLINGS JENKINS • NATALIE CLEMENS • MARK EUBANK • M
ARDLE FREDERICKSON • JORDAN MARIE GREEN • WENDY HALE MCKAY • MA
ILLER • JIMMER FREDETTE • PETER VIDMAR • KYLE WHITTINGHAM • STEVE YOUN
ARKDULL • JOSH ROMNEY • CLAYTON M. CHRISTENSEN • STEEVUN LEMON • L
EN KAPP PERRY • JULIE BELLON • GREG OLSEN • JEFF SAVAGE • RICK WALTON
HILIP N. HALE • JOHN BENNION • CAROL ANNE CLAYSON • H. WALLACE GODD
DOUGLAS THAYER • HEATHER A. WILLOUGHBY • TWILA WOOD • JULIE B. BEC
NCKLEY • JANA PETERSON STAPLES • VIVIAN MCCONKIE ADAMS • RICHARD
ARTINS • NEYLAN MCBAINE • ROBERT L. MCKAY • MIKE WINDER • GARY R. HE
HAFFETZ • MATTHEW GODFREY • MARK R. VAN WAGONER • DOUG WRIGHT • S
E SLOVER MAZZEO • BOB EVANS • SHAWNI EYRE POTHIER • KRISTINE WARDLE F
TIFFANY GEE LEWIS • GLENN RAWSON • TRENT TOONE • BRYAN MILLER • JIM
ARRIOTT JR. • ROBERT P. DOTSON • MARK ALLRED • MATTHEW DEAN BARKDULL
RICHARD EYRE • SHARLENE W. HAWKES • LAUREN JOHNSON • STEVEN KAPP P
KATHI ORAM PETERSON • TRISTI PINKSTON • JANETTE RALLISON • PHILIP N. H
ARDY • PATRICK MADDEN • KERRY MUHLESTEIN • GENE A. SESSIONS • DOUG
CK MERRILL,• SILVIA H. ALLRED • ROSEMARY M. WIXOM • RICHARD G. HINCKL
AN • SUSAN EASTON BLACK • CAMILLE FRONK OLSON • MARCUS H. MARTINS
E • CHAD B. MCKAY • RONALD C. PACKARD • HARRY REID • JASON CHAFFETZ
GS JENKINS • NATALIE CLEMENS • MARK EUBANK • MAREN ROSEMARIE SLOVE
JORDAN MARIE GREEN • WENDY HALE MCKAY • MAURINE PROCTOR • TIFFAN
PETER VIDMAR • KYLE WHITTINGHAM • STEVE YOUNG • J. W. "BILL" MARRIOTT
EY • CLAYTON M. CHRISTENSEN • STEEVUN LEMON • LARRY BARKDULL • RICHA
LLON • GREG OLSEN • JEFF SAVAGE • RICK WALTON • MARSHA WARD • KATH
NNION • CAROL ANNE CLAYSON • H. WALLACE GODDARD • GRANT HARDY
EATHER A. WILLOUGHBY • TWILA WOOD • JULIE B. BECK • GERILYN BECK MER
RSON STAPLES • VIVIAN MCCONKIE ADAMS • RICHARD LYMAN BUSHMAN •
CBAINE • ROBERT L. MCKAY • MIKE WINDER • GARY R. HERBERT • MIKE LEE •
ODFREY • MARK R. VAN WAGONER • DOUG WRIGHT • SANDRA STALLINGS JE
OB EVANS • SHAWNI EYRE POTHIER • KRISTINE WARDLE FREDERICKSON • JORD
GLENN RAWSON • TRENT TOONE • BRYAN MILLER • JIMMER FREDETTE • PETER
DOTSON • MARK ALLRED • MATTHEW DEAN BARKDULL • JOSH ROMNEY • C
HARLENE W. HAWKES • LAUREN JOHNSON • STEVEN KAPP PERRY • JULIE BELL
TERSON • TRISTI PINKSTON • JANETTE RALLISON • PHILIP N. HALE • JOHN BEN
ADDEN • KERRY MUHLESTEIN • GENE A. SESSIONS • DOUGLAS THAYER • HEAT
ALLRED • ROSEMARY M. WIXOM • RICHARD G. HINCKLEY • JANA PETERSON S
ACK • CAMILLE FRONK OLSON • MARCUS H. MARTINS • NEYLAN MCBAINE •
ONALD C. PACKARD • HARRY REID • JASON CHAFFETZ • MATTHEW GODFREY
EMENS • MARK EUBANK • MAREN ROSEMARIE SLOVER MAZZEO • BOB EVANS
WENDY HALE MCKAY • MAURINE PROCTOR • TIFFANY GEE LEWIS • GLENN RA
HITTINGHAM • STEVE YOUNG • J. W. "BILL" MARRIOTT JR. • ROBERT P. DOTSON

LIFE LESSONS FROM

Mothers
of Faith

INSPIRING TRUE STORIES ABOUT LATTER-DAY MOMS

Cover pictures of Church leaders © Intellectual Reserve, Inc.

Jacket and book design by Jessica A. Warner © 2012 Covenant Communications, Inc.

Published by Covenant Communications, Inc.
American Fork, Utah

Printed in China
First Printing: March 2012

19 18 17 16 15 14 13 12   10 9 8 7 6 5 4 3 2 1

ISBN-13 978-1-60861-748-7

LIFE LESSONS FROM

Mothers of Faith

INSPIRING TRUE STORIES ABOUT LATTER-DAY MOMS

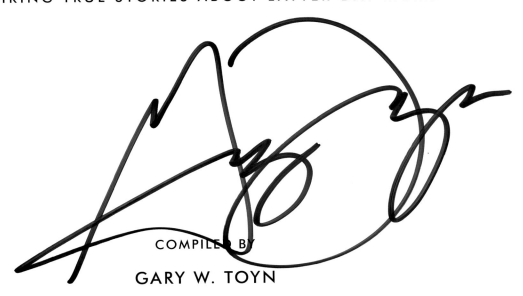

COMPILED BY

GARY W. TOYN

Table of Contents

COMMUNICATION

SPORTS

BUSINESS

ARTS & ENTERTAINMENT

EDUCATION

Foreword

The Mother of Mothers

by Jane Clayson Johnson

My mother was a beauty queen. As a teen, she was Miss Portland, and she wowed the judges with her skill as a concert violinist. She later went on to BYU, where she earned a bachelor's degree in education, and she also performed regularly with the BYU Program Bureau, which enabled her to perform around the world.

I was the oldest of three, with my sister, Hannah, and my younger brother, David, who was nearly eight years my junior. Playing the violin was a skill we all learned. As a family quartet, we would often play for various Church functions or other events. The fact that she wanted us to have the challenge of learning such a difficult instrument exemplifies my mother's skill as a mother. She had a knack for finding every opportunity to teach her children important lessons. Not only did she teach us to love music, but she knew that the process of learning to play a musical instrument would teach us patience and help us realize the rewards of learning other skills too.

I've been blessed with an expert mother who loves being a mother. She possesses a God-given gift of mothering. I've never met anyone who loves to mother more than my mom. I marvel how she revels in the minutia of mothering as she goes about it with seemingly little effort.

She embodies the best qualities of all of the best people I know. She is talented, intelligent, and wise, and has shared her wisdom with me throughout my life. I'm often amused at how much I still learn from her.

She is also my teacher and my example. Her degree was in education, but she was a natural-born teacher, in addition to the degree. She has the ability to connect her soul in quiet ways with those she teaches. I guess you could say she has a very high EQ (Emotional Quotient), as she understands why people—especially children—act as they do. If a child is feeling left out or needs some additional love and attention, she's there to help out and is always quick to give a hug or talk or listen, simply because she is completely sensitive to the needs of others.

As my children and I get older, I am especially able to appreciate her unique and innate aptitude for connecting with others, identifying their needs, and responding appropriately to meet their needs.

In addition to those abilities, I am blessed to experience a unique mother-daughter relationship with her. It wasn't until I had a child of my own that I had a deeper appreciation of this unique relationship. Consequently, my mother is my confidant. I can tell her things I would never tell anyone else in the world, things no one else would understand. I value that element of our relationship. And when I tell her something in confidence, I have complete trust in her because I know she will tell no one, as she always keeps her promises.

I was a bit late to motherhood, becoming a mother at the age of thirty-seven, but I made up for it by having an instant family when I married my husband, Mark, who brought with him three wonderful children from a previous marriage. Our two youngest children, William and Ella, came along later to complete our family. Although I may have been intellectually prepared for being a mother, I was undoubtedly surprised by the intensity of motherhood.

Quite frankly, I don't love a lot of what I must do as a mother. I can usually think of a million other things I would rather be doing than sitting on the floor playing with my son and his toys. But the other things I would be doing are not as valuable as teaching him that he is worthy of my time or helping him

> Quite frankly, I *don't* love a lot of what I must do as a mother.

JANE WRIGHT STRATFORD CLAYSON

is the mother of

JANE CLAYSON JOHNSON

Jane Clayson Johnson is an Emmy-winning journalist and author. She grew up in Sacramento, California, where she was an accomplished violinist and played with the Sacramento Youth Symphony.

She graduated from Brigham Young University in 1990 with a degree in journalism. She began her television career at KSL–TV in Salt Lake (1990–1996). While at KSL, she traveled to China to write and produce a series of stories about American doctors assisting Chinese children with disabilities. Her work there earned a regional Emmy. She also received the Radio and Television News Directors of America's Edward R. Murrow Award while at KSL.

In 1996, she moved to Los Angeles, where she worked as a correspondent for Good Morning America, World News Tonight, and other ABC News broadcasts. Her work included coverage of Senator Bob Dole's 1996 presidential campaign, the OJ Simpson civil trial, and NATO's strikes against Kosovo and the resulting refugee crisis in Macedonia.

In 1999, CBS News launched "Operation Glass Slipper," the widely publicized search for Bryant Gumbel's co-host on The Early Show, and Jane was chosen. From 1999–2002, she anchored The Early Show through the new millennium, the inauguration of President George W. Bush, and the attacks on September 11, 2001.

She and her husband, Mark, live near Boston with their five children.

learn right from wrong or a myriad other lessons I can be teaching him while we sit together on the floor.

My mother taught me that nothing is more important than what I do with my children right here and now. And although I sometimes feel the world is passing me by, I know from watching my mother's example and remembering how it made me feel that spending time with my children is always time well spent. Let the world pass me by if I can make my children feel as loved and valued as my mom has made me feel.

My mother taught me that motherhood matters. It matters to my children. It matters to my family. And most importantly, it matters greatly to God. He and I have an indelible connection and dual interest in rearing His spirit children, as I am just a temporary steward. My mother taught me the importance of trusting God and subjecting my will to His will, even if doing things His way doesn't make sense to me at the time.

I learned this lesson in a powerful way when I was eighteen years old. My brother David was ten when he woke up one morning and he was so sick he couldn't walk. Initially, we thought he had a virus, but as the days wore on, his condition worsened. After several tests, we learned the horrifying news that he had a malignant brain tumor.

His treatment was aggressive, and after weeks and months of chemotherapy and radiation treatments, he was bedridden and physically unable to communicate. Painstakingly, my mother would sit for hours, reciting letters in the alphabet, waiting for my brother to open his eyes to confirm a letter

Left: April 1968. Jane with her daughter Janie at BYU, where Jane performed regularly with the BYU Program Bureau as a concert violinist.

Middle: 1968 in the Wilkinson Center at BYU.

Right: Jane and Janie at the Clayson grandparents' home in Orem, Utah.

in a word they were trying to spell out.

Day after day, I watched and prayed for my brother, praying for what I so desperately wanted, which was that he would be restored to good health. I remember vividly the outpouring of support from friends and neighbors. Church members brought in dinners each night for months while my mother attended to David. She watched over him, lovingly dressed him, and took care of his every need. Collectively, our faith was united and determined to help him get well, and I'm confident that no other group of people had more faith that David would be made whole.

Then, one night in December, the pain medication could barely dull his pain, and my brother was given a priesthood blessing. The message was brief, but for the first time, it ended with the words, "Thy will be done." It required great faith to accept those four

She taught me the importance of not being **angry** or **resentful** when the Lord's will is *different* from my own.

words, knowing His will may not be our will. At just eleven years old, David passed away that night. It was December 21, 1985.

David's farewell was held on Christmas Eve. His gifts were still under the tree, as in the months and weeks prior, he had cheerfully encouraged everyone around him to live life to the fullest and to believe that he would be around to celebrate the holiday. To honor David, my mother, my sister, Hannah, and I played our violins, with David's little violin resting silently on a music stand next to us.

I still miss David to this day. Yet, I often contemplate the unspoken lessons my mother taught me about compassion, service, and pure Christlike love—a mother's love.

She taught me a powerful lesson of not of only subjecting my will to God's will but also of the importance of not being angry or resentful when the Lord's will is different from my own.

Clayson children (Janie, David, and Hannah) playing their violins with their mother, Jane. The four of them played as a quartet for various Church functions and other events.

She Never Looked Back

by Gary W. Toyn

Having finally finished the year-long process of writing and compiling this book, my editor has given me the daunting assignment of writing about my own mother.

I'm uplifted by the impressive abilities of our contributors, but I expect many have faced the same conflict I now face—a host of ideas and emotions but no idea of how to proceed. I now understand the challenge all contributors faced in having to condense a lifetime of memories of their mother into an essay of 1,500 words or fewer.

Joy Wood at age 19.

Having worked with such a diverse and distinguished group of contributors, I feel fortunate and blessed that each essay is different and highlights a unique maternal characteristic from which an important life lesson can be learned.

Likewise, my mother has taught me many important life lessons, and I am tempted to highlight such characteristics as her willingness to sacrifice for others, her wonderful sense of humor, her ability to listen and offer sound advice, and her insistence upon never being a burden on others, regardless of how much she must sacrifice. But the one lesson that I'm impressed to write about is that she taught me to endure to the end.

I am the youngest of six children, and I'm sure that after my mother chased five kids around, she was ready for a mellow, bookish child who loved to read and think deep thoughts. I was not that child. I was the active kid, always making a mess, getting into things I shouldn't, or running off to explore every inch of my beloved hometown of Huntsville, Utah.

My mother admits with some exasperation that growing up, I had only two speeds: fast and stop. I hated to take a bath, sit down to eat, or take care of bodily functions because they simply took too darn much time.

I've since come to the conclusion that one of my purposes in my early life was to give my mom experiences to build her faith. It seemed that even from an early age, the things I did often forced my mother to her knees.

As a young child, I fell through a storm-door window, causing a deep gash from the top of my head to my chin. I subsequently had numerous other visits to the emergency room,

Joy with her sixth and youngest child, Gary.

resulting in a unique collection of scars covering almost every part of my body. Each scar was the result of an incident or illness requiring my mom or dad to escort me to the emergency room. Each of these events surely caused my mother grief or misery to some degree or another. But these numerous hospital visits wouldn't be worth mentioning, except for the fact that many of them touched a tender nerve in my mother, who deeply feared losing a child. This fear was not unfounded, since she had already experienced the grief and heartache of burying my oldest sister, Debbie.

Debbie's brief five-year life span was spent in and out of a hospital as she suffered from cystic fibrosis. She endured multiple hospitalizations, painful therapy, and endless visits to the doctor's office. Despite it all, Debbie remained cheerful and optimistic. On a gloomy December afternoon in 1955, my mother noticed that Debbie was having difficulty swallowing, and food was coming through her nose. She called the doctor, who immediately called an ambulance to take Debbie to the hospital. In just a matter of hours, polio had stricken my sister's entire body. My mother was overwhelmed with sorrow as she watched her precious angel be placed in an iron lung to keep her alive.

After a day or two, the immediate crisis passed, and soon Debbie recovered enough to begin talking to the nurses. My mother smiled as Debbie spoke lovingly about her baby brother Rob and how hopeful she was to be home in time for Christmas.

I've come to the conclusion that one of *my* purposes in my early life was to give my mom *experiences* to **build her faith**.

Feeling a bit more at ease, my mother left the hospital briefly to see her other two children at my grandmother's house and to run a quick errand. But when she got to Grandma's, she was told to hurry back to the hospital because Debbie had taken a sudden turn for the worse. Panicked, my mother rushed to the hospital only a few blocks away. By the time she arrived, the hospital staff had determined that Debbie was going to die, and they refused to let my mother be with her to say good-bye. She was forced to sit in the waiting room until after Debbie passed away.

Both my parents were devastated by the loss of their dear little girl, but it was especially difficult because they were not active in the Church.

Although my mother was baptized when she was eight years old, she was not brought up in a home where she learned the gospel. Her parents were inactive, struggled with the Word of Wisdom, and simply didn't discuss religious matters in their home.

After Debbie's passing, my mother found consolation in the hope of being with her again but knew it would only happen if she was worthy. It took several years for my mother and father to prepare to go through the temple, but the hope of being with Debbie was a powerful motivator. On June 24, 1959, my parents and my older siblings were sealed in the Salt Lake Temple.

Without an example of how to teach gospel principles, my mom and dad did their best to teach us kids, but much of it was trial and error. Fortunately, by the time I came around, we went to church every Sunday and attended Primary, Mutual, and Scouts during the week.

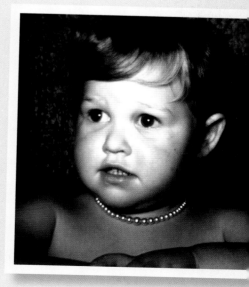

Debbie Toyn, Gary's oldest sister.

JOY WOOD TOYN
is the mother of

GARY W. TOYN

Gary W. Toyn is the son of Robert E. and Joy Wood Toyn. He is an author, writer, editor, video producer, and marketing consultant. He is the founder of American Legacy Media, a publisher specializing in American military history. He loves to travel, try new food, and meet fascinating people. In all, he has traveled to nearly fifty countries, and at press time, his favorite countries were Korea, Turkey, and France. He and his wife, Danita, have four children, a geriatric dog, and a skittish feline that sheds excessively. He is a home teacher, Sunday School teacher, ward choir director, and stake chorister in the Clinton 13th Ward, Clinton Utah Stake.

Although my mom was always known for being kind, loving, and Christlike, in hindsight, it was obvious that she struggled with a full conversion to the gospel of Jesus Christ, yet she always tried to set a good example. I don't remember my mother having many Church callings, and I don't recall her reading the scriptures, saying many prayers, or bearing her testimony. Yet she always went to church and made sure I attended all my meetings.

I realized my parents were not strong in the Church when I was a teen and they were unable to go to the temple when my brothers were married, and it hit me again when they could not attend my marriage. It was especially heartbreaking for my mother. To make matters even more challenging, she worked in a very poor environment where most people smoked and alcohol poured freely. I remember sitting in a waiting room while my mother finished working, and a man sat beside me, gulping down an entire fifth of whiskey. Within a half hour, he was completely incoherent and collapsed on the sofa with me. I remember how much I hated her working there.

It wasn't until after I was married, but I was thrilled when my mother retired from that job. Almost immediately, I saw a noticeable change in her spirituality. One day, out of the blue, my parents mentioned that they were attending the temple.

Once my mother discovered the blessings of living gospel-centered standards, she never looked back. My mother even convinced my father, who is a good man and eager to live the gospel, to go on a mission. It was a joyous day in our family when they opened their mission call and read with much anticipation that they would serve in the Nauvoo Illinois Mission. My parents were thrilled!

They arrived in Nauvoo shortly after they broke ground for the Nauvoo temple. They had many choice experiences during its construction, one of which was a spiritual confirmation to my mother that the Church was true and that she was where the Lord wanted her to be.

I remember taking my family on a vacation to Nauvoo and seeing my parents thrive in this environment. While my parents served at the Family Living Center, I watched in amazement as my mother taught visitors

Far left: Four generations: Sister Bangerter with her mother, grandmother, and daughter Julie. *Left*: Sister Bangerter holding great-granddaughter Hope, standing next to granddaughter Gerilyn and her husband, Seth. *Above:* Four generations: Sister Bangerter, her daughter Sister Beck, Sister Beck's daughter Gerilyn Merrill, and Gerilyn's daughter.

a woman with a "mother heart" but also a woman with the hands of a worker and a healer. She has blessed innumerable lives with her love and good works.

As a young woman, my mother, Geraldine Hamblin Bangerter, heard her seminary teacher say, "Welcome the task that makes you go beyond yourself, and you will grow." These words became an enlightening and motivating theme in her life. She has approached so many efforts and challenges with faith and courage. In our family we call it "stick-to-itiveness."

Although her accomplishments have been numerous and constant, no accomplishment has meant more to her posterity than being taught how to work hard, to approach life with optimism, to live with absolute faith, and to love people.

—Julie B. Beck

Always Adaptable

by Silvia Henriquez Allred

My mother was born in San Salvador, El Salvador, in 1924. As was the case with most families in El Salvador, she was raised in a devout Catholic home. She was by nature a good soul—kind, thoughtful, and giving, and although she didn't know about the Relief Society motto until later in life, she never failed to be charitable.

She was raised in humble circumstances and was forced to make sacrifices at a very young age. When she was ten years old, both her parents were forced to work to support the family, requiring my mother to quit school to tend her younger brother. This ended her formal education at fourth grade, yet her ability to articulate herself, her reading ability, and her beautiful handwriting would never reveal her limited schooling.

She was quite capable of adapting to changing circumstances, which she did throughout her life. In the 1940s, my family would have been considered middle class, but we had no car, and we lived in a rented home. All the laundry was washed by hand, and everything we ate was prepared from scratch.

My father's family ran a small shoe-making shop near our home, but by the time I was about five years old, my grandmother had assumed responsibility of the business so my father could start his own business.

Right: Hilda Alvarenga de Henriquez, 1944.

HILDA ALVARENGA DE HENRIQUEZ
is the mother of

SILVIA H. ALLRED

Silvia Henriquez Allred was born October 11, 1944, and has been a member of the general presidency of the Relief Society of The Church of Jesus Christ of Latter-day Saints since March 2007.

She was born in San Salvador, El Salvador, and served as a missionary in the Central America Mission in the early 1960s. She attended the University of Arizona, Brigham Young University, and the General Francisco Morazán Institute, where she studied mathematics. On September 7, 1966, she married Jeffry A. Allred in the Salt Lake Temple.

She served with her husband during his time as president of the Paraguay Asunción Mission and during a separate time as president of the Missionary Training Center in the Dominican Republic. Sister Allred and her husband were also public affairs missionaries in Madrid, Spain.

Prior to her call into the leadership of the Relief Society, she served as a member of the general board of the Young Women organization. Sister Allred and her husband are the parents of eight children.

He started a little store across the street from our home, but it was more like a "bazaar," featuring unique items, such as buttons, perfume, and a host of other items that were popular at the time. My mother helped keep the store clean, and she also managed the books.

They had almost **NOTHING** *left, and they had no choice but to start all over again.*

The store did well enough that they opened a second, much larger store in San Miguel, about 135 kilometers (eighty-four miles) away. Since we didn't have a car, my father would leave Monday mornings on a three-hour bus ride, stay at the store all week, and return on Sundays. This routine persisted for a few months, my mother being pregnant with their eighth child at the time. Soon after the baby was born, they decided it would be better to move the family to San Miguel and hopefully build their business and expand. My mother agreed to make the move, despite having a brand-new baby. She packed up the house and all seven children (my older brother had died in infancy), and we rode a bus to our new home in San Miguel.

We lived in a nice colonial-style home that could accommodate our large family and a second, smaller store in the front room. It was the most prosperous time of my young life, but our financial success was short-lived.

On a day I will never forget, fire ravaged through the block where our larger store was located. Having lost the store, my parents were forced to liquidate their smaller store to pay off the debt of the larger store.

They had almost nothing left, and they had no choice but to start all over again. They saw no reason to remain in San Miguel, as our families were back in San Salvador.

To my mother's credit, soon after we moved back to San Salvador, they rented a house, registered us for school, obtained the necessary school uniforms and supplies, and we were back at school the next school day. We never missed a day of school, and no one knew of our financial destitution because of my mother's incredible resourcefulness, creativity, and determination to solve our problems.

My father returned to the shoe shop, and my mother struggled to feed us, yet we never went hungry. After a while, she had saved a small amount of money and opened a little neighborhood store out of our house. She sold foodstuffs and other related items that people in our neighborhood needed. When she bought food for the family, she bought it in bulk at a cheaper price and sold the remainder in the store at a small profit. Before long, she had created a nice little supplementary income for our family. She also bought a sewing machine and made beautiful items

Left: Hilda at thirty-seven in 1945. *Above*: The Henriquez family, 1989.

that adorned our home and were also sold in her store. In addition, she made our dresses, and we were always well dressed.

My mother worked tirelessly. During the four hours of siesta time, most people either took a nap or simply relaxed after eating a big meal. My mother, however, couldn't bear to sit idle, so she embroidered or crocheted beautiful tablecloths and other fine linen items.

My mother was always giving to other people. She had a very large extended family,

and relatives would often come to her seeking financial assistance. Without any fanfare, she would end the conversation with a hug and slip some money in their pocket, trying not to let them know. She was always charitable and freely gave what she could spare.

When I was fifteen and my sister Ana Dina was seventeen, we were introduced to the LDS missionaries. We listened eagerly to the restored gospel, and when we were invited to be baptized, we agreed, but we had to obtain permission from my parents. My father readily agreed, but my mother refused. She was never rude to the missionaries, as she would invite them in and be hospitable to them, but she wouldn't stay and listen to them. After a month, she realized our determination, and she finally relented and allowed us to be baptized.

Her strong family ties and Catholic upbringing meant that important rites and ceremonies were attended by the whole family. Consequently, though my mother was somewhat reluctant to attend our baptism, she did. It was a very special occasion, one that not only my family attended but also almost all the members of our small branch.

My sister and I were asked to bear our testimonies after we were baptized, and I directed my testimony to my mother. I bore solemn witness that I knew The Church of Jesus Christ of Latter-day Saints was true and that being baptized was the right thing to do. I knew God loved me and that He was pleased with my decision. The Spirit testified boldly to my mother, and after the baptism, she asked the missionaries to teach her the gospel. She and our younger siblings were baptized only a few weeks later.

My mother was spiritually prepared to join the Church. She had few if any vices, and she embraced the gospel wholeheartedly. Likely the only change she had to make was to quit drinking coffee, which she did without hesitation and was never tempted by it again. She was a good person before she joined the Church, and the gospel only made her better.

The decision was courageous, as she had to reject many of her family's Catholic traditions, which was not easy. In fact, courage and determination were hallmarks of my mother.

I remember watching her grow in stature in the Church. Only three months after she was baptized, she was asked during a district conference meeting to come to the pulpit and bear her testimony. I prayed silently for her as she walked to the stand, but I was impressed with her ability to articulate herself in front of more than two hundred people. She spoke eloquently for five minutes and then sat down. She was impressive and convincing. Not long thereafter, she was called as the Relief Society president in our branch, and she never looked back. Service in the Church was a blessing to her, our family, and all the sisters who were in her circle of influence for good.

It must have been a couple of years after my baptism when I fully realized my mother's goodness. I was reading in Proverbs 31:10–29, and I thought to myself, *This describes my mother exactly*:

> Who can find a virtuous woman? For her price is far above rubies. The heart of her husband doth safely trust in her, so that he shall have no need of spoil. She will do him good and not evil all the days of her life. She girdeth her loins with strength, and strengtheneth her arms. She stretcheth out her hand to the poor; yea, she reacheth forth her hands to the needy. She maketh fine linen, and selleth it. She openeth her mouth with wisdom; and in her tongue is the law of kindness. She looketh well to the ways of her household, and eateth not the bread of idleness. Her children arise up, and call her blessed; her husband also, and he praiseth her. Many daughters have done virtuously, but thou excellest them all.

It's as though King Solomon had envisioned my mother when he wrote these prophetic words. How grateful I am to have been taught by such a virtuous, courageous, and devoted woman as my mother. I couldn't have been more blessed.

The Kitchen Table: The Faith of My Mother

by Rosemary M. Wixom

The kitchen table was the spiritual center of my mother's home, and when our family surrounded it, we drew from our mother's faith. She did not preach to us. She simply lived her life so we could be taught. She did not demand our presence. Her warmth was an invitation. Her service to our family was not a burden—it was the air she breathed. She was and is not perfect. She is real!

How do I know this? I observed her while I was growing up, and I still observe her today in her ninety-second year. Much of the time with my mother was spent within the walls of our family home. It is a humble home, but to her, it is a castle because it can compare to the sacredness of the temple. Each member of our family feels it when we walk through the front door. The Spirit draws us to her—then we gather at the kitchen table.

We ate and digested not only food but also *conversation.*

As a child, it was at the kitchen table that we ate and digested not only food but also conversation. The events of our day became *her* focus.

It was around the kitchen table that we would kneel on the linoleum floor for family prayer. It was at the kitchen table that we would read the scriptures. It was on the kitchen table that the bottled peaches, pears, pickles, and tomatoes would rest before they were taken to the fruit room downstairs. Mom would tediously peel, pack, and steam the fruit while she sometimes dripped with sweat herself.

It was on the kitchen table that the fresh sheets and towels, just taken from the clothesline, would be piled before they were folded and put away. It was around the kitchen table that we girls would sit while Mom would give us a perm or roll our hair in curlers while we talked and shared intimacies about our lives. Every prom dress began on the kitchen table. The fabric was laid out, and the pattern was pinned on. Sometimes the process went late into the night.

It was at the kitchen table that Mom would prepare the lessons for her current Church calling. Her scriptures and books would be piled open before her as she marked the thoughts she wanted to remember. Each school night that same table would become "homework central" for all of us children.

RELIGION

MARY CANNON MIX
is the mother of

ROSEMARY M. WIXOM

Rosemary Mix Wixom was born in Ogden in December 1948 to Robert W. and Mary Cannon Mix. She was reared in Salt Lake, attended Utah State University, and graduated in elementary education. She married Jack Wixom in 1970.

She has served as a Primary general board member, stake Young Women president, stake Primary president, and Lambda Delta Sigma adviser at the institute adjacent to the University of Utah. She also served with her husband while he presided over the Washington DC South Mission from 2006–2009.

Currently, she serves as the general president of the Primary; she was sustained in the April 2010 general conference. She is the twelfth general president in the history of the Primary.

She and her husband are the parents of six children and have eight grandchildren. She loves her kids and adores her grandchildren and considers Sunday family dinners the highlight of her week.

Above: Mary Cannon as a young child. *Middle*: Bud and Mary Mix sealed in June 1941 in the Salt Lake Temple. *Right*: Rosemary and her mother, Mary.

It was at the kitchen table that we would carve pumpkins, dye Easter eggs, and serve Christmas dinner—and there would always be dimes and nickels wrapped in foil and hidden in the birthday cakes for the lucky guests.

It was at the kitchen table that Mom would sit to pay the bills. From the way she would hold her head in her hands, one could tell the financial strain of that month. With never a word of complaint, she would close the checkbook and return to her duties of the day.

It was at the kitchen table that, as a child, I let a bad word slip; I was immediately marched to the bathroom, where my mouth was washed out with soap.

It was at the kitchen table that neighbors would come to visit and relatives would gather. Daily conversations would consistently occur and laughter could be heard throughout the whole house.

Yet, it was also at the kitchen table that life-changing conversations would occur, like the conversation with the hospice nurse when Dad was dying from cancer. Then the voices were tender and quiet, yet her faith was resilient. The table provided a physical support.

Now, years later, she spends much of her day sitting near the window at the kitchen table. When the front door opens and friends and family come in, they all head for the kitchen table. It has been a popular place for grandchildren to bring their dates, knowing full well that Grandma would entertain them. "Now you come in here and let's just see what we can find to eat," she always says as she opens the refrigerator.

Rob, a grandson, still remembers bringing his date to Grandma's home. She was

Above: Mary celebrating her birthday with her grandchildren. *Right*: Mary with Robert Wayne Mix, now deceased.

in such a hurry to answer the door that she forgot to button her skirt, and while she was searching through the cupboards, her skirt fell to the floor. There she was, standing in her slip. Grandma laughed the hardest that day.

It is said that "the Israelites were forbidden to build an altar except in the place where God should choose to put His name" (Bible Dictionary, 607). The kitchen table in our home is such a place. Although the table is but a physical object, it is the Spirit in my mother's heart that makes it sacred.

For years it was there, at the kitchen table, that I felt the love of the Savior through the life and the faith of my mother.

When the front door opens and friends and family come in, they all head for the kitchen table.

My Mother, the Great Affirmer

by Richard G. Hinckley

When I reflect on my childhood, I realize that wet garbage was my downfall. You see, there were no garbage disposals in those days, so the "wet garbage"—that is, orange and apple peels, lettuce ends, carrot tops, and other waste collected during the preparation of meals—was placed in a little strainer in the corner of the sink, and when a sufficient amount was collected, Mother would say to me, "Would you take out the wet garbage, please?" I was to dump it outside in a little compost pit, where it eventually decomposed and was used as fertilizer for the garden.

Don't get me wrong. I didn't mind mowing the lawn, irrigating the orchard at 4:00 a.m., or mixing concrete for a new retaining wall, but for some reason, taking out the wet garbage defeated me. As we grew older and I outgrew that silly obsession, Mother and my siblings would—with great glee—recount how, when asked to take out the wet garbage, I would lean against the kitchen wall, slide down it, and play dead or writhe with faux pain. Mom, ever patient, would just laugh and say, "Well, when it begins to spill out of the sink and fill the kitchen, I guess we'll just have to eat in the living room!" No coercion, no raised voice, certainly no corporal punishment; just a shrug of her shoulders and a suppressed laugh. She was not a strict disciplinarian, nor was she a hard taskmaster. And she was never very good at getting mad if we approached our tasks with indolence or even ignored her repeated requests to complete this chore or that. Eventually, I would come around and trudge out to the compost pile, feeling like the most put-upon little fellow in the world—but it was never because of something Mom did or said.

Lest you think otherwise, there were times when we pushed too far. We knew Mom was at the end of her rope when she would say, "I give up. When your father gets home, he'll have to deal with you!"

When I was very young, Mother once made a casserole for dinner. I had never seen a casserole before, and when it came out of the oven, it must have looked vaguely familiar because I said quite innocently, "Mom, why did you bake the wet garbage?" (Even at that young age, I was apparently obsessed with wet garbage.) She burst into laughter and told everyone about it around the dinner table that night. We all had a good laugh, but I remember feeling a bit silly— not nearly as silly, however, as I felt as an adult when she repeated that story to a large meeting of the Saints. She had a wonderfully cheerful disposition, seeing good in people and humor in life.

One of Mom's most remarkable gifts was her total inability to criticize others. It simply was not in her DNA. She could only see the good side of people and seemed to be blind to their faults. In "The World According to Marjorie Hinckley," everyone was good. She was the "great affirmer." As newlyweds, my wife and I came home one evening to find our house had been burglarized. Among other things, Jane's jewelry had been taken. Though there hadn't been a lot, there were a few nice pieces her grandmother had given her. We called home, and Jane talked to my mother, describing piece by piece what had been taken and how sad she was to lose them. Jane said she suddenly realized she was sounding rather worldly and, feeling a bit guilty, quickly added, "Oh well, we can't take it with us." Mother responded emphatically, "True, but it's nice

RELIGION

RICHARD G. HINCKLEY

is the son of

MARJORIE PAY HINCKLEY

Richard Gordon Hinckley was born on May 2, 1941, in Salt Lake City to Gordon B. and Marjorie Pay Hinckley. He was raised in East Millcreek, Utah, where he graduated from Olympus High School. He served a mission to the Central German Mission, and while he was away, his father was ordained an Apostle and became a member of the Quorum of the Twelve Apostles. Following his mission, Richard earned a BA degree in economics from the University of Utah and an MBA from Stanford University.

His professional career included management consultant at Deloitte and Touche in Los Angeles, California, then "Touche, Ross, Bailey and Smart," and being an equity partner in several small businesses.

His community service has included being chairman of the board of the Salt Lake chapter of the American Red Cross, past director of the University of Utah Alumni Association, and other advisory boards and charitable organizations.

Richard has served in a number of Church callings, including bishop, stake president and counselor, and sealer in the Salt Lake Temple. He also served as the president of the Utah Salt Lake City Mission (2001–2004) and most recently as a member of the First Quorum of the Seventy and executive director of the Missionary Department. He became an emeritus General Authority in 2011.

Richard and his wife, Jane, are currently serving as the directors of Church Hosting.

He married Jane Freed in the Salt Lake Temple in 1967, and they have four children and fourteen grandchildren.

One of Mom's most remarkable gifts was her total inability to criticize others. It simply was not in her DNA.

to have while you're here." Mom didn't criticize Jane for feeling bad about the jewelry; instead, she helped her see that at times it's okay to feel bad about trials in life.

After our oldest daughter graduated from high school, some friends invited her to spend several months in England living with them as a cook and nanny. These friends were serving as mission president and wife, and they needed help. Jennie sent Mother a letter from England for Mother's Day and then called her. In response, Mother wrote Jennie a long letter, typical of letters all her grandchildren received from time to time. Part of it read, "Dear Jennie, [Your] letter was warm to my heart. This was a letter to make any rough roads we might have traveled to reach the age of seventy-seven worthwhile. You gave me a Mother's Day supreme. A wonderful letter and a phone call. My heart leaped when I heard your voice. I could scarcely believe it! I ask myself what I ever could have done to deserve such a remarkable and beautiful and wonderful granddaughter. I sometimes think you are too good to be true. . . . I don't know what to say except I love you, and that seems so inadequate. Thank you for what you are and for bringing such joy into our lives." What teenage girl's heart would not burst with joy after reading such a letter from her grandma?

When Kathy and I were very young, before our siblings came along, Dad became ill, diagnosed with bronchial pneumonia. There was little physicians could do, so he lay in bed for a month, growing weaker every day. He had never been so sick. I think he had never missed a day of work due to illness. I remember thinking how pale and thin he was. One evening, Dr. Mel Davis, our family doctor, came by the house on a regular visit. After examining Dad—and I remember this very clearly—he said, in effect, "Marge, I have done all I know how to do. I know of nothing more I can do. I would like to give him a blessing." Those words carried such a sense of finality. Dr. Davis removed his white medical frock. He looked so different from the doctor who seemed to know all there was to know about medicine. Underneath, he was wearing a dark suit, white shirt, and a tie. Our neighbor Wes Osguthorpe came over to assist Dr. Davis with the blessing. Mother didn't cry, but her

Previous page: Marjorie Pay Hinckley, 1930.

Left: Marjorie, 1998. Middle: President and Sister Hinckley with Lady Margaret Thatcher, 1996. Right: Marjorie holding Richard, sitting next to Kathy, 1943. Below: President and Sister Hinckley at a U of U LDSSA Conference, 1996.

worry and anxiety were palpable. When Wes arrived, Mother took Kathy and me firmly in hand to the other end of the house and said, "Let's pray for your father." So we knelt in that room—two little kids and their mother—while Mom poured out her heart to the Lord. I don't remember what she said, but I remember the feeling of desperation and the pleading in her voice, her reliance on the Lord. I will never forget it. Dad got better and was never again that ill until the day he died.

She rarely exhibited what might be called a forceful or dominant personality, but behind those soft brown eyes, just beyond that good-natured humor, ever so slightly beneath the surface, was a layer of iron resoluteness born of a simple faith that God is in His heavens, that He knows us and our circumstances, and that by living the gospel, "things will work out." I think if she were still here, she might say, with a twinkle in her eye, "And

things will work out for you too. But often, it seems to take a very long time!"

Thanks, Mom. You really were one of a kind.

The Remarkable Vision of My Mother

by Jana Peterson Staples

BROOKIE PETERSON

is the mother of

JANA PETERSON STAPLES

Jana Staples was born in Arizona. Her father is former General Authority H. Burke Peterson, and she is the fourth of five daughters. After moving to Utah, she attended Brigham Young University, where she met Mark Staples. They were married in the Salt Lake Temple and are now the parents of three daughters and two sons. They have four grandchildren.

In addition to her current calling on the Relief Society general board, Sister Staples has enjoyed serving in various capacities in the Primary, Young Women, and Relief Society auxiliaries of the Church.

I grew up in a family of five girls. My mother and father had only brothers, so this was an eye-opening experience for them. It wasn't long before my parents realized that just like boys, their girls needed ample time, prayful guidance, and love unrestrained.

My mother was a loving, organized, strong, intelligent, and wise influence in our lives. She loved to take us to cultural events. We would often go to plays, ballets, and museums. Classical music regularly filled our home, and going to the library was regarded as a "special treat." Of course, growing up in Arizona, we had endless water parties, lemonade stands, and art projects. My mom's formal dresses from her college dances made the best dress-ups in the neighborhood.

Mom tried to give each of us some personal time with her. My needs were a little different from my sisters'. By the time I was twelve, my mom determined that she needed to give me more one-on-one time. She

She would never **promise** us *anything!*

Left: The Peterson family in 1967 in their Phoenix home. *Below:* Jana (left) and the Peterson family sing around the piano.

began sitting by my bed at night before I fell asleep. I wasn't much into visiting, but Mom would still come and sit by me four or five times during the week. If she started to give advice or counsel, I would turn over and tell her that I loved her but good night. So often she sat by me without saying anything, just being a comforting presence. This went on throughout my teenage years.

I remember one night clearly. It was a December evening and I was twenty-one years old. I had just come home from college. It was cold outside, but there was a lot of excitement in our house because the next morning I was to be married. I had finished

packing and had wrapped up all the last-minute details. I said my prayers, turned off my lights, and crawled into bed. Not long after, I saw a light come into my room—it was Mom coming in for our last visit. This time I wanted her wisdom and guidance as I was starting my new life.

As girls, we would often see her reading her scriptures, studying Sunday School lessons, or doing genealogy. She worked with us to help us learn to cook. She spent her time on those things that were essential since days were crowded with a house full of girls and emotions.

She was serious about her testimony of the gospel and always wanted to be truthful and honest with her children. Though we surely realized she wasn't perfect, there was so much good in her that we didn't dwell on any missteps. However, she did have what seemed to us a small quirk. She was afraid of promising something and failing to carry it out and then having her children not trust her. She would never promise us anything!

She would say, "Jana, go and do the dishes and that will be your last job."

"Do you promise, Mom?"

And she would say, "Umm, no."

Or she might say, "Jana, let's get the house clean and then I will drive you down to the swimming pool."

I would say, "Do you promise?"

And she'd say, "Umm, no."

As a child, I thought this was a little odd, but as I grew a little older it became somewhat of a game or challenge. My sisters and I would manipulate and maneuver many conversations to try to extract some kind of promise out of our mother, but it never worked. Whatever strategy or scheme we dreamed, she was wise to us, and she would promise nothing.

One day when all my ploys had finally failed, I asked her in frustration, "Mom, is there anything you can promise me?"

Quietly and very purposefully, she knelt down close to me so we were eye to eye. She said in all seriousness, "Jana, I promise you the Church is true."

Instead of the elation at finally eliciting a promise from her, I felt a joy and a burning feeling that she was testifying to me. I informed my sisters of my success, and for years we would still try to get her to promise myriads of things. In the end, we always asked that fateful question—if there were anything she could promise, and the words

H. Burke and Brookie Peterson.

were always the same: "I promise you the Church is true."

In later years, I have compared this experience in my life to Abish in the Book of Mormon. Abish was able to help many of the people in King Lamoni's kingdom come to know the true gospel: "Having been converted unto the Lord for many years, on account of a remarkable vision of her father" (Alma 19:16).

I, too, have had the blessing of being converted for many years because of the remarkable vision of my mother.

Fidelity and Grace Unremitting

by Vivian McConkie Adams

Some years ago, my mother, Amelia Smith McConkie, became ill during a family retreat. My father, Bruce R. McConkie, immediately took her home, and she ended up in the hospital with an illness that was never fully diagnosed. Father hovered over her there and then at home. In a way, it was almost a happy aside because mother, who had spent much of her life serving our father, was now being waited on by him. He relished this experience, but as the July vacation period ended, he was needed for conference assignments, and I went to stay with Mother until he returned. I took a large notebook, and in those ten days, I interviewed her as long as she could endure inquiry.

Hearing about her life was like reading Church history. She was the daughter of prophets, from her father, Joseph Fielding Smith, to Joseph F. Smith, to Hyrum Smith. Her mother, Ethel Georgina Reynolds, was the daughter of George Reynolds of the First Council of the Seventy and secretary to Brigham Young. She was also the wife of a wonderful husband and father who, in the course of their life together, became a member of the Twelve. She seemed to know not only by training but also by intuition the way of prophets.

She came into the world in the old Smith home that was built on property first owned by Mary Fielding Smith, the wife of Hyrum, on what is now 2nd West in Salt Lake City. Every home on the street belonged to a Smith, and the aura of the past swirled around her there. Eight days after her birth, on June 21, 1916, Grandpapa Joseph F. Smith came to their home to give her a name and a blessing. Had he not approved of the name chosen, he would have blessed her with something else, as he had done with her cousins.

Mother's father charmed his children as they grew with accounts of the great men he had known, and he entertained them at breakfast with stories from the scriptures and Church history. She was astonished to learn during a

Amelia Smith McConkie, July 1937.

Next page: Amelia as a young toddler.

Hearing about *her life* was like reading Church history.

Her father also owned Hyrum's gold watch, a gift from the Prophet, his dark glasses, and records penned by the Prophet's secretaries. These things, along with much of Joseph F. Smith's personal library, were to our family, in essence, the Sword of Laban and the Liahona.

Mother heard her father deliver hundreds of speeches at general conference and in the wards and stakes of Zion. She watched him bring forth a host of manuscripts and more than twenty books on the doctrine or history of the Church, all of which he typed with two fingers on the Underwood at his roll-top desk. He brought book galleys home in the evening and paid the children ten cents for every mistake they could find. His work was scholarly and added to the discussions in the household, which everyone loved.

His work also engendered opposition. Mother kept in her own papers a copy of the blessing her father received from Patriarch Joseph D. Smith of Fillmore in 1913. It read, "The time will come when the accumulative evidence that you have gathered will stand as a wall of defense against those who are seeking and will seek to destroy the evidence of the divinity of the mission of the Prophet

Sunday School class that he was an Apostle and went home for confirmation. She thought he was just Papa. Her first experience with him in general conference came when she was five or six years old. She sat on the stand at his feet as other children of the Brethren sometimes did in that day. Her only instruction was that she move out of the way when one of the Twelve went to the pulpit.

Her father's study contained tangible evidences of the Restoration: Hyrum Smith's wooden box, his name etched into the grain by his own hand, which was unexpectedly spelled *Hiram*, his Nauvoo Legion uniform, his blue silk Masonic apron, and a temple apron made of white doeskin with five of the nine leaves embroidered by Emma Smith. A note attached to the apron explained that she had quit on the fifth leaf because it was too difficult to stitch through the leather.

Joseph; and in this defense you will never be confounded."

When Father met Mother, he was immediately smitten, though she teased that he courted her so he could talk about the gospel with her father. His primary interest at the Smiths, of course, was Mother, who was vivacious and pretty. As to doctrinal discussions, he had been well trained at the table of his own parents, Oscar W. and Vivian Redd McConkie. Her mother was impressed because Father did not party on the Sabbath; she called him "that nice Bruce McConkie." It struck me to read in his missionary journal two sentences, one after another, that reflect what his life would become. He wrote of his mission, "The people need sound doctrine" and of Mother, "She is like my mother for her graces and goodness."

After his mission, Mother and Father were married by her father on October 13, 1937, in the small sealing room just off the celestial room in the Salt Lake Temple. It was the room where her father and mother were married in 1908 by President Joseph F. Smith and was, her father jested, "the only true marriage room in the temple."

It was of interest to us that Mother's patriarchal blessing promised her that she would

"I know the truth when I hear it."

RELIGION

VIVIAN MCCONKIE ADAMS
is the daughter of

AMELIA SMITH MCCONKIE

Vivian McConkie Adams served twelve years on the Chicago Region Public Communications Council of the Church, appearing in numerous media interviews and speaking to school, college, and community groups on LDS doctrine and history. She was then called to serve as media representative in the Midwest on controversial issues for the Church. She has been active in state and national politics and civic and public service organizations and is a recipient of the Brigham Young University Alumni Community Service Award.

She has been a presenter at BYU Education Week and BYU Women's Conference and in LDS women's conferences across the country. She has published several articles and electronic media on Church-related subjects. She serves as historian and educational outreach chairman for the Joseph Smith Sr./Lucy Mack Smith Foundation and for the Joseph F. Smith Family Association. She currently teaches Church history and doctrine in the American Heritage School Distance Education Program.

She and her husband, Carlos, have recently returned from a CES mission in Boston, where they taught Institute at Harvard and Boston College. They now teach for BYU. Brother and Sister Adams are the parents of six children, grandparents of thirty-two, and great-grandparents of an adorable little girl.

"proclaim the gospel of peace to the nations of the earth." That was a formidable promise at that time for a patriarch to give a young woman of nineteen. Father's blessing said nothing about going anywhere. In Father's thirty-nine years as a General Authority, he traveled extensively. When her children were young, Mother could not accompany him. He wrote her that he missed her and that his travels were lonely. The fulfillment of her blessing came when her family was grown, and she traveled with him to forty-seven countries, where she was often called upon to speak.

Wherever they traveled, they were greeted with affection by a humble people. While in Japan, Mother was charmed by a five-year-old girl, who smiled with pride when she laced her shoes up on the wrong feet. "People are the same," she wrote. She was grateful to be with Father at the dedication of the temple in Chile in 1983, a temple that came about in response to a prophecy he had made to the Chilean Saints in 1977. Mother noted the people had little but were beautiful and filled with the spirit of love. She was moved by the newspaper padding that covered the holes in their shoes. She watched

have been singing. Now it's your turn." It must not have taken them long to get absorbed in church life. After we moved from our apartment on the west side of Portland to the east side, Dad was put into the bishopric of the Irvington ward. Dad thrived in the bishopric, and, by the time World War II started, was made the branch president of the little Montevilla Branch. I would have been ten or eleven.

By that time, they were pillars of Mormonism. We had family prayers, and though family home evening was not much stressed, we did have evenings together when we played and enjoyed one another. I remember my mother being quite a bit of fun. She loved games and was an ace crokinole player, snapping those little rings into the cen-

Most of the family decisions were family business. We knew when Dad was about to buy a new car or when we were about to move to a new house, and we all got in on the act. The house purchases were especially major events. That is when we heard the family motto, "If it works out, it is right." It seems like a small thing now, but it summed up a deeply held attitude. We put our affairs in the hands of the Lord. It is one of those principles that has remained with me less as a theological position than as a sense of the world. I have always felt that events were a form of revelation. You work and plan and then wait and watch. I tell my children that when they are choosing a school or a job to put themselves into the hands of Providence. You can't know what is best for you. Events have to point the way.

I simply wanted her to LISTEN— and *she did*. I remember that part of the day better than I remember the actual living of my life at school.

ter of the board and knocking out the other players. She could be ruthless in crokinole play. I think she was actually quite competitive. She loved to go to movies, and one of the high points of the month was those evenings when the decision was made to go to the Hollywood theater on Forty-Second and Sandy for a double feature. A large part of the fun was her excitement at going out for an evening.

My mother wanted me to play the piano. That was her idea of an ideal young man: smart, good in school, and musically talented. I simply could not measure up where music was concerned. She tried every incentive to get me to practice, but it was torture for me, and the recitals were even worse. I rejoiced when she allowed me to stop lessons at about age sixteen. It was as if I were released from prison. I stepped away from the piano and never regretted it for a second. She never rebuked me, even though she was a skilled pianist herself. She played for the Relief Society for years when she was in her eighties. I remember her playing "Clair de Lune" when she was younger. I appreciate her willingness to let me stop lessons, whatever her disappointment.

Mother always said that she was a good critic. She had a sense of the best thing to do, whether it was how to live or how to manage an event. I suppose she was restless with my decisions sometimes, but, once I got control of my clothing purchases, I never felt she was hovering over me. She may have disagreed, but she went along. In high school, I was elected student body president and came home every day with loads of worries and experiences. As she was preparing dinner in the kitchen, I would unload all the issues I faced. When she tried to make a suggestion, I dismissed her comments with a wave of the hand. I simply wanted her to listen—and she did. I remember that part of the day better than I remember the actual living of my life at school. I have sometimes told women of the Relief Society that they have no idea of the power they have—just by listening and accepting others. That sentiment comes, I am sure, from those late afternoons in the kitchen with my mother.

She was a fighter. Near the end of her life, when she was afflicted with various illnesses, I would call to ask how she was. No matter what she was going through, she would always say, "I am feeling better." She always thought of herself on an upward track. Until the end, she had been healthy all of her life, entering the hospital only for childbirth. She was a healthy person in body and

Dorothy L. Bushman, Santa Maria, California, 1970.

spirit. Finally, my sister Cherry whispered to her, "Mother you can let go," and she slipped away.

I had reservations about the name she gave me—Richard. As a boy, I worried about being a sissy, and the name didn't help. I would have preferred Joe or even Bill, my brother's name. Eventually, I became Dick and stayed with that through most of my adult life. But I wavered as I grew older. When people asked which I preferred, I would mumble something about either one. When mother died, I made a decision. I would be Richard. Moreover, following the practice of female authors, I would include the distaff name on my writings; I went to three names—Richard Lyman Bushman. I was trying to tell my mother I was proud of her and wanted to be all she hoped.

Dolly

by Susan Easton Black

"Take care of mother" were the last words my father said to me. At the time, my mother was seventy-one, with a blue tint on her graying hair and several aprons neatly tucked in a cupboard. Other than a Cadillac in the garage and discretionary funds to address every whim, mother looked and acted like a typical Mormon housewife of the 1970s. She went to church each week, taught scripture classes in Relief Society, and volunteered occasionally at a thrift shop. She belonged to a book club, a sewing club, and enjoyed membership in a women's league in town.

I anticipated frequent conversations on the phone and occasional visits as all that would be needed to "take care of mother." I envisioned my mother transitioning into widowhood, sitting in an easy chair, skimming a favorite novel as cookies baked in the oven. I saw her continuing Church activity

RELIGION

ETHELYN "DOLLY" LINDSAY WARD
is the mother of

SUSAN EASTON BLACK

Susan Easton Black began teaching at Brigham Young University in 1978. She is a professor of Church history and doctrine and a former associate dean of general education and honors at BYU. A recipient of the Karl G. Maeser Distinguished Lecturer Award, she is the author of numerous articles and books. Susan lives in Provo, Utah, and she and her late husband, Harvey, are the parents of eight children.

and philanthropic efforts in the community and having a reason to polish the silver, knowing a few friends were coming to dinner.

Less than a month after Dad passed on, Mother dyed her hair blonde, pierced her ears, and entertained a large audience with her rendi-

Isolation on the edge of fun was getting her nowhere.

tion of the cancan in a cruise ship talent show. "Take care of mother" now did not seem easy. I had not realized that the years of caring for Dad had taken its toll on her. She was coming out of the home and, in many respects, coming out of a sequestered, if not traditional, lifestyle. She had new friends and new places to go. With diamonds dangling from her ears and party dresses replacing cotton bathrobes, Mother seemed like a different person. "What would Dad say?" I asked my brothers. "Would he recognize her?"

Gratefully, there were still consistent threads in her life that reminded me of the mother I had known—she loved her family and her church. No matter where she traveled in the world, she sent postcards and gifts to all and checked her calendar to make sure she would be at home to attend the baptisms of grandchildren and give her monthly Relief Society lessons.

During one short sojourn at home, Mother was asked to meet with her bishop. At this point in her life, such meetings were rare— like tithing settlement. At the meeting, the bishop told Mother that he felt inspired to give her a new calling—Young Women's president. At the time, Mother was seventy-eight. As she stammered to respond, the bishop

suggested that she take time to think about the calling before accepting. She had always said yes to callings from priesthood leaders, but this seemed different. It had been more than fifty years since she had worked with youth in her ward.

For a week, Mother cried a lot, and we talked more than ever. Her biggest concern was not about accepting the calling; it was, "How will the young girls relate to me?" Before the week's end, she had her answer. She would invite the young women to join her at a swimming party at my brother's house. As it turned out, the party was fun for the young women but not for my mother as she sat near the edge of the pool. She felt isolated and alone. Within the hour, however, she concluded that isolation on the edge of fun was getting her nowhere. She went inside my brother's house and put on a swimming suit. She then walked out to the swimming pool and stepped

The legacy my mother left me is one of moving forward in each phase of life.

Previous page: Susan and Dolly prepare for another journey.

Left: Dolly and Susan, 1992. *Middle*: Susan's high school photo. *Right*: Dolly, 1985.

up on the diving board. The young women watched as Mother jack-knifed into the pool.

Is it any surprise that the young women loved her? They loved her in the pool that day, at girls' camp, and at service projects. They questioned her wisdom when she honked and waved at truck drivers, but they never questioned her love for them. Mother refused to simply observe young women, not at age seventy-eight or during the ensuing years of her presidency. To some of the young women, Mother was their dearest friend. To others, she was a grandmother figure, but to all she was a confidante. Phone calls to me from Mother were now filled with news of "her girls" and their achievements.

The legacy my mother left me is one of moving forward in each phase of life. She never shed the blonde hair or diamond earrings for yesterday's apron. Mother stayed current. Reminiscing over past events, even joyful events, was not all-consuming for her. She knew that my father was waiting in the eternities, and she looked with assurance to their reunion. She was positive that he would still think she was the most beautiful woman he had ever seen. In the meantime, there was life to be lived. Mother died at age ninety-eight. She left a host of friends, all of them much younger than she, and a large posterity who miss her—none more than me.

☞ Always Knew She Knew

by Camille Fronk Olson

Identifying a single incident when my mother taught me an important lesson of faith or virtue has proved most difficult. Her lessons have been a seamless, consistent theme throughout my life by the way she has faced each day, regardless of what it has presented. She is the one unifying thread in all my memories of growing up. How can I separate an isolated teaching? I think the mothers of the stripling warriors were much the same. These young men of unshakeable faith "had been taught by their mothers, that if they did not doubt, God would deliver them" (Alma 56:47). Like my memories of how my mother taught me, these boys did not speak of a perfectly outlined and presented family home evening with lovely visual aids and stunning insights or a single learning experience where the mother clearly defined and testified of faith in Jesus Christ. More likely, such faith was taught

---

Above: Easter Sunday, Roberta and five of her six children, including Camille (age ten in orange coat).

> We got to graze off of any of the produce in the garden or the fruit from the trees for dinner . . . She called it a "garden party."

by demonstrating the same assurance and hope in a constant reality when the future was unknown and often appeared bleak. I say this because that is the way my mother taught me about faith in God and finding joy in everyday life.

My mother, Roberta Harris Fronk, loves and deeply appreciates the simple pleasures in life. She can find delight in a mundane household chore. That is why my memories of growing up are filled with so much laughter and discovery. I remember that she once invited us to the vegetable garden for dinner. She called it a "garden party." Looking back, I suppose her day had not left time for traditional dinner preparation, so she improvised. We got to graze off of any of the produce in the garden or the fruit from the trees for dinner. No preparation was

ROBERTA HARRIS FRONK
is the mother of

CAMILLE FRONK OLSON

Camille Fronk Olson is an associate professor of ancient scripture at BYU. She completed a PhD in sociology of the Middle East, a master's degree in Near Eastern studies, and a bachelor's degree in education. Her dissertation and subsequent research activities have focused on Palestinian families in the West Bank and Gaza Strip. Her current academic interests include biblical studies, women in the scriptures, LDS/evangelical dialogue, LDS doctrine, and the New Testament. She is the author of *Women of the Old Testament*; *Mary, Martha, and Me*; *In the Hands of the Potter*; and *Too Much to Carry Alone*.

Currently, Sister Olson is researching materials for a book on the women of the New Testament, considering the Greco-Roman and Jewish cultures of the time, historical background, geography, and women's roles in society. She was also involved in researching gospel doctrines with three of her colleagues for their book *LDS Beliefs: A Doctrinal Reference*.

Prior to coming to BYU, Sister Olson taught seminary and institute in the Salt Lake City area and served as dean of students at the LDS Business College. She is a former member of the Young Women general board and served a full-time mission to Toulouse, France. She currently teaches Gospel Doctrine in her ward.

Sister Olson is married to Paul F. Olson, a Provo ophthalmologist. She was born in Tremonton, Utah, and still loves the feel of rural communities. She enjoys travel, gardening, running, reading, and time spent with four grandchildren.

of the chores were complex and some rather simple; the game required us to complete the chore we drew out and then take another one until the teapot was empty. Mom played right along with us, and taught us how to do unfamiliar jobs. Thinking of it as a game, I remember the mood in the house was light and playful while we worked. We all tried to finish our chores as quickly as possible, laughing when a sibling drew out the paper that read, "Clean the toilets" and giving a whoop of delight when one of us drew out an exercise challenge that read, "Run around the block." In this way, no one felt picked on, and we all learned how to water plants, clean toilets, and have fun. Learning about God giving Adam and Eve work to do was easy for me to see as a blessing rather than a curse because of Mom's example.

needed, and no cleanup was necessary. Mom celebrated the abundance of what the garden produced right along with the rest of us. She marveled at the miracle of what a small seed could contribute to so many. Without any lesson about proper health or the Word of Wisdom, her constant appreciation for God's gifts from the earth and the efforts Dad made in maintaining a yard full of food-bearing plants made it easy for me to eat my vegetables every day.

Mom made everything a game, making it impossible for us to not want to participate. Together, we all accomplished weekly chores to clean the house by selecting individual tasks written on folded strips of paper and deposited in a brass teapot. Some

When I was still quite young, I recognized in my mother a particular gift of being able to include others in conversation and fun. I was so shy and marveled at how naturally Mom could approach perfect strangers and have them laughing with her and telling her about their lives in seconds. Mom has always seen value and potential in everyone, believing each has a story to tell. She genuinely loves people, and

---

Above: Camille and her mother celebrate Camille's high school graduation.

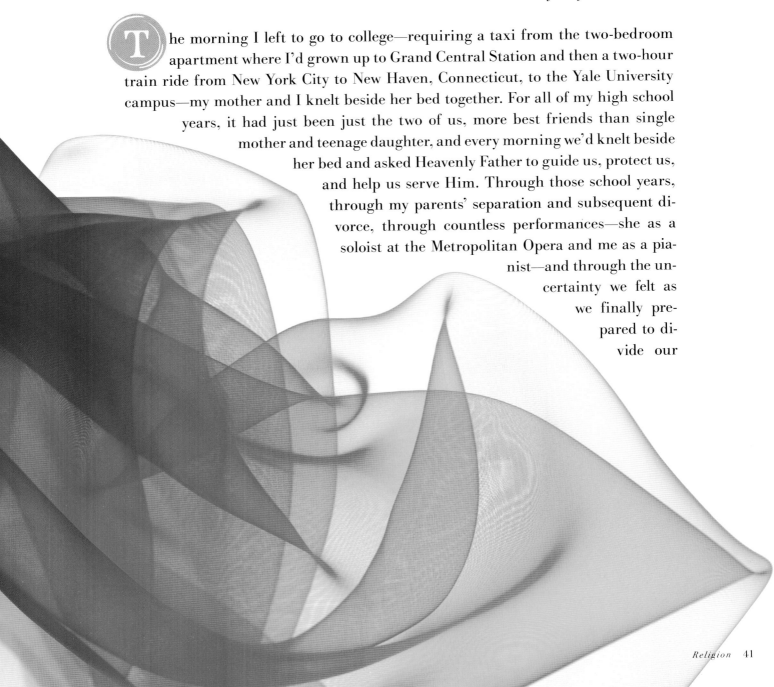

The Woman Behind the Stage

by Neylan McBaine

T he morning I left to go to college—requiring a taxi from the two-bedroom apartment where I'd grown up to Grand Central Station and then a two-hour train ride from New York City to New Haven, Connecticut, to the Yale University campus—my mother and I knelt beside her bed together. For all of my high school years, it had just been just the two of us, more best friends than single mother and teenage daughter, and every morning we'd knelt beside her bed and asked Heavenly Father to guide us, protect us, and help us serve Him. Through those school years, through my parents' separation and subsequent divorce, through countless performances—she as a soloist at the Metropolitan Opera and me as a pianist—and through the uncertainty we felt as we finally prepared to divide our

NEYLAN MCBAINE

is the daughter of

ARIEL BYBEE

Neylan McBaine grew up a member of The Church of Jesus Christ of Latter-day Saints in New York City and attended Yale University. She has been published in *Newsweek, Dialogue: A Journal of Mormon Thought, Segullah, Meridian Magazine,* and BustedHalo.com. She is the author of a collection of personal essays—*How to Be a Twenty-First Century Pioneer Woman* (2008)—and writes regular columns for Patheos.com, a premier religious information portal, and PowerofMoms.com.

Neylan is the founder and editor-in-chief of The Mormon Women Project, an expanding library of interviews with LDS women found at www.mormon-women.com. She is also a creative director at Bonneville Communications and is responsible for the female portraits in the national media campaign found at Mormon.org. She blogs at neylanmcbaine.com. She lives with her husband and three young daughters.

Many people know my mother from her public persona: Ariel Bybee, Metropolitan Opera mezzo-soprano soloist for eighteen years, singing with the likes of Placido Domingo and Joan Sutherland and performing for presidents and prophets. Or at least people older than fifty know of her in that way. If Church members of my generation know of her, it is likely because a five-foot portrait of her hangs outside the DeJong Concert Hall at Brigham Young University. Opera singers don't have the same cache with the younger set. Still, it is always glamorous to be able to tell someone my mother is an opera singer; even those who haven't been to an opera understand the respect demanded by any diva who sings to four thousand people without a microphone.

But I was the one—the only one, due to the fact that I was an only child—who got to see the private side behind the awe-inspiring voice. I got to see the morning prayers, the late night 1930s movie marathons, the Christmas mornings when she invited every stray student in our ward over for the holiday. I was the one who, at age three, interrupted a dress rehearsal of *Hansel and Gretel* (with my mom playing Hansel) because a witch with a green tongue had thrown my mommy into a cage, and I wouldn't stand for it. She was, after all, just Mom. Not Hansel, not Carmen, not Melisande. And at home, when it was just us, I had the honor of falling in step behind the woman beyond the make-up: the devoted mother, the steadfast daughter of God, the woman of faith, but most of all, the woman of power.

Right: Ariel Bybee playing the role of Hansel in *Hansel and Gretel.*

idyllic duo, we had knelt together. That morning, I was going just a short distance geographically but a world away in every other respect. She couldn't lay her hands on my head, but the powers of heaven listened to that prayer and bestowed me with the fierce protection and unreserved confidence that only a mother can summon.

My mother is powerful. At home, on the stage, when she wants to get upgraded to a first-class seat on an airplane . . . my mother conjures a no-nonsense, get-it-done, yet utterly charming demeanor that makes her the most productive woman I know. (My husband says I'm the most productive woman he knows, but he also knows exactly where I get it.) That power—the idea that through intellect, unwavering faith, talent, hard work, and feminine elegance, I could be whatever I want to be and get whatever I want to get—is the greatest gift my mother has given me.

As a single mother and having grown up with a father who eventually left the Church, it would have been easy for my mother

to feel out of place in the Church's patriarchal leadership. And yet, what she modeled to me instead was womanhood reliant solely upon God, not upon the body of a man to bring holy power into our home. While she was forever eager to feed the missionaries and invite male friends to give me priesthood blessings at the beginning of each school year, her confidence in her relationship with her Heavenly Father assured me that we were not lacking validity as a home in Zion. Additionally, I saw a woman who, through her singing, had the power to move

to tears the Apostles themselves through the power of her skill. She did not need to be a man speaking from a podium to open the floodgates of revelation. Her audiences' ears heard the potential of divine power every time she sang "Jesus Lover of My Soul" or one of her virtuosic hymn arrangements. As her accompanist for most of my youth and even now in adulthood, I still thrill at being able to go along for that ride.

But my mother doesn't just live with her head in a churchy idyll. Power to succeed in

She modeled *womanhood* reliant solely upon GOD.

the world is also my mother's legacy to me. Partly because she lived in New York City for twenty-five years and partly because my father was a highly accomplished man of the world who had a profound influence on her, my mother values the abundant life, embracing a world-class standard in everything she endeavors. For example, when tasked with directing a roadshow video for our ward's youth program, she didn't settle for a hack job in the cultural hall. Instead, she called the South Street Seaport maritime museum, and soon my friends and I were filming our skit about pirates-gone-good on the *Peking*, one of the largest sailing vessels ever built from 1911 and which is now docked in a New York Harbor.

This drive to live fully in the world set me aflame too. I remember the specific moment I caught fire. As a senior in high school, I had been accepted to Yale, but I had also been invited to visit BYU as part of a scholarship program there. After a weekend of being wined and dined (or, shall we say, fed mint brownies from the Cougar Eat) by the BYU faculty, I enthusiastically reported on my experience to my mom. "You wouldn't believe the caliber of professors we met with, Mom," I gushed. "It seems like all the professors are Ivy League graduates. The English professor got his PhD from Harvard, and the biology professor has also taught at Stanford. If I go to BYU, I could study with these people!" My mother responded slowly, careful not to dampen my

excitement for what had been a wonderful trip.

"But, lovey," she started, "you don't have to just be *taught* by those people. You could *be* one of those people." My fire was lit. I went to Yale. (And, yes, I even found a fine young Mormon classmate to marry me.)

Like so many mothers, my mother also taught me the power of love. But unlike many other mothers, her loving power came from a place of lack rather than abundance: often misjudged for having "only" one child so that she could emphasize her career, the truth was that my mother had wanted five children but, before the days of IVF, could have only one. She never tired of telling me I was her "five-in-one," everything she had wanted all rolled into one. I was her pearl that grew from the grating of a bad marriage and disappointing pregnancies. I was the legacy, the Samuel to my mom's Hannah, the summation of her hopes and dreams. I grew up knowing I was that special.

Today, I run a nonprofit organization called the Mormon Women Project (www.mormonwomen.com), which is a continuously expanding digital library of interviews with LDS women from around the world. I publish an interview every week, exploring in the women I feature the wide range of unique yet faithful choices our women make in their lives. I'm often asked why I started such an endeavor. I usually give a lengthy answer about trying to create a safe and welcoming place for all women in the Church, not just those who fit a cultural stereotype. The truth is actually much simpler. In my own way, through the stories of powerful, talented, and faithful women everywhere, I'm simply paying forward the gift my own mother gave me: the gift of having a woman to admire.

I'm simply *paying forward* the gift my own mother gave me: the gift of having A WOMAN TO ADMIRE.

Previous page: Ariel as Jenny in the 1984 production of *The Rise and Fall of the City of Mahogonny* (Courtesy Metropolitan Opera). *Above—Left*: Neylan and Ariel, 1990 (courtesy Gideon Lewin). *Right*: Ariel, Neylan, and Neylan's two daughters, 2010 (courtesy Justin Hackworth).

RELIGION

ROBERT L. MCKAY

is the son of

EMMA RAY RIGGS MCKAY

Robert L. McKay was born in Ogden on September 4, 1920. At the age of two, he and his family moved to Liverpool, England, while his father presided over all the LDS missions in Europe. Upon returning to Utah, he attended Lafayette Elementary, Bryant Junior High, and West High School.

He attended the University of Utah, majoring in speech. He was president of Pi Kappa Alpha and was involved in many theatrical productions for the Fine Arts Department.

Upon graduating in 1941, he served a mission to Argentina. Just six months into his mission, WWII broke out. Despite the unrest in Argentina, he completed his thirty-month mission. Upon returning home, he enlisted in the army and served as a medic. He was awarded the Bronze Star for action in the Ryukyus campaign.

He was sealed to Francis Allen Anderson McKay June 28, 1946, by his father, David O. McKay. He and his wife operated McKay Jewelry on 157 South Main in Salt Lake City for sixty-one years. He served his community as president of the Sugarhouse Rotary.

He served in five different bishoprics, as the president of the Temple Square Mission for ten years, and as the first counselor of the Salt Lake Wilford stake presidency for ten years.

He and his wife, Francis, have been married for sixty-seven years. They have four children, eight grandchildren, and thirteen great-grandchildren.

The Art of Motherhood

by Robert L. McKay

My father, David O. McKay, served in the First Presidency and the Quorum of the Twelve for more than sixty-three years—longer than any other General Authority of this dispensation. He traveled more than a million miles as an ambassador of Christ, and through all those years, my mother was at his side, a part of everything he accomplished.

My mother, Emma Ray Riggs—or Ray, as she was called—was born in Salt Lake City on June 23, 1877. Her father said she was named for a ray of sunshine, a fitting name for her. She grew up a quiet, pretty girl, determined and resourceful. One of her teachers at the University of Utah told her she was too shy to ever be a social success. The same day her teacher told her that, they both attended the same evening party. It started out dismally, so Ray went to the piano, improvised some popular songs, and got the young people there singing and playing games. The evening was a great success. The teacher came to her later and apologized for his poor appraisal of her character.

Right: Emma Ray on her wedding day, 1901.

$\mathscr{F}$ly High above the Trees

by Mike Winder

My mom often called me her "Bicentennial Baby" when I was growing up because I was born during America's 200th anniversary year. She loved me and nurtured me as well as one could ever hope. I remember her getting books for me when I began to ask questions about the world, and she would read poems and rhymes, fables and stories, and, of course, the scriptures to us kids.

Mom was terrific to treat my inquisitive nature seriously as a boy, and I remember having deep doctrinal discussions with her at a relatively young age because she would take me seriously. She didn't just brush me off with the simplest Primary answer she could think of but rather engaged with me like an equal. I learned tons that way.

My mom was very organized, and the routine she brought to my small world was very comforting and created an environment where I could learn and have fun. Each day for our chores, she would make a job list and have the kids take turns picking what job they wanted to do. Boys picked first on odd-numbered days, and girls picked first on even-numbered days. We had two jobs on weekdays, four jobs on Saturdays, and no jobs on the Sabbath, birthdays, or holidays. Mom would make up fun names for our jobs. "Feed the tiger" was code for putting the dirty clothes in the clothes hamper, but "feed the dragon" was transferring the dirty clothes from the hamper to the long-necked laundry chute.

In this systematic vein, Mom would give us our allowance each month and, at the same time, give us a tithing envelope in case we wanted to pay tithing on that increase

Right: Sherri with six-week-old Mike, her "Bicentennial Baby."

"We've been asked to **avoid** the very *appearance* of evil, and it is *always* SAFER to fly HIGH above the trees."

then walk around the house pretending to smoke. My mom saw me doing this, but rather than holler at me, she calmly asked me if I thought it was bad to "smoke" crayons. I replied that of course it wasn't bad because they weren't real cigarettes; they were just crayons. My mom then taught me something I have remembered for the rest of my life. "You know, President Kimball has asked us to avoid even the appearance of evil," she calmly said, "and it is always safer to fly high above the trees." That's all she said and all she needed to say. Mom left, and I looked at the cigarette-like crayons in my hand. Even though I was only six or so, I remember going through the logic in my head, *These crayons do look like real cigarettes, so I shouldn't even pretend with them.* I then threw them away. I remember pondering Mom's other advice, "It is always safer to fly high above the trees," and I had in my mind the image of an eagle soaring barely over the tops of the pine trees and then disastrously crashing into them when he wavered one bit and was tripped up in the nearby treetops. The metaphor was clear to me.

Despite the ups and downs that every mortal experiences, I have felt my mom's love and her cheering me along life's journey. She is one of my biggest fans as I try to fly high above the trees. Even now that I'm an adult, I know she never ceases to take an interest in my latest adventure.

Mom passed away in a tragic car accident on September 11, 2011, at the age of

(which we always did—not because Mom made us but because she'd taught us that it was the right thing to do). We learned about budgeting by watching Mom work her cash envelope system each month, with envelopes for haircuts, eating out, groceries, etc. She even had an old sour cream container that held dollars and quarters she used to pay babysitters, because Mom also taught us the value of a weekly date with your spouse and a monthly trip to the temple.

Yes, Mom was an exemplary teacher and looked for teaching moments any chance she got.

One teaching moment still sticks out in my mind. In early grade school, I was at the age where I wanted to look cool with everything I did. I was at home this particular evening, and I thought it would be cool to peel the wrapper off the white crayons, color the end a bit with red and yellow, and

SHERRI JEPSON WINDER

is the mother of

MIKE WINDER

Mike Winder is an American historian, businessman, and politician. He serves as the mayor of West Valley City, Utah's second largest city, where we was recognized as Utah's Best of State mayor in 2011. He was also elected by his peers as president of the Utah League of Cities and Towns.

As a historian, he is the author or coauthor of nine published books on Utah and LDS history, including *When the White House Comes to Zion* and the regional bestseller *Presidents and Prophets: The Story of America's Presidents and the LDS Church.* In 2005, Winder was appointed by Governor Jon Huntsman Jr. to a four-year term on the Utah Board of State History and was reappointed in 2009.

As a businessman, Mike Winder is a strategic advisor for Winder Farms, one of West Valley City's oldest businesses. He was named one of "40 Rising Stars Under 40" by *Utah Business* magazine.

Winder holds a master's degree in business administration and a BA degree in history from the University of Utah. He has also completed executive leadership programs with the Walt Disney Institute of Management and Harvard University's John F. Kennedy School of Government.

Winder is married to the former Karyn Hermansen, a native of West Valley City and a piano teacher. They are the parents of four children: Jessica, Michael, John, and Grace.

fifty-seven, and I take comfort in the many lessons she taught and that she will continue to cheer me on from the other side. I love you, Mom. Or as we kids used to say for years on end when she would drop us off at school, "Bye, Mom, love you, thanks for the ride, see you after school."

Above: Sherri with Mike in 1969.

Work Will Win When Wishy-Washy Wishing Won't!

by Gary R. Herbert

Born in American Fork, Utah, my mother endured a life of challenges. Growing up, her parents were divorced, remarried, and divorced again, and the turmoil associated with those events had a great impact on her life and her faith.

Above: Carol, age five. *Next page*: Carol (left) and her family, about 1945.

Her father (my grandfather) struggled emotionally throughout most of his life. He was raised in an abusive family, in a tough environment where his stepmother made him eat off the floor and locked him in a closet for periods of time. He carried that emotional baggage as an adult, which resulted in him living a selfish, rebellious life that only made him more miserable. He drank too much and turned a cold shoulder to the Church, although he was at times kind, generous, and tenderhearted. My grandmother tried to focus on his good qualities but divorced him twice because she couldn't put up with his poor decisions. Despite his choices, my grandmother chose to be sealed with her children to him after his death. Through all these challenges, my grandmother continued to have unwavering faith, and all four of her children followed her example and remained strong in the gospel.

From an early age, my mother learned to depend on the Lord for protection, guidance, and peace. She believed in what she called her four steps to happiness:

First, stay close to the Lord

Second, pray every morning and every night

Third, pay a full tithing

Fourth, keep the commandments

She reminded us often that these were the essentials to happiness, but more importantly, she convinced us they were all easy to do. She had faith in following this inspired counsel, and it has served her well throughout her life, despite her frequent tests and trials.

My mother was always quiet, but she worked hard and tried to do what was right. She graduated from American Fork High School in 1947, where she and my natural father, Paul Peters, were teenage sweethearts. He was a star athlete; she was in the pep club, and her beauty caught his eye. They attended church together and were married right out of high school. My mother went to work at Geneva Steel as a receptionist and secretary. However, Mom and Dad were both very young, and their marriage ended in divorce after three years. I was their only child, and my mom became a single mother. It was another

CAROL BOLEY HERBERT

is the mother of

GARY R. HERBERT

Gary Richard Herbert is Utah's seventeenth governor. He was born in American Fork and raised in Orem, Utah. Gary attended Orem High School, where he was very active in sports, including football, baseball, and basketball. He also played the trumpet in the band (and still plays the piano to this day). After graduation, he served a two-year mission in the Eastern Atlantic States Mission.

After returning from his mission, Gary attended Brigham Young University. He then met and

married his sweetheart, Jeanette Snelson, from Springville, Utah. Shortly before his marriage, Gary joined the Utah National Guard and served for six years as a staff sergeant, working with target acquisition, artillery, and ground survey.

Gary began his professional career in real estate, founding Herbert & Associates, based in Orem. Along with his real estate career, he and Jeanette opened a commercial child care center, The Kids Connection Daycare, which Jeanette managed for more than twenty years.

Prior to becoming governor, he served as lieutenant governor to Governor Jon M. Huntsman Jr. from 2005–2009. Governor Herbert's public service also includes fourteen years as Utah County commissioner, president of the Utah Association of Counties, and president of the Utah Association of Realtors. He also serves as the chairman of the Economic Development & Commerce Committee for the National Governor's Association.

The governor and his wife have six children and, to date, thirteen beautiful grandchildren.

Left: Carol, age twenty. Middle: Carol with her son Gary. Right: Carol and Duane Herbert's engagement, 1952.

Next page—Left: The Herbert family, 1970. Middle: Herbert family with spouses, 1988. Right: Governor Herbert and his mother at the Governor's Mansion, 2010.

tre-mendous challenge for her, but she remained faithful, and lived by her four principles of happiness.

My mother later married her second husband, Duane Herbert, who adopted me and changed my last name to Herbert. They were a great team! My father eventually started a real estate and construction business, but they both worked hard to make it succeed. In turn, they taught their children the value of hard work. Our family motto was: "Work Will Win When Wishy-Washy Wishing Won't!"

Together, they built a successful business. In their marriage, my mother was a co-equal, a "help meet" (Genesis 2:18), and together they developed a wonderful partnership. Dad built the business; Mom paid the bills, kept the books, and reared and nurtured six additional children: Brent,

Connie, Linda, Susan, Tom, and Holly. They also raised a Navajo foster son named Emerson Jimmy, whom my dad often lovingly called "a really good Indian!"

Money was scarce when my mother was growing up. Her father was frequently gone, and the little money they made was often gambled away. Consequently, my mother learned to be very frugal. Food at home was never wasted. I remember watching her scrape the egg whites out of the egg shells and the remaining butter off the wrapper. Even after my father became a successful businessman, she was hesitant to spend money on anything but necessities.

My mother was also a good steward of her talents and worked hard to develop her natural musical abilities. She learned to play the piano without any formal training. She also taught herself to play the organ and became so proficient she became the ward

She believed wholeheartedly that life's challenges were temporary, and because the Lord wanted her to succeed, things would always get better.

organist. With near perfect pitch, at the age of eighty-two, she could still play piano and was called upon often to share her talents. I was thrilled to be able to show off my mother's piano skills at a Christmas event at the governor's mansion. She played an impromptu piano solo of "White Christmas" and brought down the house!

Mom was always an exceptionally great cook—nothing fancy but always cooked to perfection. Her homemade rolls were the envy of the town. She loved being a homemaker and kept an immaculate house.

My mother's faith is an inspiration to me. Remarkably, she told me that despite enduring many trials throughout her life, she was never sad. She believed wholeheartedly that life's challenges were temporary, and because the Lord wanted her to succeed, things would always get better. She is the most positive and hopeful person I know. Her faith was rock solid, and she inspires

me to be faithful and remember that God will always be there to help me. I, like the young stripling warriors, have been taught by my mother to remain faithful to the end, and "that if [I do] not doubt, God [will] deliver [me]" (Alma 56:47).

I am greatly blessed to have a mother who has set such a great example of faith and obedience. Someday I hope to have as much confidence in the Lord as she had. Someday I hope to be as faithful as she was when asked to endure life's challenges. Someday I hope I can rely on the Lord's protection and love like my mom, who strived to be obedient, for no other reason than "the Lord commanded me" (Moses 5:6).

My mother lived alone as a widow after losing my father to cancer in January 2010. Her last words to him were, "I love you, Duane." Then kissing him on the forehead, she whispered, "Don't take too long to come and get me!" Just eighteen months later, he did.

Assuming the Best of Others

by Mike Lee

My mother was born in France in 1938. Her parents, both of whom were born and raised entirely in Ogden, Utah, had moved to France five years earlier when my grandfather secured a job with the U.S. Treasury Department. His first duty station was at the U.S. Embassy in Paris. The family left France when my mom was a toddler (shortly before the outbreak of World War II) and spent the next two decades moving from one Treasury Department duty station to another. By the time my mother married my father in 1959, her family had lived in France, Michigan, New Jersey, Texas, Mexico, and Japan.

Because her family moved often throughout her childhood—each time to a place and culture very different from the previous one—my mother is familiar with the painful awkwardness of being a stranger. That aspect of her upbringing, coupled with her innate sense of compassion and love for others, has made her an unusually kind friend to all around her. She is the rare type of person who can instinctively sense when someone is ill at ease, quickly ascertain why, and then figure out a way (often within minutes) to alleviate that person's discomfort. She assumes the best of everyone and considers it her duty to stand up for those who find themselves under attack.

As a child, I sometimes found the latter propensity frustrating. I would occasionally come home from elementary school angry, and expecting to find a sympathetic

Mike Lee and his mother, Janet, 2010.

audience in my mom, I would start complaining about another student or express my frustration with a teacher who I felt was being unfair. My mother was always sympathetic but never at the expense of others who were not there to defend themselves. She would invariably articulate every plausible reason why the target of my complaint might have had a perfectly legitimate (or at least understandable) reason to do whatever he or she did to annoy me. I did not always appreciate her keen and unwavering sense of fairness, especially because I wanted my mother to be on my side.

It was not until I was an adult that I fully understood my mother well enough to know that in those instances, she was not disregarding my legitimate concerns; she was simply teaching me that the world is a better place when we assume the best and not the worst of those around us. Through her subtle, consistent example, she taught me about compassion, empathy, and the importance of trying to evaluate life's experiences through the eyes of others. It is an important lesson that has served me well to the extent that I have followed it.

Her approach to life is rooted fundamentally in the kind of optimism that can be explained only by a firm belief in an all-knowing, all-powerful God who loves His children and wants them to be happy. Her ability to see the good in life is a gift that, like other gifts of the Spirit, can be made available to each of us in due time if we ask in faith. My mother sees it as her responsibility to cultivate her contagious optimism as a means of blessing her family. "And all these gifts come from God, for the benefit of the children of God" (D&C 46:26).

The fact that my mother has been blessed with the gift of optimism does not, of course, mean that her life is always easy. She has faced some gut-wrenching challenges in her life, one of which arose when my late father, Rex E. Lee, was diagnosed with stage-four, non-Hodgkins lymphoma—an advanced, aggressive, and often deadly form of cancer. Needless to say, the summer of 1987 was an extremely difficult season for both of my parents. But my mom somehow managed to make it seem less difficult than it really was. In addition to taking care of my father during his illness, she nobly helped all seven of her children deal with the seriousness of this life-and-death situation. Of her seven children, three were married. I was sixteen at the time and was the oldest of the four still living at home—the

> I did not always appreciate her keen and unwavering sense of FAIRNESS, especially because I wanted my mother to be on MY side.

youngest, Christie, was seven. Patiently and skillfully, she helped all of us realistically confront these difficult issues, yet she saw no point in dwelling on the negative. She led

JANET LEE CHAMBERLAIN
is the mother of

MIKE LEE

Mike Lee was born in Mesa, Arizona. He attended BYU and served as student body president his senior year. He graduated with a BS degree in political science in 1994. He later graduated from BYU with a law degree and served a clerkship for Judge Samuel A. Alito Jr., now a Supreme Court justice. He served as assistant U.S. attorney in Salt Lake City before serving as general counsel to Utah Governor Jon Huntsman Jr. He specializes in appellate and Supreme Court litigation and has a legal background in constitutional law.

He ran for the U.S. Senate in 2010, defeating incumbent U.S. Senator Bob Bennett in a primary election. He won the general election to become Utah's junior senator. He was born in 1971 and is the youngest current U.S. senator.

He served a mission to the Texas Rio Grande Valley Mission, returning in 1992. He and his wife, Sharon, were married in 1993 and have three children. They have a home in Alpine, Utah.

us toward hope and peace amidst the turbulent times—to God's eternal plan and the comforting prospect that our Heavenly Father's love would extend into the eternities. My mother's faith strengthened us all. With the variety of emotions associated with my father's illness, for nine years, my mother's example brought constant comfort during uncertain times.

My family's strength and enduring vision throughout my father's disease-ridden years can be attributed to the character of my mother. By 1996, my father's illness had worsened, and he needed to be hospitalized. At the time, he was preparing to argue a case before the Supreme Court and asked my mother to bring his briefcase to the hospital. Willingly and lovingly, she helped my father prepare a case she knew he would never have the chance to argue. Her faith endured through my father's passing and still provides the same vision that continues to bless my family today.

True to her character, she continues to serve the Lord. She has since married Wayne F. Chamberlain. Together they served a mission in Europe and now preside as president and matron of the Jordan River Temple.

I am grateful for a mother who has taught me the importance of compassion, a positive outlook, and charitable service to others. Through her example, I have learned to look for the good in life and be hopeful in the face of adversity. Just like the army of Helaman, I have been taught by my mother that if I do not doubt, God will deliver me (see Alma 56:48).

Family gathering, 2010.

$\mathcal{G}$ive Something Back

by Jim Matheson

About my mother—former Utah First Lady Norma W. Matheson—my father (two-term Governor Scott M. Matheson) always said, "She has the best political instincts in the family." She was, however, an accidental campaigner who grew into the role. Her experience was grounded in a value imparted by one of her teachers, J. Hazel Whitcomb, whom Norma often quoted to her children: "Because we have the privilege of living in this country, we have the obligation to be a participant and to give something back."

Norma was the product of small-town Utah. She lived as a child in Nephi before graduating from high school in Salt Lake. She recalls going door-to-door with her mother, selling paper poppies benefitting veterans for Memorial Day and even donning a poppy costume as she waved from a parade float. Her father, Leo, was an obstetrician; her mother, Ardella Sabine Warenski, was an active community

Norma Matheson, Utah Governor's Mansion, 1981.

Jim and Norma, 2002.

volunteer and medical auxiliary leader. Her father's profession no doubt influenced her love of science. Norma graduated from the University of Utah with a degree in zoology. Both parents shared their enjoyment of the West's beautiful natural environment with their children during trips to parks, mountains, lakes, and canyons.

Through her upbringing, Norma saw first-hand what a difference one individual could make in his or her community. To this day, constituents often approach me by saying, "Your grandfather delivered me," or, "Dr. Warenski was my obstetrician." At times, it

seemed to me as though Grandfather Leo single-handedly brought everyone in Salt Lake County into this world.

I was fortunate to grow up in a house next door to my grandparents' home and across the street from my aunt and uncle. My father supported us as an attorney for Union Pacific Railroad. All the Matheson cousins and friends were one big pack of neighborhood game participants. One time my grandparents—seeing our front lawn turned into a miniature golf course constructed of flattened appliance boxes—worried about the grass surviving our game. Mom reminded them, "I am raising children, not lawn." Norma was the neighborhood mom—actively participating in the local PTA, teaching Primary in our ward, and serving as a Cub Scout den mother.

Drawing on her education and her volunteerism in her children's schools, she worked with my father on a law-related education project that was geared toward

"I am raising CHILDREN, *not* lawn."

secondary school students. It highlighted the role of the judiciary as one of the three co-equal branches of government and featured a "mock trial" competition. Their effort began as a pilot program that was eventually adopted by the Salt Lake School District.

My mother was forty-seven years old when my father was elected governor. That was when she entered an entirely new phase of her life. As that first term in office unfolded, she discovered the joys of traveling around the state with the governor, he to preside over some official function or state meeting and she filling her hours with visits to schools, hospitals, and senior centers. In just two years, she visited every senior center in Utah. That was her introduction to her passion for the cause of Utah's elderly residents—a passion that remains with her to this day. She was an excellent and empathetic listener, whose sincere interest in their lives prompted them to confide in her and share both the joys and the struggles they faced as senior citizens. She has remained a staunch advocate for seniors her entire adult life.

Conversation at the Matheson family dinner table often centered on public affairs and—of course—politics. The conversations were animated and covered a wide range of topics. It was a second pillar of my mother's core values—often emphasized in these discussions—that you must always tell the truth, which strongly sculpted my public service. In fact, both my parents made it clear to their children that honesty was the only acceptable policy.

My father died before I entered political life. Thankfully, my mother was and continues

NORMA MATHESON
is the mother of

JIM MATHESON

Jim Matheson is a sixth-generation Utahn. He was born and reared in Salt Lake City, where he and his sister and two brothers attended Salt Lake City public schools.

He earned a bachelor's degree from Harvard University and his MBA from the UCLA Anderson School of Management. His father, Scott M. Matheson, served as governor of Utah from 1977–1985.

Jim has served five consecutive terms representing Utah's Second Congressional District. During

his time in Washington, Matheson has championed bipartisanship, looking to "reach across the aisle" for commonsense solutions to issues. He is a member of the Blue Dog Coalition—a group of fiscally conservative House Democrats. He serves as the co-chair of the Blue Dog Energy Task Force.

Before his election to Congress in November 2000, Jim worked in the energy industry for thirteen years for several local companies and in his own firm. His wife, Amy, is a pediatrician, and they have two sons, William and Harris.

to be a strong supporter of my decision to campaign and to serve in Congress. She is the one person I talk to every day about issues and the consequences of public policy decisions on Utahns' lives. Her deep and abiding love for this state and its citizens found its most lasting expression in her commitment to J. Hazel Whitcomb's admonition to "be a participant and give something back."

Oatmeal and a Prayer

by Chad B. McKay

Donna grew up in Salt Lake City. She was the great-granddaughter of the prophet John Taylor.

Donna was the second oldest of nine children and was no stranger to work. In her early twenties, Donna dated regularly but was in no hurry to get married. One night she was invited to serve at the wedding reception of her friend Lucille Gold McKay. Donna was hesitant to go, but her mother said, "You might meet Mr. Right"—and indeed she did.

She met Gunn McKay from Huntsville, a strapping young man who was both a farmer and a returned missionary. They dated and eventually married, but she could not have suspected that someday he would be a United States congressman. She couldn't have known that she would host delegates and political dignitaries from around the world. Nor could she have guessed she would attend Christmas parties at the White House or spend a weekend with her husband as guests of the president of the United States at Camp David.

Indeed, she traveled the world on assignment with her husband, who was a member of the powerful House Appropriations Committee. She accompanied him as an "unofficial ambassador" and was expected to act with decorum and statesmanship in support of her husband.

She bore the blessing and burden of being a "mission mom" when her husband became a mission president in Scotland, managing the affairs of the mission home, hosting General Authorities, and caring for large groups of hungry missionaries as they routinely came and went. She was committed to standing by her husband's side and supporting him in his national and international responsibilities.

Donna Biesinger McKay, as the wife of a five-term congressman, dutifully played her part, much the way Abigail Adams did for her husband, John Adams, usually serving quietly in the background, sustaining, supporting, and managing the day-to-day affairs of a busy home.

Together, Gunn and Donna raised ten children. Most of Donna's daily life was consumed with diapers and dishes, dinners and duties. Before microwaves and cell phones, before disposable diapers and gas dryers, Donna spent her days happily enduring the often-mundane tasks of a homemaker. But she did it masterfully, always leaning on prayer and scripture study to make the duties lighter.

I was seventeen years old, sitting in a high school biology class, when I finally came to understand how wonderful my mother was. I was busy talking and was unaware of the topic of discussion until my teacher turned to me and asked, "Chad McKay, what did you have for breakfast this morning?" Looking back, I think my teacher was attempting to teach us about nutrition. I answered

DONNA BIESINGER MCKAY
is the mother of

CHAD B. MCKAY

Chad Biesinger McKay was born in the Olde Rock House in Huntsville, Utah, and enjoyed the country life such a beautiful landscape afforded. At age nine, he was uprooted from country life and moved to a city in Virginia when his father was elected to be a congressman from Utah. You can take the man out of the country, but you can't take the country out of the man, and school years flew by as Chad anticipated spending his summers back in his beloved Huntsville, where he wrangled horses,

hauled hay, and slept on balconies with his many cousins. An amazing turn of events led him to purchasing the Olde Rock House from his parents. During a remodel on the home and while serving as bishop of a large ward, he stopped to change the sprinkler pipes on his hay field and was critically electrocuted with 7800 volts. Through the miracle of priesthood blessings, fasting, and prayer from family, neighbors, and strangers, he lived to raise his large family. Three weeks after the accident, he was allowed a visit home where he cooked his children breakfast from his wheelchair. That tradition continues—minus the wheel-

chair. An attorney by profession—but a farmer by choice—when groans fill the air, he quips, "We aren't raising cows and horses; we're raising hard-working kids." He brings flowers home regularly and shows his children how to lovingly treat a wife with regular date nights, getaways, and temple service. Following the examples of his parents and in-laws, he hopes to give a tithe of his life, living out his life in the mission field with his lovely wife.

Above: Donna Biesinger in high school, 1943.
Right: McKay family with Osmond family at the National Music Awards gala in Washington DC, 1972.

Each challenge I faced was preempted by the FAITH of a loving mother who had armed her teenage son with the proverbial *hug* of a **warm meal** and a *kiss* in the form of **gentle conversation.**

calmly, "I had a bowl of homemade oatmeal mush with brown sugar and raisins. Then I had a glass of orange juice, two slices of homemade wheat bread with butter, and homemade jam. I also had two pieces of bacon and two eggs overeasy, and to wash it all down, I had a tall glass of milk." (Teenage appetites know no bounds.)

As I spoke, the class grew strangely silent. They could not believe my mother would take the time to prepare such an amazing banquet, but little did they know that this type of meal was the norm, not the exception—even for my mother, who always chose to care for us on her own instead of hire household tasks for such duties.

The teacher finished asking the rest of the students what they had eaten for breakfast. Most of the responses were, "I didn't have breakfast" or "I ate cold cereal" or "I stopped by McDonald's for an Egg McMuffin." At Langley High School, in McLean,

just to get us through the winter until the next harvest. It was a monumental task, requiring all of us kids to work very hard alongside her.

She demanded that we obey the rules of the house and keep God's commandments. The consequence of our disobedience was usually that we had to go out and find a willow, which swiftly found its way to our tender backsides. On one occasion, my older brother Von and my sister Donna were herding cows along a dirt road and found a smoldering cigarette. Unable to resist the temptation, they gave in to their curiosity and took turns smoking the cigarette. When they came home, my mother immediately smelled the cigarette smoke on their clothes. She told both of them to go out and find a willow for their spanking. However, when they returned, she took them aside and stated her sadness and disappointment that she had failed to teach them the importance of keeping the Word of Wisdom. My mother insisted that she was the one who needed to be spanked for failing to teach them this important lesson. Von and Donna reluctantly and halfheartedly swatted my mom, but the lesson was powerfully taught. Although I wouldn't recommend such an unconventional approach in today's world, the end result was that each of her children thought long and hard before giving into such temptations to break the commandments.

In the summer of 1941, I was ten years old, and thirteen of us were still living at home. My parents were like many others who struggled financially during the Great Depression. Despite their best efforts, it was clear they wouldn't be able to make their annual payment on the farm. After much prayer and fasting, my father

> My mother insisted that *she* was the one who needed to be spanked.

Left: Taken in 1923 shortly after Forrest Packard left for his first mission in California. Esther C. Packard is holding her son Forrest Elder, who was born April 19, 1923, and died one year later, April 7, 1924.

Right: Esther & Forrest with children Dee, Beth, Cleo, and Jay. Picture taken after the death of baby son Carter in December 1924.

She *never* doubted in that priesthood blessing . . .

signed a one-year contract as a construction worker for the Morris Knudsen Company based in Boise. He figured that during the year, he could make enough money to make the payment on the farm. They gave him a choice of working on Guam, Midway, or Wake Island, and he selected Wake Island, the island closest to home.

My mother recalls receiving a letter from my father, reporting that he had landed in Hawaii on his way to Wake Island. While there, he went to the Hawaii temple and asked the temple president to give him a blessing. He reported in his letter that he was blessed that "he would live to return to find his family chain unbroken." My mother had great faith in that priesthood blessing, and she enjoyed great peace after receiving that letter.

On December 7, 1941, the Japanese attacked Pearl Harbor and simultaneously attacked Wake Island. After a protracted fifteen-day battle, the Japanese prevailed, and all the Americans were captured. For many months after the fall of Wake Island, we didn't know if my father was dead or alive. We relied greatly upon my mother's faith, and she never doubted in that priesthood blessing given to her husband.

Upon learning about the attack on Wake Island, my mother had a feeling that my father wouldn't be coming home soon, so she immediately took matters into her own hands. It wasn't until nearly eight months

later that we received a bulletin from the Red Cross stating that my father was a prisoner of war being held in Japan. So with my mother leading the way, we all pitched in to help support the family. Many times, my mother was out to the barn in her "gum boots" to help us milk nearly fifteen cows each morning and night. Every day we would send the milk to the creamery, and at the end of the month, we received a small payment, yet it simply wasn't enough to pay the bills. Realizing the desperation of the situation, my mother took the only job she could get, selling women's corsets door-to-door. Day in and day out, she would weather the elements, facing rejection after rejection selling women's underclothes.

After nearly eight months, we received a bulletin from the Red Cross that my father was being held as a prisoner of war in Shanghai, then part of Japanese-occupied China. We later learned that he was blessed because he wasn't among the ninety-eight Americans who were left on Wake Island as forced laborers. In 1943, as the Americans threatened to retake Wake Island, all ninety-eight Americans were executed by the Japanese in one of the most notorious war crimes of World War II.

It was a very difficult time, and we struggled greatly during the first year of my father's imprisonment. But my mother didn't quit. It wasn't long before she had sold enough corsets to make the overdue payment on the farm. Within a year, she had eventually saved enough money to rent a small shop twelve miles from our home, where she opened up a dress shop and sold women's clothing. After four and

he remained very weak. My mother traveled to San Francisco to escort him home, and eventually, she nursed him back to health. Meanwhile, she also managed to keep her dress shop open and keep the farm operating.

After a few years, all of my brothers and sisters were sufficiently independent, and my parents prayed to know how they could best serve the Lord. Shortly thereafter, the Lord called my father to serve another full-time mission, taking him to the Eastern States Mission for another two years. Ever faithful, I never heard my mother utter a peep of complaint; her unfailing support was remarkable. Through her faithfulness, our family thrived while my father served the Lord.

My mother took every opportunity to teach us the gospel. Although the Church hadn't officially adopted the family home evening program, my mother set aside a night each week as family night. We had a lesson, played games, and learned the gospel from each other. We had deep gospel discussions, and my mother would

a half years of my father being a POW and despite the difficult wartime economy, Mother had not only made the payments on the farm, but she was also able to pay off both the house and the farm.

When my father was liberated in 1945, he weighed about 120 pounds. He spent a few weeks in a rehabilitation hospital, where they helped him regain his strength, but often play devil's advocate, making us defend our beliefs. She would challenge us to make an effort to learn the gospel as she had and to discipline ourselves to read the scriptures every day. I remember distinctly when she challenged me to read the Book of Mormon, and she promised that if I did, she would give me a handsome reward of ten dollars. I eagerly read it, and she quizzed me often to follow my progress. It was the best ten dollars I've ever earned because I have spent a lifetime reading and rereading that marvelous book.

My mother's incredible diligence and perseverance eventually gained her quite a reputation. She was nominated and won the title of "Idaho Mother of the Year" and went on to compete for the national title, where she was the runner-up.

Upon my father's return from his mission, they agreed to sell my mother's dress shop and move to Bountiful, Utah, where several of my brothers and sisters were living. My older brother had a pilot's license, and he shuttled my parents back and forth to Idaho as they completed the sale of their home and business. On a cold, stormy spring day, March 30, 1957, the plane iced up and crashed. My father was left an invalid for the rest of his life. My mother was gravely injured and subsequently died three days later.

Her funeral was held on a Saturday afternoon, April 6, 1957. It was conference weekend. President David O. McKay was so touched by my mother's incredible story and was so heartbroken by the circumstances of her death that he asked Elder Henry D. Moyle of the Quorum of the Twelve to skip conference and preside at her funeral.

My mother never held a so-called "high office" in the Church, but she served diligently in all her callings as a visiting teacher, instructor in Sunday School, and president of the YWMIA in her ward, among many other assignments. Yet the attendance of an Apostle at her funeral indicates the honor and respect she gained for her lifetime of dedication to serving the Lord.

As I reflect on the countless things I learned from my mother, I believe the most important life lessons she taught me are these:

Follow the brethren;
you'll never go wrong if you do

Keep the commandments—
each and every one of them

Work hard every day
(even in your Church callings)

Be faithful; God will never abandon
you

Be self-reliant

Study the scriptures daily

As a family, we followed my mother's advice. If the accomplishments of her children are any indication of my mother's effectiveness, then she did exceptionally well. In all, six of her children went on to obtain graduate degrees (PhD or equivalent), and all of us became successful in the trades we pursued.

Spiritually, she prepared her children to become leaders in the Church. Among her children are many sister leaders, several

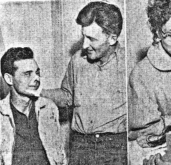

WRECKED IN LANDING—A mountain top crash landing severely damaged this light plane Saturday. Only the pilot walked away as three of the four occupants were seriously injured when weather forced the craft down near the Utah-Idaho border. (Picture by A. H. Reiser Jr.)

PILOT AND RESCUER—D. R. Packard, left, pilot of the downed plane, talks with rancher Chester Kunzler who assisted in rescue after Packard hiked 13 miles for help.

FRACTURES BACK — Brother of the pilot, William (Ace) Packard, suffered a fractured back in the crash landing. He is comforted by his wife, Joyann Packard, in hospital.

On March 30, 1957, Esther and Forrest Packard were being flown by their son between Idaho and Bountiful as they completed the sale of their business and home, when the plane iced up and crashed.

Below: This truck carried the injured bodies from the airplance crash. Notice the blankets in the back—they were used to cover the injured bodies. This was the only 4x4 truck in Park Valley (Box Elder County) at the time.

Bountiful Plane Victims Improve

FORREST L. PACKARD
... hurt in crash landing

TREMONTON—Two men and a woman, members of a Bountiful family who were injured Saturday when their light plane crash landed on a Utah mountain top near Idaho, were reported in "fair" condition and "improving slightly" Monday.

The trio, passengers in the small plane, were hospitalized in the Bear River Valley Memorial Hospital.

Pilot of the plane, D. R. Packard, 39, Bountiful, was treated for lacerations and released to his home Saturday.

Injured were Forrest Packard, 64, and Mrs. Esther Packard, 62, parents of the pilot, and William Packard, 22 a brother.

The forced landing occurred Saturday about 8:30 a.m. while the Packards were flying from Bountiful to Boise Idaho. low clouds and rain caused ice to form on the wings of the plane and the craft had to crash land.

After the landing, the pilot was the only one able to leave the plane. He walked 13½ miles to the J. J. Kunzler ranch in Park Valley to get help.

The elder Mr. Packard suffered a possible dislocated hip and internal injuries. His wife suffered a possible skull fracture and lacerations, while William Packard sustained a fractured back.

The rancher, Mr. Kunzler, drove to Snowville to telephone the Box Elder County sheriff's office for help and his two sons returned to the plane with blankets and food about 2 p.m. Chester and Darrel Kunzler climbed the mountain to the site of the downed plane where they

chopped down saplings and made stretchers with their coats and transported the injured down the steep mountain.

The victims were taken to the Kunzler ranch and then to the Lawrence Carter ranch, where a Salt Lake physician, Dr. A. Hamer Reiser Jr., and his wife, a nurse, were visiting relatives.

The Reisers treated the injured until help arrived to remove them to Tremonton. They arrived in Tremonton about 6:30 p.m.

The pilot, a Bountiful building contractor, said he took off from the Bountiful Sky Haven airport about 6:30 a.m. Saturday.

"The weather was clear until the Utah-Idaho border, when heavy clouds and rain reduced visibility to zero and iced the plane's wings," Mr. Packard said.

"I circled a small settlement in Park Valley trying to make up my mind about what to do, then decided to try the other side of the mountain to the west and north," he continued.

"But the wings iced up, and I just couldn't hold altitude," the pilot explained.

Mr. Packard set the plane down on a mountain top on Dove Creek Divide.

bishops and stake presidents, three mission presidents, and three temple presidents.

Yet despite the accolades and successes of her children, she remained unpretentious and never assumed any credit for preparing us for any of our achievements. It wasn't until the last day of her life, as our family tended her at her bedside, that she quietly and reluctantly admitted, "I've been a good girl."

Indeed, Mom, I think you've been a very good girl.

[1] Neal A. Maxwell, "The Holy Ghost: Glorifying Christ," CES Broadcast, 2 Feb. 2001.

We Can. We Will. We Must.

by Harry Reid

Every generation makes the same promise. We strive and struggle to give our children a better life than we had. That includes sharing our values with them so they will one day work to make their children's lives even better than their own.

That's the promise of America and, for me, the purpose of public service.

I'm not quite sure when or where I learned that lesson or who taught it to me. I wish I could say I grew up in a house where we sat around the kitchen table and talked out our problems and our dreams. I wish I could say my moral compass as a boy had a true north. But it wouldn't be honest for me to say so.

When I grew up in Searchlight, Nevada—a desolate desert mining town years past its prime—religion was as hard to come by as hot water. You could count thirteen brothels in town but not a single church. And inside my family's tiny home, the closest thing we had to a religious symbol up on our wall was—a pillowcase. No picture of Christ, not even a cross.

a pot-bellied pig, she understood the lessons to be learned from taking care of animals. I learned responsibility and what it feels like to have others depend on me. I wasn't always responsible in taking care of my animals, so my mom did play backup for me at times, but the lessons I learned were invaluable.

Despite my protests, my mother knew exactly what she was doing. Little by little, my rough edges softened, and before long, I had unknowingly become a little less self-centered and a bit more kind and loving, like my mom.

When I turned sixteen, we were living in Arizona, and my parents allowed me to choose a special gift to celebrate this milestone birthday. Although I might have asked for a new car, I surprised my parents (and myself) by asking to go visit my ailing grandfather in Florida.

"Mac," as he was known, was my grandfather on my dad's side. He was an iconic figure, having served for decades with the FBI. Both his size and impeccable reputation made him a true man of stature.

My mom and dad allowed me to travel alone for the first time, and I didn't notice their concern when they nervously put me on a plane. After arriving safely in Florida, I had a great reunion with my step-grandmother at the airport.

My mother had warned me that Mac was suffering from some type of dementia, but I didn't know the seriousness of his condition until I walked into his room at the nursing home. I was stunned to see that he had nearly withered away, lying in his bed, somewhat incoherent and unable to walk.

PEGGY ANN WOOD CHAFFETZ
is the mother of

JASON CHAFFETZ

Congressman Jason Chaffetz was elected as representative of Utah's Third Congressional District after mounting a grassroots campaign that stressed fiscal discipline and included no paid staff, no polling, no free meals for potential voters, no campaign office, and refusal to go into debt to finance the campaign.

He grew up in California, Arizona, and Colorado, and was invited to Utah in the mid1980s by legendary BYU football coach LaVell

Edwards to be a placekicker. He drove to Provo with a few hundred dollars in his pocket and everything he owned piled into his car. At the time, he had no idea how much his experiences at BYU would shape his life. He set two school records at BYU as a starting placekicker and earned a degree in communications.

He served as campaign manager for Utah Governor Jon Huntsman Jr. and worked as the governor's chief of staff. As part of his assignment in Congress, he is the chair of the House Subcommittee on National Security, Homeland Defense, and Foreign Operations.

He has been featured in the national press for his fiscally conservative practices. He appeared on *The Colbert Report* in 2008, where he was defeated by Stephen Colbert in a leg wrestling match. He is also known for sleeping on a cot in his Congressional office rather than paying for living quarters in Washington DC.

He and his wife, Julie, have three children, Max, Ellis, and Kate.

In fact, he was completely incapable of taking care of himself.

It suddenly dawned on me that while I was there, it was my responsibility to help him as much as I could. He had a day pass to leave the nursing home, and I decided to get him ready. He had lost so much weight that I easily scooped him up from his bed and set him in his wheelchair, then wheeled him out to the waiting car. I also took care of his other physical needs throughout my visit.

It was a humbling experience, and I amazed even myself by stepping up to care for him during my visit. It was also a life-changing event as I realized I could be a man and still be tender and loving at the same time. Frankly, I didn't know I had it in me, but I credit my mother for teaching me that a real man is both meek and powerful.

I'll never forget saying good-bye to him. Looking into the eyes of my helpless dear grandfather, for a brief lucid moment, we connected with each other. I saw through his pained gaze an understanding of the seriousness of his condition, but because of his inability to communicate, we recognized that these were our last moments together. This event remains a difficult and emotional memory, but it also helps me remember the strength my mom gave me to figure out who I am and be proud of it.

Even more painful, I lost my mother in 1995 after an eleven-year battle with breast cancer. To this day, if I've had an especially good or bad day, for a split second, I think to myself, *I need to call Mom and tell her.* But instead, I get on my knees and thank my Heavenly Father for giving me a mother who taught me to love.

I miss her terribly.

I credit my mother for teaching me that a **real man** is *both* meek and powerful.

Wedding of William and Carol Jeanne Godfrey, 1964.

Through Adversity, Strength

by Matthew Godfrey

Mom always dreamed of having eight children. She married Dad, William Godfrey, at nineteen, which certainly seemed to pave the way for her plans. They quickly had four children, each of them about two years apart. They had their fifth child, Rebecca, in July of 1976. Twelve days after Rebecca was born, Mom and Dad awoke to a lifeless baby. They started CPR and immediately called a neighbor, who was a nurse, to assist as they drove to the hospital. In the end, they were unable to revive baby Rebecca.

Mom and Dad came home from the hospital to inform us, their four young children, that Rebecca was not going to be able to grow up with us. We knelt and prayed together as a family, and then they reassured us that because of their temple marriage, we would all get to be with Rebecca again. It was an understandably difficult time for us all, but life quickly resumed as normal.

Less than a year later, Mom became pregnant. We were excited and a bit nervous for the new addition to the family. Mom and Dad were blessed to have a healthy baby girl. Then, two years and one miscarriage later, Mom was six months pregnant again, but something didn't feel right, and Mom was rushed to the hospital. The baby was coming early, but the joy quickly turned to sorrow when the baby was stillborn. While dealing with a mother's grief for a baby that had been carried for so long, the doctors and nurses became alarmed at her loss of blood. The

GOVERNMENT & POLITICS

CAROL JEANNE GODFREY

is the mother of

MATTHEW GODFREY

Matthew R. Godfrey is the youngest person to be elected mayor in the history of Ogden, Utah. Recently completing his third term, Mayor Godfrey opted not to run for a fourth term. During his tenure, he helped rebuild the city, and Ogden is fast gaining a reputation as a high-adventure destination. He and his wife, Monica, have five children: Natasha, Harrison, Danielle, Tyler, and Grant.

Born and raised in the Ogden area, Matthew

attended Weber County public schools. He was awarded a scholarship to Weber State University, where he earned the distinction of being an NCAA All-American in track and field. He graduated with a bachelor's degree in finance and a master's in professional accounting. He later taught courses at WSU in quantitative analysis, business calculus, and finance.

An avid adventurer, Matthew enjoys skiing and hiking; he rides his bike to work most days in the summertime and has been known to play Frisbee in the park. He is also a regular participant in the Ogden Marathon.

doctor called for freshly donated O+ blood in hopes that it would coagulate and stop the bleeding. She was given all the hospital had.

Hospital staff called our family to tell us there was a significant chance Mom would not live. The family gathered for prayer and knelt for an extended time, pleading with the Lord that Mom would be permitted to stay with her five children and husband that were here on earth. Mom later tracked the time of the family prayer to the time the hemorrhaging abated, and it didn't surprise her that the times matched.

We grew up in a home of faith and closeness. Mom would often refer to spiritual experiences that transpired as a result of her trials. Her faith in the Savior grew with each earthly challenge. The gospel was the center of our lives and Mom exemplified it with near perfection.

Malinda, the oldest, was married in the temple, and Jason, the oldest boy, left on a mission to Puerto Rico. On a warm July evening in 1988, the family received a visit from Bishop Shurtleff, who, with his head

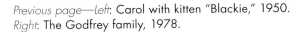

Previous page—*Left*: Carol with kitten "Blackie," 1950. *Right*: The Godfrey family, 1978.

Above—*Left*: The Godfrey family, 1989. *Right*: Carol upon winning Utah Mother of the Year, 1985.

lowered, informed us that Malinda, who lived in a new condo in a nice neighborhood in Costa Mesa, California, had just been murdered in her home.

Shock and disbelief surrounded our family as we gathered once again to pray for strength and understanding from Heavenly Father. During that prayer, we made many requests. The petitions I remember most were those for the person who had committed this horrific act and that he would not do this to anyone else. And we prayed for his soul. There was also a blessing requested for the family of the perpetrator, that they might feel peace and comfort and know that there wasn't animosity toward them but rather a desire for their healing as they came to discover this tragedy.

This dramatic event was hard to comprehend for our family because we had always lived in the small town of Harrisville. It was peaceful, and our home was a home absent of arguments and profanity, much less violence.

Quick healing came to all members of the family except Dad, who had a tenderness for this loss for some time. In many ways, it was a positive change for him personally and spiritually.

She never defined herself by her challenges.

Over the years, there were many economic challenges as well. Dad worked diligently to provide for the family but always worked on commission, and there were many months without much, if any, income. Years later, Mom told the family about how she would go to the empty fridge and cupboards to try to figure out what she could make for dinner. A creative thought would come to mind about something she could make from nothing, but she knew this meal would be the last she would be able to provide. She commented that there were many times when she would go through that routine for weeks at a time. Someone might drop something off, or in some way a door would be opened that would allow the family to eke out one more meal. We chikdren were largely unaware of the oft-destitute circumstances.

The nurses . . . emerged from the room in *tears*, amazed by the POWER and SWEETNESS of her FAITH.

There were Christmases when there wasn't money for both food and presents, but not wanting their children to go without in any way, Mom and Dad would go to the DI and, for a few dollars, cobble together a Christmas. We children never knew.

Mom was asked to speak all around the area about how she was able to deal with so many losses. These requests surprised her because she never defined herself by her challenges. She never assumed that she had any more than anyone else. Her talk theme was "Joy Through Adversity," and everyone who heard it received it well, especially all who had known her personally and had seen her remarkable faith and resilience.

On September 2, 2007, Dad was in a terrible car crash. Mom was rushed to the hospital by a Harrisville bishop and ran into a frantic emergency room, where a team was working desperately to keep Dad alive. The pace soon slowed as the physician, a family friend, came out of the ER with tears streaming down his face to inform Mom that they had done all they could to save him. She was invited in to say her good-byes. During that time, she talked to Dad as though he were still alive and listening and asked him to send her love to their three children who were now greeting him on the other side. She hoped the reunion would be sweet with his parents, who had died many years earlier. She told him that she would be fine and that he needed to stay focused on the work ahead of him. The nurses that were still attending to things in the emergency room heard this marital epilogue and emerged from the room in tears, amazed by the power and sweetness of her faith.

Mom never got her eight children but did help parent thirty-six other children through foster care. Her biological children remain very committed to the gospel. The boys all served missions, and all her children married in the temple. She lives alone today but continues serving and lifting those around her. Mom's testimony of Jesus Christ and His restored gospel is stronger because of a life of trials.

*Y*ou're Home

by Mark R. Van Wagoner

My favorite memory of my mother was an evening we spent together at the Utah premier for the motion picture *Annie*. It was an incredible evening; it started with a fully catered and luxurious dinner at the estate of the late O. C. Tanner and then moved to the old Villa Theater to see the movie.

I noticed tears in my mother's eyes several times during the movie, which was unusual because my mother never cried. Afterward, I asked her why she was so moved by this story. I knew before she answered.

"Because this is my story," she said.

Joy Beck was born April 16, 1928, to a mother and father I never knew. They were both severe alcoholics and abandoned their five children regularly for weeks at a time.

One of my mom's first memories is that of her older brother sawing pieces of wood from under the little house they lived in for firewood just to stay warm. Another memory is that of her father breaking down the motel door, where she was staying with her mother, and almost killing a man that was in the room with her. Those early childhood memories made quite an impact during my mother's formative years.

COMMUNICATION

JOY BECK VAN WAGONER

is the mother of

MARK R. VAN WAGONER

Mark Van Wagoner has been a professional broadcaster, emcee, on-air host, and radio personality for almost forty years. He is best known by his on-air nickname, "Mark in the Morning." He attended the University of Hawaii in Hilo, and he first entered broadcasting in Hawaii in 1969. He then came to Utah in 1971, where

he was hired as a deejay at KRSP, a popular hit radio station in Salt Lake City. He spent close to fifteen years at KSL radio and television, where he hosted a popular morning radio show; most recently, he was the morning host at KDYL AM 1060. He currently works with the LDS Employment Resource Services as an instructor for career workshops and as part of their professional resource staff.

Eventually, in 1932, the State of Utah came in and took the children away from their parents and put them in an orphanage. Her three brothers were adopted quickly because local farmers in the area could use them to help with the chores and running a farm.

Her sister was adopted a year later, and my mother was left behind. Her housemother told her, "You're a bad girl. You wet the bed and will never be adopted."

Mom remembers hiding behind trees and bushes at the orphanage while prospective parents came in and chose a child to take home with them. She believed that she was unadoptable and unlovable. But like Annie, there was always a dream.

After more than three years in the orphanage, a beautiful car pulled into the driveway, and the man who emerged from this vehicle asked for little Joy Beck. His name was Vernal Huffaker, a farmer from Midway, Utah. Vern had adopted my mother's sister two years earlier and had come to get my mom. To my mother, he was "Daddy Warbucks."

My mother had never been in a car like that one and remembered that drive from American Fork to Midway as an astronaut would remember a trip to the moon. It all seemed too unreal for her. Mom's insecurities from a horrific childhood prevented her intelligence (she was a certified genius) from comprehending the change that was about to take place in her life.

She believed that she was unadoptable and unlovable.

It became real when they arrived at her new home. Shep, Vern's dog, ran out to the car and barked at young Joy. Vern scooped little Joy into his arms and scolded Shep, saying, "You will never bark at my princess again," and then he wrapped both arms around her and said, "You're home." My mother's heart melted, her self-protective shield dropped, and she knew then that dreams can come true.

"Uncle Vern" was chided by several neighboring farmers who asked why he would adopt girls when boys could be more useful helping on the farm. He simply said, "They need me."

Mom's life did change. She was treated like a princess, and her intelligence became evident almost immediately. It was hard for them not to notice her constant questions, her nose always in a book, and her love of learning. Uncle Vern dubbed her "My Wise Little Owl."

My mother excelled in school all the way through the University of Utah, where she was president of the Tri-Delts (Delta Delta Delta), and her goal was to finish her graduate work in England. She loved everything English, and Cambridge was her ultimate wish, but love got in the way.

She fell in love with the handsome head cheerleader at the university, an incredible athlete, fellow student, and active Mormon. Mom had been baptized a member but, like Uncle Vern, was not really active in the faith.

That all changed with her marriage to my dad, and they were sealed in the Salt Lake Temple. Mom put aside her dreams and had six children within the following ten years.

My father had wanderlust, and mom followed him whenever and wherever he decided to move. Her dreams were put aside for her new husband and family.

Everywhere we moved, Mom was always asked to be the Primary or Relief Society president, and she served faithfully from California to Kansas, New Jersey, Hawaii, and Salt Lake City. She also taught in the high school everywhere we moved. Our family's longest stay was in Salt Lake City, where Mom became head of the English Department for South High School.

She was a school district star, always serving on committees and boards, promoting education and teachers' rights and needs. However, tenure is the name of the game in education, and whenever we would move, Mom would have to start from the bottom—but she would always rise to the top.

I can't tell you how many times I'd be with my mother and someone would run up to her and embrace her tightly and through tears exclaim, "You were the best teacher I ever had." She was the best teacher I ever had. She was also my confidant, my counselor, my friend, and my coach.

Mom was my speech coach, and we would enter every speech contest we could find—and won our fair share. The highlight was winning the *Reader's Digest*/Boy Scouts of America "Report to The Nation" National

contest. It made the headlines in Hawaii, where we were living at the time, and we became quite the speech contest team.

High intelligence can be a blessing and a curse. It was both for my mother. She would see things differently and always questioned the status quo. She taught us children to always question life, to question our leaders, and to know that there were always two sides to every story. She taught us to never judge anyone.

She also taught us to never make anyone feel small and that "all men are created equal." She taught us to love nature and all living things. (Needless to say, we were not hunters or even fishermen. Taking any life, even spiders, was taboo in our home.)

She taught us to avoid mediocrity and always do the very best we could. I remember having to memorize and recite a poem in a seventh grade speech class and asking my mom if she had any ideas. I ended up memorizing and reciting a portion of Geoffrey Chaucer's *Canterbury Tales* in Old English! Modern pronunciation of Chaucer's works is one thing, but to recite in Old English? (Ask me if I received an A on that assignment!)

Mom hated contention and confrontation of any kind. She was a champion of the underdog, and her love of learning never ceased. She loved "real" conversations, where people would truly open up and share their deepest thoughts. She had no time for shallowness. She loved politics and discussing the turmoil in the world and what we could do to be better citizens.

After all the children had grown and were launched into the world, she accomplished her dream and did finally get to Cambridge in England for her continued education. She loved every second of it! Besides being an incredible teacher, she was a great writer. (I wish I could share some of her essays with you.)

She was about to write a book when tragedy struck—Alzheimer's. The worst thing that could have happened to my mother did happen. She started losing her beautiful mind, and she knew it. That knowledge, plus her early childhood trauma resurfacing because of the disease, made the last few years of her life a living hell.

We would sit together and recite the poems she could remember, especially "Invictus" by William Earnest Henley. That was her favorite. Later, her anxiety increased to inhuman levels, and the facility we had to put her in did everything they could to make her comfortable.

The last day of her life, she became Mom again. Instead of her overwhelming fear and anxiety, she was calm, happy, and even singing! (Mom never sang around her children; it was not one of her talents.)

The amazed staff asked her what was going on and why the total reversal in her demeanor. She told them, "Uncle Vern is coming. He is going to take me home!"

They attributed it to a new medication they had put her on and considered it gibberish, not knowing Mom's childhood history.

But Mom knew. The next morning, they found her on the floor, with her shoes on her feet and a smile on her face. Uncle Vern did come to take Mom home, again. I know this.

Mom was definitely part of the "greatest generation"—living through the Depression, rebuilding this country, and always putting her family and society first. She taught me that seeking the greater good would benefit us all more than individual desires to "follow one's own star." She put aside her wants and desires and put her energy into the rising generation, and we are so blessed because of her selflessness.

I know where my mother is. She is teaching, writing, and serving beyond the veil. She is the "master of her fate and the captain of her soul." I miss you, Mom. So very much.

> She started losing her *beautiful* mind, and she knew it.

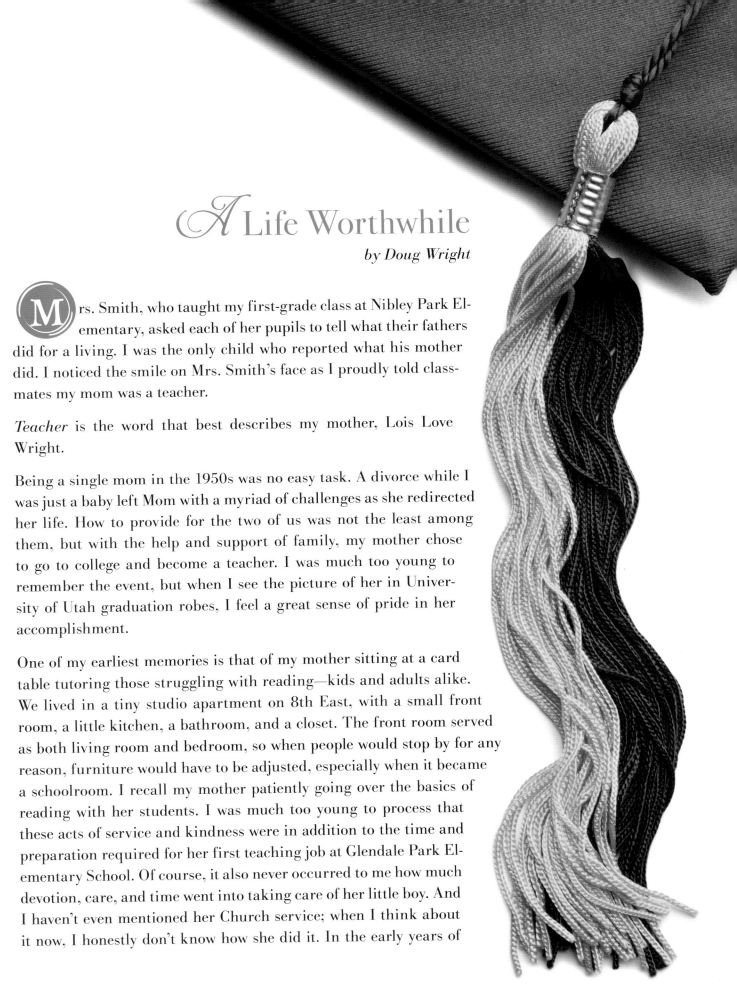

A Life Worthwhile

by Doug Wright

Mrs. Smith, who taught my first-grade class at Nibley Park Elementary, asked each of her pupils to tell what their fathers did for a living. I was the only child who reported what his mother did. I noticed the smile on Mrs. Smith's face as I proudly told classmates my mom was a teacher.

Teacher is the word that best describes my mother, Lois Love Wright.

Being a single mom in the 1950s was no easy task. A divorce while I was just a baby left Mom with a myriad of challenges as she redirected her life. How to provide for the two of us was not the least among them, but with the help and support of family, my mother chose to go to college and become a teacher. I was much too young to remember the event, but when I see the picture of her in University of Utah graduation robes, I feel a great sense of pride in her accomplishment.

One of my earliest memories is that of my mother sitting at a card table tutoring those struggling with reading—kids and adults alike. We lived in a tiny studio apartment on 8th East, with a small front room, a little kitchen, a bathroom, and a closet. The front room served as both living room and bedroom, so when people would stop by for any reason, furniture would have to be adjusted, especially when it became a schoolroom. I recall my mother patiently going over the basics of reading with her students. I was much too young to process that these acts of service and kindness were in addition to the time and preparation required for her first teaching job at Glendale Park Elementary School. Of course, it also never occurred to me how much devotion, care, and time went into taking care of her little boy. And I haven't even mentioned her Church service; when I think about it now, I honestly don't know how she did it. In the early years of

COMMUNICATION

LOIS LOVE WRIGHT
is the mother of

DOUG WRIGHT

For more than two decades, Doug Wright's name has been synonymous with KSL radio in Salt Lake City. He has long been recognized as a trusted voice on the airwaves of the Intermountain West, and faithful listeners depend on his knowledge of worldwide political and current events to keep them informed.

Doug is a Utah native, is proud of pioneer roots tracing back to the 1840s, and was raised in the Salt Lake City/Sugarhouse area. He began his broadcast career while still a high school student and has been honored with many awards for his professional and community efforts, including induction into the Utah Broadcast Association Hall of Fame.

He is an avid reader who loves history, coin collecting, his historic home in Eureka, movies, and, of course, his family. Married for almost thirty years to D. Wright, the Murray City School District public relations specialist, they are proud parents of three unique and interesting young adults: Katy, Ian, and Eric.

her career, she didn't even have a driver's license and traveled by bus, complete with transfers, for the commute to work every day.

For thirty-three years, my mother taught in the Salt Lake City School District, most of those years in the northwest part of the city. Former students have often approached me and asked, "Was your mom the Mrs. Wright who taught at Jackson Elementary?" Sometimes they would ask about Riley, Riverside, or even eastside schools like Clayton, Hillside, or Indian Hills. Answering in the affirmative, I'd be treated to a story about my mother, usually telling of a very tough teacher but always including how much she cared and what a difference she made. Some even told of the times my mom wento to bat for them, including appearances in court.

I'm truly impressed that with all of the difficulties my mother faced, she provided an incredible childhood for me. She always looked for fun and expanding opportunities. On a very limited budget, she provided piano lessons, tickets to plays, swimming lessons, and more. She was always ready for little excursions around the state that often included my grandparents and cousins.

Recalling our several little apartments affectionately dubbed "the cracker boxes" and finally our home east of the Villa Theater, I remember them filled with music and books.

Reading has always been a love and a priority for our family. Curling up in my mother's lap as she read to me is an indelible memory. Going hand in hand with appreciation of literature is the love of music—a consistent source of happiness in my mother's life. From her girlhood to today, she has always shared her musical talents. I doubt there is anyone who knows her who hasn't directly benefited from those talents through her singing performances at events that range from weddings and funerals to various choir recitals. To this day, hearing certain songs and stories will immediately transport me back to those years.

Today, when I walk through the front door of my mother's home, odds are I'll still

find her absorbed in simple acts of service and kindness. Sometimes she'll be sitting on her couch surrounded by books and papers, all being distilled into a lesson plan. Often I'll find her out on the breezeway carefully cutting, gluing, and assembling thoughtful gifts destined for family and friends. Frequently, she'll be in the kitchen preparing a meal or treat with a special destination in mind.

My wife, D., and I, along with our three children, Katy, Ian, and Eric, have been blessed by my mother's profound love. Affectionately known to my kids as "Grammy Lou," her home has always been a haven. Every holiday, birthday, or special occasion calls for

Previous page: Lois Wright graduating from the University of Utah.

Right: Doug and his mother, 1957.

decoration and celebration that is sure to include extended family and friends. Somehow she always comes through, whether it's wielding a paintbrush at our home in Eureka or staying up late to help a grandchild or cousin with a school assignment, Mom has always been willing to drop everything in order to help.

When I think of Albert Einstein's famous quote, "Only a life lived for others is a life worthwhile," my mother immediately comes to mind.

Above: Lois Wright missionary photo, 1949.
Below: Lois with Doug's children, Katy, Ian, and Eric, in 1988.

No Substitutions

by Sandra Stallings Jenkins

The best part about coming home from school every day was finding my mom and giving her a hug. She was the center, the hub of our family, where things happened. Once I had checked in with her, I would fix a piece of home-made toast. Mom made four loaves of delicious bread every Saturday. I would slice through the golden buttery crust and slide the thick bread into the toaster. Meticulously, I'd spread the butter from edge to edge and then saturate it with honey. Watching Gilligan's Island and eating my toast was the perfect way to relax.

Living on a farm, our lives were very scheduled and so were our meals. If it wasn't time to feed the animals, it was time to feed the family. Mom cooked three meals a day every day of her married life—and what a cook she was. She was determined that her girls would learn to cook while they were young, but I certainly proved a challenge for her. It wasn't that I was unwilling—I was just a slow learner. And lucky for me, I now have a bread mixer because kneading bread was something I never got the hang of. I would end up with big mittens of dough stuck on my hands instead of a nice smooth ball of dough. My mother would try to give constructive advice, but in the end, she would rescue the bread from me while I tried to get the mittens off.

On dark winter nights, we'd make taffy, and Mom would always pull the biggest, hottest piece. Flaky piecrusts would surround fruity fillings for holiday treats, but the crown jewel of Mom's creations was a spice cake with brown sugar frosting.

Only special occasions would warrant the effort this cake took. Mom usually made this to celebrate their wedding anniversary because it was Dad's favorite cake. I think it seemed even more special because Dad would ration the pieces to make sure it lasted. Only one medium-sized piece was allowed, so it had to be savored.

When I finally merited enough confidence in my mother's eyes, she would let me help with the cake and watch her make the frosting. We would get the recipe out before going

to the grocery store, which was half an hour away, and Mom would say, "See what we need to make the cake and the frosting because with this recipe, there are no substitutions!"

Butter and heavy cream were the items she was talking about. In some recipes, you can cut down on the butter and use milk instead of cream, but with this frosting, it just wouldn't turn out. "It's not worth the bother of making it if you aren't going to make it right," she'd say. Once we were into the project and my interest and attention were waning, she would encourage me instead of let me go: "You've got to stay with it. You can't leave it once you've started." I often hear her voice of encouragement, as if she were sitting on my shoulder, coaching me to do my best. "Stay with it!"

That pretty much summed up her philosophy of life, too. Do it right the first time, stay with it, and no substitutions. No substitutions for integrity, honesty, hard work, or devotion to family.

"I learned my lesson about getting things right early on in my married life," she would say with a genuine shiver, bracing herself as if a cold bucket of water was about to hit her in the back. Only a time or two did she tell the story,

but you could see the pain from the experience even years later.

"Your dad had farmed with his dad his whole life, but he wanted to start out on his own. We

"With *this* recipe, there are **no** substitutions!"

had saved a little money, all that we could, and we put all of it into some registered Holstein cows. Just about everybody had a few cows but not registered Holsteins. They were expensive but good milk producers and not so much butter fat. We were on our own now, and your dad worked so hard," she recounted.

COMMUNICATION

MARGARET STALLINGS
is the mother of

SANDRA STALLINGS JENKINS

Sandra Stallings Jenkins introduces four-year-olds to foreign cultures through the beauty of music and art. She served an LDS mission in Bolivia and earned a degree in print journalism from BYU. She dabbles in freelance writing; grows raspberries, pumpkins, and herbs on the family farm; and is a passionate beekeeper. She loves having her three children in the kitchen, each talented cooks who have perfected their skills at making chocolate chip cookies and can fix a tasty dinner.

Every now and then, she makes her mother's spice cake and wishes her mother were still here to offer advice and encouragement.

She had twice as many children to get ready as I do while my dad served in demanding callings, yet she showed her dedication to the Lord each week as she took us and sat next to us on the pew alone. Now that I'm older, I realize she probably couldn't focus on more than half of what was said during those meetings while she wrestled us crazy kids. But she took us anyway. And by taking us to church, she instilled in me the importance of religion and showed me the blessings that come from dedicating our lives to the Lord.

My mother and I developed a strong relationship early in my life. She made time to listen. It was important to her that she was home waiting for us when school got out. It was a time when we opened up to her, and she found that if she wasn't home, the opportunity was lost. I remember many times sitting next to her in our kitchen, giving her minute-by-minute updates of everything that had happened from the time I had left for school that morning. My relationship

She is a bright LIGHT that shines on my life *every* day.

with her blossomed as she listened open-mindedly to my elementary school drama.

Today my mom works harder than anyone I know. She works long hours as an assistant manager at a busy retail superstore. She serves her customers and coworkers with the same love and dedication she does her own family. She supervises many employees whom she considers friends, not subordinates. They can feel that she genuinely cares and turn to her when they need help on the job. She often takes calls on her days off to help with difficult situations at work.

Although I no longer live at home, she still serves me with unwavering dedication.

There isn't a day that goes by that I don't talk to her two or three times on the phone. Many of those calls involve me soliciting her help in some way.

She picks me up when my car breaks down, takes me to lunch when I'm feeling blue, and babysits my boys whenever she can.

One of her favorite things to do is spend time with her grandchildren. She often invites them to sleepovers where she ends up staying awake half the night on a blow-up mattress giggling next to her five little grandkids. Not too long ago, she bought an outdoor mud-making station. The grandkids love squashing their fingers and toes in the cold, wet mud while making her pies that she pretends to eat.

Yet, with all she does for others, she still finds time to serve me in a very personal, exceptional way. Sometimes I wonder if anyone else thinks about the baby I buried last spring. Then I drive to the cemetery to visit his grave and find I'm not the only one who has been there. I see a little toy horse or sword or gun or another carefully positioned trinket next to his granite headstone—treasures left for Luca by his grandma Debbie. Although her life is very busy, she finds time to show love for my little one in heaven. She is still supporting me through my darkest trial.

She is a bright light that shines on my life each and every day.

Now that I am older, I am starting to realize what she has sacrificed in order to be a great mom. She has always put her needs and wants last, and I will be forever grateful for her selfless service.

She is my mentor, my cheerleader, my friend, and I am proud to call her my mother.

> She ends up staying awake half the night on a blow-up mattress giggling next to her grandkids.

Velaine with Mark on the beach, April 1943.

Confidence in Me

by Mark Eubank

My mother came from pioneer stock. Her great-grandfather, William Flint, crossed the plains in 1847 with Brigham Young. When the company got to Wyoming, Brigham asked William to forego going on into the Salt Lake Valley, retrace his steps, and lead another company the following year—which he did. These were the kind of people my mom came from.

When she was born in Salt Lake in 1915, she had a heart valve that didn't close fully. All her life, she was told not to exert herself too much and to build up her strength. But my mother had an irrepressible spirit. She was an energetic, lively person who was full of fun. Because of this heart defect, the doctors advised her to never have children, as giving birth could easily stress her heart so much that she would not survive. However, at age eighteen, she received a patriarchal blessing and, among other things, was promised that her name would live "in the lives of her children." My mother demonstrated the same unyielding faith as her grandfather, William Flint. She believed in that promise and put her belief into action. When she married, she and my father wanted a family, and despite the doctors' warnings, she didn't hesitate to have children, and she gave birth to two sons.

At night, my mother would often come into the bedroom where my brother and I slept, sit on my bed, and sing songs as she rubbed my back. Listening to her voice and feeling her hand on my back at the quiet end of a day made me feel secure and cared for. I knew she and my father loved each other and would take care of my brother and me. Everything was going to work out for the best. It was a feeling she radiated. I knew she cared about me, loved me, and was pulling for me. She never had to say those words; I simply noticed how she spent her time. It has been more than sixty years, and I still remember those feelings.

I never forgot the careful way my mother listened to my idea and the trust she placed in me.

She had a rare ability to trust and encourage her sons. In the early 1950s, televisions were relatively new. My dad had saved to acquire a wonderful new television set for our family. We were in awe of the black-and-white picture on its round picture tube that was less than twelve inches in diameter. But one day the television quit working. I poked around the set for a little bit and told my mother I thought I could fix it. She asked me how I would do it. Instead of transistors or circuit boards inside the television, there were eight small glass vacuum tubes that helped produce the visual picture. I told her I would take the tubes out of the set and take

Mark, about six years old, with his mom and brother.

them to a repair store where I had seen a tube tester. After testing them one by one, I would know which tube was defective and could buy the proper part. She smiled at me and told me to go ahead.

When my father found out that his fourteen-year-old son had dismantled the wonderful new television set, he was more than upset, but my mother calmed him down and told him I had a good idea and we should see what happened. I carefully rode my bicycle with a sack full of the vacuum tubes to the repair shop. I was able to find which tube was defective and buy a replacement. Once home, I reassembled the television, and—to the surprise of my father and to the relief of my mother—it sprang to life once again. I never forgot the careful way my mother listened to my idea and the trust she placed in me.

When I graduated from high school, I wanted to go on an adventure. I asked my parents if I could take my fourteen-year-old brother and drive from our home near Los Angeles, California, to Carlsbad Caverns in New Mexico. My father hesitated. I'm sure he was thinking of all the things that could go wrong. But my mother showed that trust in us by giving it serious consideration. The trip was almost a thousand miles, and it would take two days just to get there. Finally, with my mother's encouragement, my dad said we could do it. We were elated! We drove through Indian lands and saw young boys like us tending sheep. We visited the interesting caverns. I witnessed one of the most impressive rainstorms of my life in Bryce Canyon National Park. The memorable part wasn't so much what we saw on that trip—it was the independence we felt. My mother fostered trust and helped us have experiences that taught us we could believe in ourselves in the same way she believed in us.

Financially, my parents struggled for many years. They were married at the height of the Depression in 1938, and they had some serious financial setbacks. However, my mother was skilled at budgeting and planning and made certain things happen—even if it took some time. When I was about sixteen, she showed me how to make a budget box. She took a carton a little smaller than a shoebox and helped me put dividers into it. I carefully labeled each part of the grid, and then when I got my paycheck from a summer job, I would put cash in each of the various slots. You could move money around, but you had to be careful to cover necessities. My mother taught me in a very concrete way that planning was as important as the money. If you didn't plan, money disappeared. But if you earmarked where it should go and were patient, you could do almost anything you wanted to do. Now I use a spreadsheet on the computer, but that lesson of planning for the future and being patient is still with me today.

The experiences with my mother that taught me about trust, independence, and planning

eventually helped me get my first job in weather. I wanted a profession with weather in the worst way because it was so much a part of what I loved. I couldn't imagine doing anything else for a living. I applied at a small local television station in California that didn't have a weatherman. They asked me what my weather background was? I had dropped out of UCLA. They said, what is your TV background? I didn't have any. Not surprisingly, they told me no thanks.

VELAINE FLINT EUBANK
is the mother of

MARK EUBANK

Mark Eubank is a retired Salt Lake City television broadcasting meteorologist. He most recently worked for KSL–TV Channel 5. Eubank joined the KSL news team in 1990 as their chief meteorologist. Prior to KSL, he was employed as a meteorologist for KUTV Channel 2 in Utah, a position he'd held since 1967.

Eubank began his meteorology career at age twenty-four in Redding, California, at television station KRCR. He attended UCLA and  graduated from the University of Utah in 1972 with a BS in meteorology. Eubank also owned and operated a weather consulting firm, WeatherBank, Inc., for twenty years. He was the chief meteorologist for the 2002 Winter Olympic Games. On November 29, 2006, Eubank signed off the air for the final time. He passed on the reins and his trademark white coat to his son Kevin Eubank. Shortly after retiring, he and his wife, Jean, served a mission at the Laie Hawaii Temple Visitors' Center. They have seven children and seventeen grandchildren.

But my mother had taught me all my life that if I wanted something enough and was willing to do what it took to make it work, then it could usually happen. About a year later, I met a man who worked at that same TV station. He told me, "If you ever want an audition, I can help you get one." From my previous interview, I knew I had no prior experience to recommend me, so my audition had to be compelling. I practiced over and over before even asking for the audition. I knew with the camera in the studio, my nervousness and inexperience would show. My way of overcoming those feelings was to imagine that my wife and my mother were sitting just beyond the camera and that I was explaining the weather to them. I knew my mother loved me. I knew she had always been interested in what I had to say. I knew she would not judge me if I made a mistake. After practicing like this many times, it was much easier to talk to the camera during the audition and to feel relaxed. I attribute my success in getting that first job to the faith and trust my mother placed in me. She didn't even have to actually be there for her confidence to inspire me.

My mother didn't just give these gifts to my brother and me. She had an amazing ability to love people for who they were and not judge them. She accepted people, even when they were unusual and required unreasonable amounts of her time. She spent endless hours listening to various individuals who were sad or who had serious problems. She wouldn't hide from them or ignore them, even when it was inconvenient for her. We would tease her a little. "Why do you allow yourself to get drawn in?" But she would answer that the person was lonely and needed someone to talk to. My mother never talked to a person and then said something different or less flattering when they were gone. Whether the person was present or not, she was consistent. Her conversation to me could always have been said in front of the person we were discussing. She was positive and merciful. She knew how to be a good neighbor. She made people feel at ease and, at the same time, inspired them to do better. As a young boy, I thought all mothers were like this, but as I look back now, I see what a rare combination of gifts she had. She influenced for good everyone with whom she came in contact.

Above: Mark at KRCR.

Below: Mark with his parents and brother.

Choosing Your Blueprint

by Maren Rosemarie Slover Mazzeo

I don't know how to build a boat.

Neither did Nephi.

Neither did the brother of Jared.

As I make daily decisions in raising my children, I try to look to the future and the fruits I hope my care will bring. When I try to know what I should do each day, it's easy to feel overwhelmed, as though I'm being asked to build a boat when I don't know the steps. It's hard to see how what I am doing today fits into the thousands of things that need to come together in the right way to make my boat watertight, strong, and functional—or, in other words, to help my children have testimonies, confidence, and the skills to survive in a competitive world.

When I feel overwhelmed by the enormity of my role as a mother, I try to turn my mind to the scriptures and the responses of the faithful. Like Nephi, I do not need to ask for the entire plan right away. I need to determine the first step to be taken, ask for my daily task, and do my best to fulfill my assignment with faith. The first step for Nephi, and for all of us, is to somehow acquire the tools we need for our daily work.

Left: Robin Baker as a child. *Below—left*: Robin studying during medical school in 1975. *Below—right*: Dr. Slover speaking with elementary school kids in Korea around 1980. *Right*: Robin shortly after giving birth to Maren.

I believe one of the first things we need to recognize is that the process will be different for each mother, and for each mother, the process will probably not be what she expected. Though both were built under the direct guidance of the Lord, the boat of Nephi wasn't the same design as the boat of the brother of Jared. Once on the sea, one was directed through the use of the Liahona, and one was a dishlike barge directed by winds and waves. Maybe you think you're building a sleek and streamlined yacht and look up one day to see your yacht is looking more like a tugboat. That's okay. The Lord knows the blueprint He's giving you, even if you don't. But it's not easy to realize your perfect dreamboat isn't what you're getting.

I've heard a story about a man who buys a new car, drives it home, and whacks the door with a baseball bat. He surveys the dent in his new car and knows now that he won't have to worry so much about avoiding any future damage to the car—perfection has already been breached. I could have found a way, I suppose, to do that with parenting. At the hospital, on the way home, in the first week or so, I could have done less

than what I felt driven to do and accepted the fact that my life as a mother was not going to be without mistakes.

I didn't make any deliberate efforts to take myself out of the running for Flawless Mother, but it happened on its own soon enough. Mothering was a joy to me, but making decisions did not come easily or even naturally. I didn't have any experience with newborns, and as I didn't have a stay-at-home mother, I had no idea what a day of staying home with my baby should even look like. I agonized over schedules, poured my heart into every decision-making process, and worked harder at mothering than I had ever worked at anything else in my life.

Even with the uncertainties, I felt successful for my first few years as a mother. Then came the day when I decided to clean the couches. We had just moved into our first house, my husband was in the first weeks of his new job, and we were all adjusting to life in a new home, new city, and even a different country. I was five months pregnant with our third child and had been

Left: Family picture of Robbie, Michel, Robin, Maren, Melora, Sasha, and Rob. *Above*: Robin looking at guide book at a Korean Buddhist temple around 1979. *Right*: Wedding day, Maren and Robin.

hard at work unpacking boxes. My parents had generously given us some older furniture, including two white leather couches I well remember coming into my childhood home brand new. A decade, several pets, a few moves in a U-Haul, and many spills, bumps, and scratches later, they didn't look quite the way I had remembered them. I was up to my elbows in foaming leather cleaner, scrubbing hard. My children were bored with the activity I had given them. They ran into me, into the couch, into the foam, and I raised my voice in frustration. And I fell from the high standards I had placed for myself as a mother.

I never wanted raised voices in my home. I'd lost my patience, and I felt terrible. I still feel bad, but I've since slipped in that and other areas again. I have striven, but I have not been the perfect mother I started out believing I could be. Sometime between the three children in three years, somewhere between the foaming cleaner and my aching back, I had changed into a mother who was doing her best and had to adjust her plans and expectations.

I wonder what Sariah's plans were before she was commanded to leave Jerusalem. What were her dreams for her children? How did she spend her time? What did she do to nurture her growing family? And how did she think their lives would turn out? Because of her obedience to the Lord's commandments, I would imagine many of the dreams, plans, and goals she had as a mother were forever set aside. What remained, however, were surely the essential desires of her heart: to raise a righteous posterity and to demonstrate love to her children and dedication to the Lord. She was a supportive wife, a hard worker, and, clearly, a very strong woman of faith. As in Sariah's life, the plans of a mother are often changed through circumstance and obedience to the counsel of the Lord. Did Sariah's neighbors, her friends from the synagogue, question the wisdom of her path and the future of her children as she branched out on an entirely new line of parenting—wilderness survival parenting?

I am grateful for her efforts
in **BUILDING ME . . .**
and helping me have the strength to
CRAFT and NURTURE
the *next* generation in our family.

My own mother is an exceptional woman whose life pattern hasn't always fit the standard blueprint for a Latter-day Saint mother. After years of staying home with her children, she felt she needed to complete her training as an anesthesiologist and practice medicine. My father is also a physician, and between their long hours, Church callings, and five children, life was pretty busy in our home.

My two oldest brothers were diagnosed with manic depression when I was still a young child, and the added pressure of trying to help them through their challenges took a lot of my parents' energy. There were many times when I wanted more time with my parents, but it wasn't possible. Being stressed and busy, however, didn't stop my mother from doing her best and giving her best to each of us. She got creative in the ways she would spend special time with us. I spent many nights at the hospital, dressed in scrubs far too large for me, trailing after my mother as she went on rounds. We would eat our picnic dinner in the doctors' lounge, and she would even sometimes bring me into an operating room to see a procedure.

My favorite experience was standing on a step stool watching a quadruple bypass heart surgery. The room was very warm, and my scrubs went well past my shoes. The surgeon was kind and wanted me to understand what was going on, so he talked to me about everything he was doing. He scooped up the heart and held it—still connected to the patient's body through veins and arteries—closer to me to inspect. My mother was standing behind me the entire time, monitoring the patient's vital signs and enjoying my fascination. And that's how it was. She wasn't there for track meets or soccer games. She didn't get me dressed for the homecoming dance. My mother took me to conferences she spoke at and let me choose activities for the end of her workday. She took me with her grocery shopping to let me chat with her in the car. She tried to help me help myself in pursuing my dreams.

Maren at Bear Lake in 1985.

COMMUNICATION

ROBIN BAKER SLOVER
is the mother of

MAREN ROSEMARIE SLOVER MAZZEO

Maren Rosemarie Slover Mazzeo was born the youngest of five children to Drs. Robert and Robin Slover in Denver, Colorado. Maren spent the first sixteen years of her life living in Colorado, enjoying the outdoors, keeping pet birds, and participating in imaginative games with her siblings. Her status as youngest and smallest usually earned her interesting roles, like Roo in *Winnie the Pooh* or the dinghy boat in *Pirates of Penzance*.

Maren next lived in Asia, where her father presided over the Korea Pusan Mission. She graduated from Wellesley College with a bachelor's degree in English in 2004. While an undergraduate, she married Brian, an MIT student who impressed her with his love of reading. Maren left Cambridge, Massachusetts, for Cambridge, England, where Brian became a doctoral student. While living in England, she bore her two oldest children and fell in love with the fens and the college choir. Maren returned to the United States in 2008 and currently lives Provo, Utah, where Brian teaches at BYU and Maren stays home with their four young and active children. She currently serves in the Relief Society of the Edgemont fifth ward.

My own time as a mother has been different from what I envisioned. My blueprint seems to be very different from my mother's so far, but she is still an example to me. She made decisions she felt were right, even in the face of misunderstanding or disapproval from some around her, perhaps even in the midst of her own feelings of inadequacy and confusion over where her decisions were taking her and her family. Now that I've left home and set sail on my own sea of experiences, I am grateful for her efforts in building me, building my testimony, giving me knowledge and experiences, and helping me have the strength to craft and nurture the next generation in our family. I may not see the pattern my decisions are part of, but I am able to know that if I have faith and do my best, I can trust that my efforts will see my children safely and confidently leave my harbor to travel their own paths to their promised lands.

JERRY JORDAN SHAW EVANS

is the mother of

BOB EVANS

Bob Evans has been co-anchor of *Fox 13 News at Nine* since October 1995. Previously, he worked as an anchor/reporter for KUTV and at stations in Kansas City, Spokane, and Boise.

He has won numerous awards in his career, including two Emmys, two Telly Awards, and many Society of Professional Journalists and Utah Broadcasters awards. He has had the opportunity to report on a wide variety of issues and events.

Bob enjoys meeting viewers in person, saying that it is a privilege to take part in the station's community events. Over the years, he has represented Fox 13 at functions such as The Great Salt Lake Council of the BSA Silver Beaver Awards, the Governor's Office on Volunteerism Silver Bowl Awards, the Combined Federal Campaign Kick-off Luncheons, Utah's Safe Kids Coalition, the American Lung Association of Utah, the Days of '47 Celebration of Utah's Cultures, the Granite Education Foundation "Excel" Awards, Utah Regional Ballet, and many others.

Bob graduated from Brigham Young University with degrees in broadcast journalism and music performance. He met his wife at BYU and describes their union as follows: "We were both in the broadcast journalism program and had on-air assignments. She had come back to get her master's degree in broadcast management. And as it turned out, she's managed this broadcaster and our family very, very well for the past twenty-six years. And I could not be more grateful to her. We've been blessed with wonderful children. We love the mountains, skiing, sports, and music. But mostly, we like just being together."

Only on Days That You Eat

by Bob Evans

The fact that her parents spelled her name with a *J* instead of a *G*, as in Geraldine, has always annoyed my mother just a little, particularly when mail would come for "Mr. Jerry S. Evans." She isn't annoyed at the spelling of her name but rather at those who think she's a man. To her, Jerry with a *J* makes perfect sense. She has never understood why anyone would be confused, despite the fact that Jerry with a *J* is almost always a man's name. And, no, her given name isn't Geraldine. It's Jerry. *J-e-r-r-y.*

My three other siblings and I grew up knowing that Mom was in charge . . . until Dad got home. And there were plenty of times she warned us of what would happen when he did arrive. Not that anything really did happen. But when you're just old enough to get yourself in trouble and not old enough to know it isn't really serious, the prospect of ultimate authority paying you a visit is enough to make you straighten up and fly right.

Jerry Jordan Shaw was born in Hollywood, California, on October 4, 1931. She was the eldest of two children born to Edward Lufkin Shaw and Mary Nelson Shaw. Jerry spent most of her growing-up years in Long Beach, just southwest of the airport. Her father was a bank executive with Security First National, managing the branch in downtown Los Angeles. He was also a member of the Lion's Club. Her mother was active in the community and volunteered for many years at the local hospital.

Mom's interest in music led her to try out for the orchestra in junior high school. She wanted to play the violin, but the orchestra teacher needed someone to play the string bass and enlisted my mother to try it out. When her mother came to pick her up at school that day, it was quite a sight—the two of them struggling to get this funny-looking, overgrown instrument into the back of the sedan. But Mom took to the string bass and wound up going to the University of Washington on a music scholarship.

It was there that she met my father, Robert E. Evans, who was also on a music scholarship. Piano was his principal instrument. But he also played the sousaphone in the UW marching band. As it turned out, Mom was also looking for a way to be a part of the marching band. She auditioned and won a spot playing the bells.

Dad didn't date a lot, but he was looking for someone to take to a fraternity dance and had begun to notice Mom. It was at marching band practice that their paths literally crossed, and while they were standing there on the football field during a break, he asked her to the dance. And she accepted.

They began seeing each other off and on and really started to like each other. But Dad was raised as a Latter-day Saint, and Mom was Episcopalian, so there were some religious issues that needed to be resolved. To that end, Mom started studying the restored gospel, taking the missionary discussions, and attending Church.

Dad went slowly with their relationship because he didn't want Mom to join the Church for the wrong reasons. But about a year after her baptism, it was clear her testimony was founded in the Savior and the principles of His gospel, and the wedding bells started to ring.

Mom was the only daughter of Ed and Mary Shaw. They were not religious people but respected those who were. While Mom and Dad were determined to be married for time *and* eternity in the temple, the thought of not being able to attend their only daughter's temple wedding didn't just sit poorly with the Shaws—it was *unbearable*. So Mom and Dad were married for time in the Long Beach ward chapel by my grandfather, Elvin E. Evans, who was a stake president at the time. Three days later, they were sealed for eternity in the St. George temple.

That whole episode impressed my sister Lauri, who related the following:

Above: Jerry Jordan Shaw, five years old.

When I visited St. George several years after my own wedding, I couldn't help but think of my mother's wedding. She was a young bride in Long Beach, California, in 1954 and had to travel to St. George in order to perform the sealing ordinance in the temple there. She had been a member of the Church only a couple of years at that point, and she was the only member of the Church in her family. With the exception of my dad, she was alone for that experience.

We are much better now at preparing our members for the kind of eternal work we do in our temples, but in 1954, there were no classes in place or coursework to be completed in order to attend the temple. I'm sure at that first visit, things must have felt foreign to her. The only thing for her to rely on at that time, besides the love and testimony of my dad, would have been her own testimony and faith.

As I walked around the temple grounds in that peaceful, warm, Utah Dixie town, I pictured her entering, doing her own temple work, and leaving the temple. She must have had questions ringing in her mind, maybe even some concern about the level of commitment she had taken upon herself. Yet, hand in hand, she left the temple grounds with my dad and forged ahead with her new life.

I reflect on that picture in my mind, and I marvel at the faith, courage, and devotion she demonstrated that day. She has always maintained her worthiness to enter the temple, from that day until this day, remaining ever true to her covenants there. She has found great peace and joy by serving in many temples and has a circle of friends and loved ones all over the globe that all share her lifelong temple service history. She is not alone anymore.

Mom and Dad are highly trained, highly accomplished musicians. And along with the foundational principles of the restored gospel of Jesus Christ, we grew up with music as the lifeblood in our home. Everyone seriously studied an instrument. Karen plays the cello and still teaches privately. I play the violin. Ed plays the trombone, football, and the radio, and Lauri plays and teaches violin privately. All of us had the finest private music teachers Tacoma had to offer, and with the exception of Ed, all of us graduated in music from BYU. (For a trombone player, Ed turned out to be an excellent doctor.) Mom was the principal string bassist in the Tacoma Symphony and spent her early years playing in the Seattle Symphony. Dad was not only the band and orchestra teacher at Woodbrook Junior High just south of Tacoma, but he was also the leader of the family band and accompanied all of us on the piano. In addition, we all sang together, like the Von Trapps—only not nearly as famous.

I can't tell you how many times rehearsals for the various programs we'd be asked to perform

Bob and Jerry Evans' wedding, 1954.

would degenerate into fits of laughter so intense we'd have to quit rehearsing altogether just so we could breathe. It's funny how music and laughter make such fond memories.

But I dare say, those memories would not be nearly as sweet without the comforting knowledge that our loving eternal relationships are solidly in place, a foundation laid by a mother and father who knew and lived correct principles and expected nothing less from us.

Bob and Jerry Evans are still spoken of with great affection among their dear lifelong friends and associates in Tacoma, despite having moved to the Atlanta area for Dad's ending fight with prostate cancer. We lost him in 2005, ushering him out of this world to the strains of his beloved "Clair de Lune," videotaped at his last recital just two months earlier.

As my brother, sisters, and I contemplate the great gifts our parents gave us, so many examples of simple but firm faith emerge.

Our earliest years were spent in much want, although we didn't know it as little children. 1618 North 8th St. in Tacoma had a roughed-in attic, where all four of us children slept. Dad installed an intercom that sat in the rafters of the attic so we could call to them downstairs in the middle of the night if we needed them.

> "Daddy? . . . Daddy??! . . . Daddy!???! . . . DADDY!!????!!"

> "What?"

> "Potty."

Dad worked three jobs to try to put food on the table. He sold insurance and real estate for his father, taught private piano lessons, and was the seminary coordinator for the Church for all of western Washington, which at the time was a paid position.

Mom stayed at home with us, overseeing our basic needs and making sure we didn't fall out of the windows of the attic, get lockjaw from a rusty nail, or run into the street. We spent many days driving to the store or on errands, with the Pacific Northwest drizzle accumulating on the windshield, the gray skies acting as a backdrop, the car heater blowing in our little faces, and the faint classical music of KIXI–AM playing on the very crackly car radio.

We said our prayers over breakfast—usually eggs, toast, and milk. On special occasions, we got real butter. For lunch, we took turns blessing our peanut butter and honey sandwiches and apples. Sometimes we had potato chips. At dinner, Dad would thank Heavenly Father for all our blessings—before we ate our cottage cheese and home-canned fruit.

After dinner, Dad, a Korean War veteran, would line us up for "inspection," give us some marching commands, and play a Sousa march on the piano while we soldiered our way, single file, around the living room, the dining room, and the kitchen, through the hallway, and back into the living room.

Tuesday and Wednesday nights, while Mom was away at Mutual or symphony rehearsal, Dad would make popcorn and we'd all sit on the couch and watch *Combat, 12 O'Clock High,* and *Rat Patrol.* Then off to bed in the attic and prayers by the bedside, with Dad scratching my back until the end of my little-boy prayer. ("Amen. Keep on scratching, Dad.")

I remember when Karen and I discovered that there were other kinds of music out there besides classical and Perry Como. It was almost scandalous when we somehow obtained our first 45 rpm record. It was the Beatles. "I Want to Hold Your Hand" on side A. "Day Tripper" on side B. Mom would only let us listen to it for about five minutes at a time, just long enough for both sides of the record.

But that was enough.

With that new rock n' roll beat lodged in our little brains, our desires to make music were born. It's hard to find a better example of just how primal music really is.

Mom's newfound challenge became channeling those primal desires into the kind of music she could (1) tolerate and (2) give us a much broader base for, paving the way to make all kinds of other music for the rest of our lives—namely classical. While we loved and played lots of rock n' roll, the foundations of our most meaningful musical experiences remain in the countless orchestra rehearsals and concerts we played in growing up. Respighi's "The Pines of Rome," Bernstein's "Overture to Candide," Tchaikovsky's "1812 Overture," the brilliance of anything by Bach, the grandeur of Beethoven, the sweeping romanticism of Brahms, the divine inspiration of Handel's "Messiah."

While I self-administered my daily dose of Top 40 hits, the genesis of all the greatest musical gifts my mother gave me came in a myriad of other ways: listening to the Tacoma Symphony rehearse and waiting to carry Mom's bass back out to the car; a bike trip to the University of Puget Sound library with a note from my mother, where, at eleven years old, I sat in a cubical and listened on old World War II–style headphones to Bach's "Brandenburg Concerto No. 4" for the first time while following along in the score; or the near-constant ambient sound in the house of Mom and Dad's

practicing or lesson teaching. I think she knew exactly what she was doing. And it worked.

My life became music. All kinds of music. And because I came to understand and appreciate so much about music, the power of that medium provided the bedrock on which my most important convictions regarding divinity and life were formed.

So when, at six years old, I was taught the alto line of "How Great the Wisdom and the Love" to sing at Karen's baptism, I not only learned the principles of harmony, but the principles of the Atonement. And when we sang with the congregation "Abide With Me" or "Come, Come Ye Saints" or "How Firm A Foundation" or "We Thank Thee, O God, For a Prophet," those words sank indelibly into my soul. To this day, some of the most stirring feelings of heavenly influence to course through me are so often accompanied by the hymns of faith.

We didn't know it at the time, but many of the principles of musicianship we learned while young are universal and have divine implications. My sister, Karen, related the following:

"Today in sacrament meeting, Kristina Burrell Dooley gave a talk. She was asked to speak on President Uchtdorf's general conference address entitled 'Things that Matter Most.' She said that when she was young she was one of Mom's violin students. She remembered two things that Mom always told her. One was, 'You only have to practice on the days you eat.' The other was, 'Perfect practice makes perfect playing.'

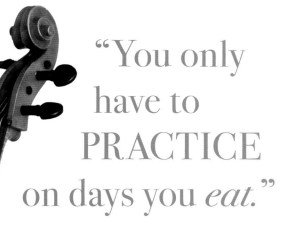

"You only have to PRACTICE on days you *eat.*"

"Kristina said that she applied these lessons to her music at the time. As she grew, however, she found that those phrases Mom had taught her applied to many other areas in her life, especially her study of the gospel. 'You only have to read your scriptures on the days you eat,' and 'You only have to pray on the days you eat.' Perfect practice of the commandments, for example the law of tithing and the Word of Wisdom, were things she gleaned from what Mom taught her. I was amazed and humbled by how a simple lesson applied in Mom's life had infused gospel principles into the lives of those she taught.

She said that the lessons Mom taught her changed her life."

Indeed, many of the things Mom has taught us have broad application, especially along gospel lines.

She and I were in the car one day when I was in the middle of the eighth grade. I had been first chair violin of the Jason Lee Junior High School orchestra for a year and a half and was contemplating that accomplishment.

I turned to her and said, "You know, I think I'm going to quit playing the violin."

She said, "Oh, really? Why's that?"

I said, "Because I've become good enough now that I don't need to play anymore."

And I'll never forget her response: "Okay, I'll make you a deal. When you turn eighteen, you can quit playing the violin."

Realizing what that meant, I said, "Yeah, but if I wait until I'm eighteen, I'll be so good I won't want to quit."

Smiling, she said, "Isn't that interesting."

Just before my eighteenth birthday and as concertmaster of the Tacoma Youth Symphony, I, along with the rest of the symphony, was privileged to attend the International Festival of Youth Orchestras in London, England, and Aberdeen, Scotland. Following the festival, TYS concertized for two weeks all over Scotland, England, and Wales. Because of my continued study of music—the violin, the piano, guitar, and drums—by the time I was twenty-one, I had experienced more in life and had traveled more places around the world than most others my age.

But the principle she taught at the corner of Sixth and Alder was, again, universal. Continued practice of gospel principles from infancy and through our formative years laid a foundation for my siblings and me that has guided and blessed our lives ever since.

Continued *practice* of gospel principles laid a FOUNDATION for my siblings and me that has *guided* and *blessed* our lives.

Mom is the epitome of determined commitment. In the early 1970s, she saw that the University Place School District in Tacoma had no orchestras and no curriculum to teach stringed instruments. Singlehandedly, she started the program, first in the four grade schools and then at Curtis Junior High and Curtis Senior High School. For more than a decade, she was the only person running the burgeoning orchestras in that district. During her tenure, literally thousands of students came under her direct tutelage, receiving the same life lessons and love of music that we received as her children at home.

To this day, lives are being touched in numberless ways because of what she established. Forty years later, the tens of thousands of students who have come through the extensive orchestra programs in the University Place School District have my mother and her tireless efforts to thank for the blessings of music and musicianship in their lives. But beyond that, the blessings those students have passed on to others because of what they experienced at the hands of my mother and those who came after her cannot be counted. Truly, you can count the seeds in an apple, but you can't count the apples in a seed.

But Mom has always had determined commitment, especially when it comes to following the promptings of the Spirit. And she has passed that trait on to her children. My brother Ed related the following:

"When I was in college, I had determined that I wanted to apply to medical school. I felt that there were things in this life that I wanted to do and things I felt I had to do. This was an instance of 'had to.' But there were those who felt the time commitment required for schooling and a career in medicine would be far too great and that I would not have time for my family, my church, or myself. Regardless, I still felt this overwhelming impression that medicine was what I needed to do.

"As I prepared for the exams necessary to enter med school, Mom was there with sound advice: 'Stick to your guns!' I have never forgotten that since she said it more than thirty years ago. The principle that she taught was to not squelch the impressions of the Spirit and to follow those impressions regardless of those around you who may feel otherwise.

"Mom has always had an uncanny sensitivity to the Spirit. When I was in high school, I remember very distinctly the night that one of my uncles, her brother, was killed in a midair collision over Long Beach, California. Mom came to my room to talk to me before the call came. She told me that something had happened to my Uncle Ted. She didn't know what . . . just that something was wrong. Shortly thereafter, the call came that he had been killed. I was very touched by how she was sensitive enough to already know."

And even now, Mom is certain of the times when Dad has a moment to let her know he's close by.

Left: Linda and Shawni, 2010. *Right*: The Richard and Linda Eyre clan, 2010.

I do wish the geneticist would have at least told me to sit down, or find a quiet place. . . . I mean, she must have been able to hear the chaos going on around me on a Friday afternoon when my house was filled with the whole neighborhood. I felt like my whole world was suddenly swimming around me.

The syndrome is called Bardet-Biedl, and among a myriad of other health issues, it causes vision loss, slowed learning, and obesity. We went through a period of mourning (and still come up against those periods here and there). But my mother has been by our side to help every step of the way, to help fight against the many varied things that can go wrong. She was the one behind founding the "I Love Lucy Project" that we started to help contribute to foundations fighting vision loss and other needs Lucy may face. She tirelessly delves into any kind of research she finds that can help Lucy. She buoys us up when we become emotionally drained. She is truly a partner to help us help our daughter. And for that, we can never thank her enough.

My husband and I recently took our children on a tour of the Conference Center.

Part of the tour expounded on the king truss, the main support beam for the entire massive building. We found out that the king truss, with its strength and power, can hold up the entire weight of the Conference Center.

My mother is, in a way, her own sort of king truss, supporting the weight of everything around her in her own beautiful way.

I love my mother. Yes, I do have her genes . . . and they give me hope that someday I can develop some of those amazing attributes I love so much.

For now, I'll bask in the fact that I read street signs aloud and love newborns so much. Maybe I'm on the right track.

*D*evotion and Prayer

by Kristine Wardle Frederickson

**ESTELLE SCOVILLE
WARDLE WARREN**

is the mother of

KRISTINE WARDLE FREDERICKSON

Kristine Wardle Frederickson earned a PhD at the University of Utah and currently teaches British, European, and world history, religion, and women's studies at both Brigham Young University and Utah Valley University. She has written and presented widely on Victorian England, Mormon history and historiography, and women's issues.

KEITH JOHNSON,
DESERET NEWS

Along with many other activities, she helped cover the 1970 World Cup soccer games in Mexico City and the 1972 Munich Olympics for United Press International, and she currently writes a weekly column for the *Mormon Times* portion of Salt Lake City's *Deseret News*.

Among her nonacademic interests are tennis, swimming, running, biking, basketball, softball, volleyball, carpentry, calligraphy, and jewelry making, as well as politics and current events, travel, and family.

My mom was only eight when word came that her father had slipped while walking a round pipe and had fallen thirty feet to the ground at the beet factory where he worked outside Raymond, Alberta, Canada. His back was broken, among other injuries. They put him in a tight body cast, and seven days later, he was dead. Mom's mother, Blanche, was left to raise eight children on her own in a tiny two-bedroom home. She used the one thousand dollar insurance payout to put in a bathroom, replacing the outhouse thirty yards from the house.

With four older sisters, my mother wore only hand-me-downs for the first sixteen years of her life, so it was no surprise that she developed a love for fashion and clothes and a gift for making people look good that led to her own successful dress store and work in the clothing industry.

It was no surprise either that Mother learned early in life to work hard, do her best, trust God, be resourceful, and "buck up" when life proved challenging. I possess a letter my mother wrote at age thirteen to her older,

Young Estelle.

married sister. It reads, "Boy, Lenore, I have more work to do since . . . everybody has gone. Last Friday I got up early, got breakfast, and [did] dishes. Then I did all of the washing myself. Mama never came down. [She was ill.] Then I scrubbed all the steps down, mopped out the hall, etc. Then I came upstairs and mopped and waxed and polished the kitchen floor and cleaned the bathroom. Then I came in and did the front rooms. Well, I got finished at 6:30 p.m. I was surely tired. Saturday we got up and put up preserves and gooseberries and went through the front room again. The last few days, I have done my work and then gone out and hoed the garden. . . . Well, I must close now. I have something to do."

Is it any surprise that even today, although an octogenarian, my mother still keeps a spotless house, a flower-filled, well-manicured yard, and has no trouble entertaining upwards of twenty people for dinner. There were six children in our family: Bruce, me, Stacie, Clark, Thomas, and Lucy. Even her boys call regularly and love to spend time with her in her home.

Besides teaching us about unconditional love and besides her ability to listen and empathize, mom taught us the gospel of Jesus Christ. I'll never forget the time she lost some important papers. After searching, she went into her room, offered a prayer, and, when she came out, walked to a desk drawer and began rummaging until she found them. I don't know that she verbally told us at the time about prayers being answered, but she didn't need to; her example spoke for itself.

My dad, Jack Wardle, had the capacity to make and spend lots of money. Everyone loved Dad—his great sense of humor,

Estelle grew to womanhood very familiar with hard work.

smarts, and resourcefulness. However, money was often tight or nonexistent. Mother patiently managed and taught me about persevering, taking the good with the bad, and "hanging in there." Her example continues to empower me today.

Whatever her Church calling, mom fulfills it. Currently, she serves weekly at the Joseph Smith Building in Salt Lake City. She initiates many acts of selfless service. She regularly picks up a ninety-year-old woman in her ward, drives her to sacrament meeting, and takes her home afterward because the woman can't stay longer.

Mother's is a living testimony. Sure, I've heard her bear her testimony, but more importantly, it's been the day-in, day-out living and loving the Savior by serving her family and others that has drawn me back when I've faltered and that has led me to my own testimony.

One experience that had a lifelong impact occurred when I was a senior in high school. My brother Bruce had completed his freshman year at BYU, and Mom flew out to help him drive his VW Beetle home. On that endless, monotonous, straight stretch of road in Nevada, the temperature soared to 110 degrees with no air conditioning. Bruce was asleep, and Mother was cruising along at sixty-five mph. She fell asleep too. The car rolled two-and-a-half times, coming to rest upside down. Bruce's gear, previously crammed in the car, littered the desert floor. The police could not understand how they survived.

Dad drove out to bring them home. Two days later, Bruce and Mom arrived to banners and balloons. We excitedly awaited their arrival. When the station wagon pulled into the garage and Bruce emerged, a painful

silence descended. Bandages covering stitches crisscrossed his forehead, both eyes were mottled black and blue, and his nose had disappeared in his swollen face. Mom, ashen-faced, sliced up, equally mangled, and grimacing from an eight-hour car ride with an as yet undiagnosed broken back, had to be carried to bed.

That evening as I hovered, before Mom disappeared in the middle of the night in an ambulance to the hospital, she explained that during the accident she awoke disoriented, in terror, to the tumbling nightmare of crunching metal and cascading debris. She began to pray and petitioned, "Please don't let me break my arms or legs. I have six children to raise. Please let me live to raise my children." The Lord heard her pleas.

Another indelible memory was the night my father died. Dad had diabetes. A call came shortly after Mom took Dad to dialysis one day. His fistula had collapsed yet again, and he needed to go the hospital to have a new shunt carved into his arm. Mom couldn't get him into the car and to the hospital on her own. My husband and I transported them.

Left: Thirteen-year-old Estelle (top left) with her family.
Right: Estelle, age twenty.

Above: Estelle and Jack on their wedding day.
Right: The Wardle family.

After spending some time with Dad, his physician emerged and invited us into the room. He and Dad explained that Dad had decided to stop dialysis. We were stunned but not ignorant of the misery, the constant pain and humiliation, Dad felt in the face of this vicious disease. It had finally overwhelmed him.

We got Dad home and called hospice. A sweet woman came and explained that he would probably only live for about five more days. We called family members. Some were already there. My sister and I decided to take turns caring for Dad through the night. We had no idea he would die in the early hours that next morning.

Mom hovered over him, doing everything she could to make him comfortable. As the evening progressed, my sister went to bed to rest before relieving me at four in the morning. Although physically and emotionally drained, Mother was constantly at Dad's side. His breathing became so labored and difficult he couldn't breathe without sitting up. Soon he had to raise his arms and drape them around Mother's and my shoulders. I finally went into the family room to drag

She awoke disoriented, in TERROR, to the tumbling *nightmare* of crunching metal and cascading debris.

Jack and Estelle, 1999.

Above: BYU graduation, Estelle, Kristine (center) and sister Stacie. *Below:* Kristine and her daughter Rachel and Estelle in London, 1998.

in his recliner, hoping he could sit comfortably upright and gain some respite. As I returned, I will never forget the picture

Her look begged for RELIEF—*not for herself* but for my father's tortured SUFFERING.

that met me. Mother was tenaciously by his side, straining to prop him up as the weight of his desperately heaving body sagged against hers. Tears streamed down her face, but she said nothing. Her look begged for relief—not for herself but for my father's tortured suffering. We got Dad into the recliner, though I'll never know how. I finally cajoled Mom into bed. Shortly after 4:00 a.m., Dad passed away. But my mother remained strong in the face of this trial.

My mom is a best friend. We have traveled the world together, crafting memories that will last forever. On one trip to Paris, Mom misjudged the steps during a tour of the bell tower at Notre Dame Cathedral. My sister and I were at the rooftop scrutinizing the gargoyles and the city. We came down to see Mother sitting on a bench. She explained she had twisted her ankle.

We walked and walked and walked the rest of the day. And Mother limped. Back at our fourteenth-century hotel, after climbing three stories to our room, Mom took off her shoe. Her ankle was black and blue and already oversized and was swelling before our eyes. My sister and I went in search of an ankle brace. For the next five days, Mom trooped all over Paris. Morning, evening, and breaks in between, she was on her knees or silently praying that she would be able to walk. Amazingly, she did. Her only real travail was the embarrassment of having to wear flat, sturdy, athletic shoes instead of stylish pumps—in Paris. In the gardens at Versailles, she even refused to have her picture taken until she had covered her feet in leaves, successfully hiding her unfashionable footwear.

In large and small ways, with constant fidelity, Mother is devoted to family and to the Savior Jesus Christ. Her example has sustained me through the highs and lows of life. Her rock-solid testimony and her faith in the power of prayer persuaded and gave me courage to plant the seed and develop my own testimony. Mother's life has given me, each of my brothers and sisters, and grand- and great-grandchildren the courage to meet the challenges of life.

At Notre Dame Cathedral in Paris, France.

Home Is Where the Mom Is

by Jordan Marie Green

L et's face it—life for a girl between the ages of thirteen and fifteen is hard enough, with a large load of homework every night, the sudden importance of impressing the opposite sex, and hormone levels all over the place. Add in a relocation of 7,500 miles, being surrounded by German street signs and French store advertisements, and the feeling of extreme homesickness . . . and you're just asking for a meltdown. To top it all off, I was the only member of the Church in my school, and I faced a language barrier with the German-speaking members of our ward.

When I was a teenager, my family had the unique opportunity to move from Hawaii to Switzerland, two completely different worlds for me. For two years, we called Basel, the third-largest city in Switzerland, our home. Because my father was offered a job at a pharmaceutical company in that area and because we were avid travelers, a chance to live abroad was something my family couldn't pass up. Looking back, my experiences in Basel were incredible, but at the time, the adjustment was a little difficult. Luckily, I had my mother as a constant friend and confidant.

My mom didn't (and still doesn't) exactly fit the mold of the gentle, nurturing, Little House on the Prairie mother type. She was opinionated, blunt, and authoritative.

She was somewhat of an oxymoron—she lifted weights with manicured fingers, she watched both soap operas and criminal investigation shows, and she traveled on expensive excursions to South America but scoured for coupons in the Sunday newspaper. But Mom was willing to listen to stories about my eccentric art teacher and my friends' ever-changing lineups of boyfriends—and on any subject I brought up, I could always count on her to offer her two cents (usually more).

When I was in tenth grade, Mom was a teacher at my high school, a private English-language school in Basel, whose alumni include NBA star Kobe Bryant. She taught English as a second language to students from all over the world: the quiet boy from Poland, the petite girl from Russia, the lanky soccer player from Sierra Leone. And because the school was only two kilometers from our apartment, sometimes we walked together in the mornings. Weather permitting, Mom and I would walk from Aeschenplatz to Karl Barth-Platz. We would talk about our next trip, whether it was to the Loire Valley in France, Toledo and Barcelona, Istanbul, or Egypt. She would ask me about my history project on imperialism, the latest Josh Hartnett film, my upcoming violin recital.

Sometimes a light rain would force us to huddle under a tiny umbrella and walk close together. In either sunshine or drizzling rain, I would clutch the crook of her arm.

"You're the only teenager I know who would hold her mom's hand," she

COMMUNICATION

ROBYN WILLIAMS

is the mother of

JORDAN MARIE GREEN

Jordan Marie Green was born and raised on the North Shore of Oahu but has also lived in Utah, New Jersey, and Switzerland. She has been fortunate enough to travel to more than thirty countries so far, with Egypt and New Zealand being two of her favorite destinations. After graduating as one of her high school's valedictorians, Jordan studied at Brigham Young University, where she graduated in 2007 with a BA in English. She has always focused on creative writing, winning several writing competitions in various publications. Jordan has worked and written for *LDS Living* magazine and what is now MormonTimes.com. She currently writes at www.jordanmariegreen.blogspot.com, and she also contributed to the compilation *Life Lessons from Fathers of Faith*. She currently lives in California with her husband, James, and their children, Eden and McKay.

Jordan and her mother share an umbrella in Warsaw, Poland, 2005.

would say, adjusting her pair of our matching gloves.

"I just don't want you to slip and break your hip," I'd tease.

Along the way, we would cut through a strip of a city park, a little garden oasis in the concrete jungle of Basel. Every day in the spring, it seemed a new flower would appear. "Look at the crocuses," she would say. Every day would pass by with the arrival of more flowers: daffodils, tulips, and many others we couldn't name. Our favorites were the miniature daffodils, or as we called them, "baby daffodils." The emerging flowers marked the passage of time, when we, the former Hawaii residents, would soon be able to feel beach sand on our toes again.

Closer to the school, we would pass a typical Swiss bakery. The warmth and aroma from the small shop would envelop us for a mere second on the sidewalk. The strudels and semmels seemed to glow from the windows. "They don't even need a sign," Mom would say. "The smell is advertisement enough." Then we would joke about hijacking the store's delivery truck and hoarding the stolen pastries in our apartment.

As we walked by the bakery one morning, I tentatively suggested, "We should have breakfast there some time."

My low-carb mother stared straight ahead. "Yeah, maybe. Looks pricey though."

After a few minutes of silence, we reached the tram stop closest to our school. I caught up with some friends, as I normally did, and left Mom to walk the rest of the way to school alone.

"You're the only teenager I know who would hold her mom's hand."

It was nice seeing my mom in the hallways. Because she's five foot nine, I could easily spot her among the sea of filing students. Even if she tried to hide, I would be able to detect her mahogany, Mormon-helmet hairdo. I never felt "too cool" to walk up to her and give her a hug between classes; neither did my friends, who also called her "Mom."

Above: Jordan, age fourteen, with mother and younger brother, Zach, in Madrid, Spain. *Middle*: Robyn and Jordan, 2007. *Right*: Jordan and daughter, Eden, with Robyn, 2009.

I could always count on her if I forgot my lunch money or if I needed a form signed. I always knew where she hid her bag of fun-sized Snickers for her students in her classroom. I remember one time, after a big fight with my friend Sarah, I came to my mom, tears falling down my cheeks. Mom explained the situation to the school secretary, who agreed that I could go home for the rest of the day.

I realized it didn't matter where we *lived.* HOME was wherever MOM was.

Spring turned into summer, but the weather never got quite warm enough for us. As we walked through the park on the last day of school, I said, "I can't believe we're wearing jackets. It's the end of June, for heaven's sake."

Mom smiled and pointed. "Look at the lilies. Oh, and that hydrangea is beautiful."

"They always reminded me of little butterflies."

As we neared the bakery, Mom asked, "Are you still hungry, Jordan?"

I stopped on the sidewalk and turned to face her. "You want to go in?"

"Well, why not?" She grinned. "It's our last day. When else are we going to have a chance?"

As we sat at a tiny table inside, stuffing ourselves with strudels, I said, "I'm going to miss it here."

"Only two more weeks until we move home," she said.

Home. The word conjured up images of plumeria and hibiscus flowers, certainly not crocuses pushing through the wet Basel dirt. I saw a two-story duplex on Hukilau Beach, not a second-floor apartment in the city center. Hadn't Basel been home for the last two years? Hadn't we made this walk, passed this bakery, a hundred times? Now that Basel was finally starting to feel like home, it was time to leave for the home I had always known.

I brushed the flaky crumbs from my face with a napkin and looked at my mother's smiling face. We walked out of the shop, and I reached up to hold on to the crook of Mom's arm. I realized it didn't matter where we lived. Home was wherever Mom was.

As I turned back to glance at the bakery one last time, I noticed the bakery delivery van idling in an alley. Mom said, "We really should have hijacked that truck."

Barbara in high school, 1958.

Standing Ovations

by *Wendy Hale McKay*

Make a joyful noise unto the Lord . . . serve the Lord with gladness.
—*Psalm 100:1–2*

Everyone come look! Isn't it spectacular?" was a common exclamation around our home. Mom doesn't just enjoy sunsets or rain freezing on branches—they take her breath away. She "oohs" and "ahhs" over nature or a four-year-old's drawing and calls to tell you about it. Though sweet and dignified, she is not a bystander quietly enjoying events of this life. No, she is up on her feet, applauding and joyful, sending us "Hallelujahs" for each of our children's accomplishments.

She has always seen the hand of God in everything around her, and her passion and appreciation for it is a gift she shares with others. She sees it in the people she meets, the creation of this world with its music, landscapes, and opportunities, and in the restoration of the gospel of Jesus Christ. Like charity, she never fails in wanting to enrich others with her belief that God can be found in the details if we will just look.

Blessed with a can-do attitude, intelligence, and love, she could have been an asset to any chosen career outside of the home, but my mother fiercely believed that being a mother and raising good, faithful, productive children was the most important thing she could do.

Below: Barbara in 1962.

Right: Hale family in London, England, 1966.

Above: Grandson Hudson McKay graduation, 2010.

Above: Temple day with missionary grandson Jacob. Left: 50th wedding anniversary, 2010.

Mom doesn't just *enjoy* sunsets or rain freezing on branches— they **take her breath away.**

In this world of self-fulfillment, Mom filled her own bucket by filling the buckets of others. By asking our elderly neighbors to teach skills to her daughters, she eased their loneliness and formed lifetime friendships. She rarely took a gift or food to a neighbor without one of her sons or daughters to carry it in, teaching compassion. She started a book club so friends of every religion and persuasion would feel part of a group, and they came to love her dearly. They nominated her, and she was elected by her peers, to be Utah's Mother of the Year 2000. She is an elect lady in every sense of the word.

Music played a huge part in mom's childhood; she practiced her violin upwards of four hours a day until her instrument became a voice for her love of music. My life should have ended as a six-year-old when I disobeyed the "no balls in the house rule" and kicked a ball into her beloved violin, shattering it. Though clearly crushed, she showed great restraint in sparing my life. She was probably in shock. She didn't even yell at me, which made me feel great remorse.

The shock eventually wore off, and a couple of years later we moved to our Huntsville home, where she and Dad installed intercoms in all the bedrooms. Each morning at five thirty we would be jolted awake to the loud strains of Mozart's *Symphony no. 40* in G Minor or other classical marches and Mom sunnily singing, "Good morning to you! Good morning to you! Please join us for scriptures . . . in our bedroom!" As several blanket cocoons trudged their way down the hall, I'm sure I was not the only one silently cursing Mozart's and Beethoven's mothers.

One of their other inspired parenting successes came from a failure of sorts. In an

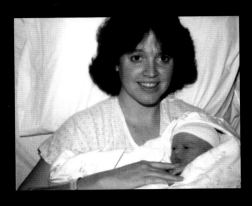  

Mom called up my grandma.

"Tiffany will be getting married in the Portland temple," she said. "It would be such an honor to have you there." There was a pause on the other end.

"We're already working on it," Grandma said quietly.

It was a sunny December day, cool and windy. As a young and fresh-faced bride, I

stepped into the sealing room and looked around at so many loving faces: aunts and uncles all married in the temple; a mother and father who remained steady and faithful—and those grandparents of mine, who came back to full activity in the twilight of their lives.

In the end, this story is really about my mother and my grandmother. It's about all the laborers in the kingdom, as Christ spoke about in His parable. Some day laborers, like my indefatigable mother, come early to the field and sweat under the heat of a noonday sun and on into the night. Others, like my grandmother, arrive as the sun begins to dip. But as the parable goes, both receive the same wage.

In the temple that day, I didn't even need the mirrors that show both the past and the future generations. We were all right there, roots and branches, and right in the middle of that family tree was my mother, solid and immovable.

Above—Left: Janice holding newborn Tiffany, 1979. *Middle:* Janice and Tiffany, 1981. *Right:* Grandmother June Arvidson at Tiffany's wedding, 2000.

Left: The Gee family, then living in Buffalo, NY, 1983.

Glenn and his mother, Janice, 2011.

I Could Always Come Home

by Glenn Rawson

I remember coming home from school one spring day when I was just a little boy, and as was my habit, I called my dog, Stockings, and we went off to explore. Living on a ranch in a remote part of Idaho provided plenty of wilderness for my adventures. I loved to wander through the trees, along the creeks, and across the hillsides. I loved it then and still do. The problem on this particular day was that I lost track of time. When I realized it was getting dark, I was miles from home. I knew I couldn't make it back before it was too dark to see my way, and where I grew up, there was no such thing as street lights or signs; it was mountain country. I looked around and saw that I was closer to a neighboring ranch than to my house. So I set out for their place, arriving just after dark. When I explained my situation to them and asked them to take me home, they didn't seem all that interested. They said they would, but they moved slowly, and it got later and later and darker and darker.

I kept thinking, I'm in trouble. My dad is going to have my hide. Time dragged on, and my fear increased. It was dark and cold, and I was scared, nearly in a panic. Then I saw headlights coming up the rutted road. It was my dad. I was saved. But the look on his face quickly made it clear that I had made a big mistake. He didn't yell at me; he just pointed back down the mountain and said, "Start walking."

I thought he must be joking. But he wasn't. Terrified, I walked a few hundred yards and sat down by the side of the road, my arms wrapped around my dog, and began to cry. Dad pulled up a few minutes later and told me to get in. I climbed into the warm pickup, and he took me home. He didn't say much. He didn't have to. I thought I knew what I had done wrong, but as it turned out, I had no idea.

We walked into the house. The lights were dim, and my mother was sitting in a front room chair, crying like I had never seen her cry. When she saw me, she came out of the chair with a sob, threw her arms around me, and cried with relief. She thought her little boy had fallen into the flooding creek behind the ranch and drowned. I will never forget that night and the pain and worry on my mother's face. It hurt so much that I tried never to do it again. I couldn't bear it. My dad quietly allowed me to learn that hurting my mother was one of the worst things I could ever do. It was a lesson I never forgot.

It's hard for me to pinpoint one story or instance in my life that would describe what my mother means to me, so I would like to share a number of them.

My earliest recollection of my mother was that she was the loveliest woman alive. I thought I had the prettiest mother that any little boy could have. As I matured, that opinion did not change. I used to brag that my mother was barely five foot two and weighed one hundred pounds—that she still had the figure of a cheerleader. We used to

go on dates when I was in my early twenties, and people would comment that she looked more like my girlfriend than my mother.

I remember on more than one occasion, coming home from school and finding my mother exercising in the front room, and that was in the days when exercise was not a popular fad. Then there were those pleasant summer evenings when, after supper, Mother would go for a walk down through the fields on the ranch. Once in a while, I would tag along on my bicycle. She did it for the exercise. I went along because I was bored.

COMMUNICATION

JANICE LEE SMUIN RAWSON

is the mother of

GLENN RAWSON

Glenn Rawson grew up on a ranch. His love of the outdoors remains strong to this day. It isn't unusual to find him outside in his free time, running, bird watching, hiking, or just taking a deep breath. Professionally, he has been a teacher for nearly thirty years, and that brought him to telling stories, which he does weekly  on his *Sounds of Sunday* radio show and on the *History of the Saints* television and radio programs. He borrowed this philosophy of telling stories from Abraham Lincoln, who said, "They say I tell a great many stories. I reckon I do, but I have learned from long experience that plain people . . . are more easily influenced through the medium of a broad and humorous illustration than in any other way."

He loves people and especially his family. Glenn and his wife, Debbie, have seven children and two grandchildren. They live in Idaho.

Below: Janice on the night of Glenn's graduation from high school. *Right*: Debbie, Glenn, Jed, and Janice at a family gathering in 2001. *Far right*: Janice on vacation in Montana. *Next page —left*: Janice and Orson at granddaughter Dawni Jo's wedding, 2010.

Those moments with my mother are deeply imprinted, and to this day, when I find myself out running on a little-used road in the sagebrush, I remember with fondness those times with her. For most of my adult life, I have been an athlete because of my mother's example.

Hurting my mother was one of the worst things I could ever do.

My mother and I were friends. We still are. I could tell her anything and often still do. I never remember her once betraying my confidence. As a teenager, when I was looking for excitement, I would sneak into the kitchen and come up behind my mother while she was cooking at the stove. Before she could react, I would grab her by the elbows, lift her up, bump her head (gently of course) on the ceiling, and then drop her and run for my life. She would grab the first thing she could lay her hands on and chase me all through the house, pretending to be furious. Usually, I was laughing so hard

that she would catch me without a problem. She would pound on me and scold me, but we always wound up laughing together.

One has to be careful, though, in doing such things with my mother. She is a fireball. There was that day, for example, when Dad did something similar, and she turned, swung her fist, and broke his nose. She may be small, but she could keep all of us in line. She even mastered the talent of punching me on the point of the shoulder and paralyzing my arm (when needed). I loved my mother for those times of fun and banter, but I always knew not to mess with her. She was a tough lady and could hold her own. Because of her, I still love to tease and play with my own children and grandchildren.

One day, when I was just a boy, I connected that wonderful fragrance that seemed to emanate from her with a small bottle of perfume I found in her room. It was Chanel No. 5. She laughed when I asked her if

Growing up, I was usually bigger than most of the other kids my age, but because my mom had taught me the golden rule, I had no inclination to use my size to intimidate others, and she made it very clear to me that gaining a reputation as a bully was probably the worse thing I could do.

But she also took it a step further, teaching me to keep an eye out for people who were teased and encouraging me to go to their rescue if necessary. She taught me to never judge people who were different.

On one occasion, I tried to help a kid who was being teased at school. I was a team captain, and we were choosing teams for a game. Trying to remember what my mother had taught me, I chose this kid first. He wasn't the best player, and everyone knew it, but suddenly, everyone began to treat this kid like he was their friend. Later that day, my teacher dropped by my house to tell my mom about the incident. My mom later took me aside and told me how proud she was of me and that I had made a big impact on that kid. It was a great lesson to learn, and I credit my mother for teaching me to have compassion for others. I would have never learned it without her great example.

When it comes to similarities, my mother and I are very much alike in that we don't like people making a fuss over us. It's obviously a lot harder for me, given my chosen career, but my mom is very shy and hates being in the limelight. I remember when I was nearing the end of my career at BYU, many

of my teammates had never met my mom. Most of them didn't know who she was and certainly weren't aware that she had been to almost every home game throughout my college career. They all knew my dad; he was always out front, interacting with the players and joking around with them. My mom, however, chose to remain in the background and out of view.

During the NCAA tournament, the television cameras would often show my family when something dramatic happened. Inevitably, they could find my dad or my brother, TJ, but my mom learned to sit as far away as possible from them because she didn't want to be on camera. She was always content with being at home, doing her thing with our family and her friends. When she's with our family and close friends, she is very charming and charismatic, but she simply prefers to avoid the spotlight.

I am grateful to my mom for teaching me how to be more Christlike. I hope I can follow her example and live up to her high expectations. It's the least I can do to show how much I love and appreciate her.

$\mathcal{L}$ike Clockwork

by Peter Vidmar

Of my mother's many admirable traits, none has impacted my life more than her consistency. Like a finely honed Swiss timepiece, my mom was unfailingly reliable.

In a world dominated by confusion and chaos, it's difficult to establish a home environment of structure and order, but that's exactly the type of home I enjoyed growing up. Only in retrospect do I comprehend its impact on my life and any success I may have achieved.

My parents were products of the Great Depression and therefore embody the stereotypical down-to-earth, quit-your-belly-aching-and-get-it-done mindset.

My father is Slovenian but grew up in Los Angeles in the 1930s. He spent many long days at Muscle Beach, where famous fitness people, like Jack LaLanne, were often seen working out. My dad was a natural athlete, and gymnastics was among his favorite activities; he performed some impressive strength-related stunts. At night, he worked hard washing dishes at a local restaurant until he joined the navy during World War II. He met my mother at a USO function while he was stationed in upstate New York.

Without any support from friends or family, he came to Utah, found a job, and was doing his best to afford the costs associated with physical therapy and learning to walk again. He was alone and needed guidance, and my mother went out of her way to help Andrew as much as she could.

Little did my mother know that stopping to help this young man would be the beginning of a friendship that remains strong to this day. Her willingness to take a risk and stop to help a total stranger is indicative of her courage, compassion, and love for others.

My mother is one of a kind. She's suffered through many trials, hardships, and heartbreaks, yet because of her willingness to show kindness to others, she is one of the most Christlike people I know. She's my friend, my confidant, and my life-long cheerleader. And I'm grateful she's my mom.

Her *willingness* to take a risk and stop to **help** a total stranger is indicative of her courage, compassion, and *love* for others.

Sacrifices

by Steve Young

Kids have no clue about the sacrifices their parents make on their behalf.

When I was about ten years old, my dad was offered a job in New York City. Both my parents are Utah natives, so they were quite apprehensive about moving across the country to a new and unknown environment to raise their kids. My parents prayed about every aspect of the move. Should they uproot their family? Which house and neighborhood should they select? It was a difficult decision and one that required significant sacrifices. Both of them not only left the comfort of their familiar surroundings but also their network of family and friends.

Fortunately, our situation in Greenwich, Connecticut, was ideal. The only problem was the ward meetinghouse was about forty minutes away. Faithfully, my mother drove us to and from the church many times each week. It was especially burdensome, since during that time, we had two meetings on Sunday, in addition to Primary and Mutual during the week.

To add to that, when I was in high school, my mother taught my early morning seminary class, which meant four times per week we had to leave at five in the morning in order to make it to the church with enough time to open the building for the other students.

The first years in Greenwich were great for us kids but very hard on my mom. She did her best not to let us know how much she struggled. My dad traveled often, and she was

left at home to fend for herself and a house-
ful of five kids, four of whom were very active
boys. My mother was never one to complain
much about anything, even though we may
have given her many reasons to do so.

It rained far more often than it ever did in
Utah, but my mom often took us on long walks
in the rain, and the younger kids thought
it was great fun. I didn't know it until I was
older, but I figured out that my mom used the
rain to hide her tears. Fortunately, her faith
sustained her despite the heavy burdens she
had to bear.

The early years in Connecticut found my parents adjusting to the cost of living and a new
house, which meant they were "house poor"
and financially challenged. Despite that, my
mom always did what she could to get us kids
involved in almost any activity we wanted to
do. Each of us was heavily involved in sports,
and she drove us to and from practices and
competitions. Despite it all, she always managed to have a great family meal on the table,
and each night we sat and talked about the
events of the day and our plans for the next.

Many people may attribute my athletic ability
to my father, who was an outstanding football
player at BYU and is known to most as "Grit."
But if you ask my dad, I'm sure he'll admit
that although his genetics helped, I inherited
speed and coordination from my mom. In
elementary school, I remember my mom always winning the "mom's race" at our annual
field day event. And when we were involved
in swimming and track, my mom had the

SPORTS

SHERRY ANN STEED YOUNG

is the mother of

STEVE YOUNG

Steve Young was born October 11, 1961, and
grew up in Connecticut. He is best known for his
time with the NFL's San Francisco 49ers. He also
played for the Tampa
Bay Buccaneers and
the Los Angeles
Express of the USFL. He
was named MVP of the
NFL in 1992 and 1994
and MVP of Super Bowl
XXIX. He was inducted
into the Pro Football
Hall of Fame in 2005,
where he was the first
left-handed quarterback
to be so honored. He
ranks third in NFL his-
tory in career passer rat-
ing among NFL quarterbacks who have thrown
at least 1,500 passing attempts (96.8). He also
won a record six NFL passing titles.

He earned a juris doctorate degree from BYU
and an honorary doctor of letters from Utah
Valley University. He is a commentator for ESPN
and appears regularly on radio and television. He is the founder of the Forever Young
Foundation, a nonprofit organization dedicated
to serving children with significant physical,
emotional, and financial challenges. He is
involved in many other philanthropic activities
and regularly speaks to young adult and other
Church groups around the country.

Steve and his wife, Barbara, were married in
2000 in the Kona Hawaii Temple. They have
two sons and two daughters.

of the things she can do, and I wonder how many other talents she has yet to show us.

I should have recognized her flashes of creativity when I was younger. I remember my brothers and sisters being impatient when she tried a new-fangled recipe from the latest women's magazine. I don't recall any of her experimental recipes tasting bad, but we were more content to have her stick to a few basic meals and rotate them accordingly. We had no clue we were stifling her abundant ingenuity. She chose to forego her own desires in lieu of her children's.

Her creativity was also evidenced in how she was always able to make do, regardless of the challenges she faced. Nothing seemed to overwhelm her.

I figured out that my mom used the rain to hide her tears.

skills to boost everyone. In those days, parents used stopwatches to record times. It seemed everyone wanted to be in my mom's lane because her eye-hand coordination was so good that our times were always the fastest when we were in her lane.

As I look back on those years, I get a glimpse of the sacrifices she and my father made for our family. It wasn't until most of her children had left the nest that we learned she was a gifted writer, revealing to us a talent she had suppressed while raising her family. She started her writing career with an article for a Greenwich, Connecticut, newspaper. Now she writes a regular lifestyle column for the *Deseret News.* She often amazes me with some

Consequently, my mom has always thought fast and acted fast. She seemed to be a mile ahead of everyone, thinking ahead and anticipating her next move. It must have been an adaptation she developed as a way of managing her cadre of rambunctious kids. Sometimes she moves so quickly or talks so fast that she'll say something that makes sense in her mind but doesn't come out quite right, and we all laugh together. Other times, she'll be going at such a pace that she'll forget something important, and she'll laugh at herself. It's become such a familiar occurrence that our family has adopted my mom's name as a verb. When someone says something out of context or does something funny, we'll often say, "You Sherry'd that one!"

My mother's passion for life and for her children has never waned. I remember a time playing little league football when I was hit hard enough to knock the wind out of me. As I lay on the ground gasping for air, my father came on the field to help me catch my breath. If that wasn't embarrassing enough, I saw out of the corner of my eye my mother rushing to the field. I was mortified! A host of embarrassing thoughts ran through my mind as I envisioned my mom rushing to my side to kiss me or do some other goofball thing that my friends would never let me live down. Instead, she came toward me and nearly stepped on me to get to the kid who hit me. She grabbed him by the facemask and scolded him, saying, "Don't you EVER hit my son like that again." Then she calmly walked off the field. This incident was such a longstanding joke in our family that during my playing career, we threatened to never give my mom lower-bowl tickets, just in case she ever felt the urge to rush the field.

Although at times my family makes light of some of the things my mom does, we have a great respect for her, especially because she doesn't take herself too seriously. Her warmth, intellect, and ability to adapt are her hallmarks. I've always been amazed at her ability to make proverbial lemonade out of lemons by simply finding the good in whatever happens. Her good-natured optimism is rooted in her testimony of the gospel of Jesus Christ.

She has engendered a competitive spirit in each of her children because she understands the eternal principle of opposition in all things (see 2 Nephi 2:11). She has taught us that being a Saint is like an athletic event, in a manner of speaking. As Saints we must be spiritually athletic, emotionally athletic, and labor diligently like an athlete. We cannot be passive or carefree about the commandments, our covenants, or our commitment to becoming all that God wants us to be.

Like mother Eve, my mom has an understanding of her own value, not only to her family and those around her but to God. She understands the eternal nature of families and the plan of salvation. I know it gives her perspective and purpose because she taught us through her example that her life has meaning. My mother has always acted in accordance with her knowledge that she is a woman of true purpose.

She has also taught us the eternal principle of charity and that without charity, we "cannot inherit that place . . . prepared in the mansions of [our] Father" (Ether 12:34). And since she understands that motherhood is

Previous page: Steve, with his parents and younger brother, visits the NFL Hall of Fame, 1974.

Above: Young Steve wants to be like his father, "Grit," 1963.

Left: The Young family in 1974.

Right: Sherry and her boys.

Far right: JJ, the dog, and the Young children

Below: Sherry with her family.

Happiness and **joy** come when we make personal, Christlike *sacrifices* on behalf of those we **love.**

the essence of charity, it influences most everything she does throughout her day.

I am lucky to have been taught by goodly parents about God's eternal plan of happiness. I am the man I am today because I have a mother who taught me to laugh at myself, to patiently endure my trials, and to know that happiness and joy come when we make personal, Christlike sacrifices on behalf of those we love.

Alice and J. W. Marriott Sr. inspecting a Hot Shoppe restaurant.

The Leveling Influence

by J. W. "Bill" Marriott, Jr.

My mother grew up in Salt Lake City, where her father was bishop of the Salt Lake thirty-third ward. During the great flu epidemic of 1919, he helped attend to scores of sick and dying members of his ward. The result, however, was that he also contracted the deadly virus and fell victim to the epidemic. He left behind his widow; a sixteen-year-old son, Walter; and my mother, Alice, who was only eleven years old.

My mother was given great responsibilities to manage the home while her mother worked to support the family. To further make life a challenge, Walter was stricken with polio, and it fell upon my mother to take care of him as well as manage the affairs of the home.

Allie, as she was known, met my father when she was only eighteen years old, and she had already been in college three years. She was an honor student at the University of Utah, majoring in Spanish. She had an extraordinary intellect and had great capacity to juggle many tasks and responsibilities simultaneously. When my father asked her on their first date, she was a member of Chi Omega sorority, served as an officer in both the French and Spanish clubs, practiced piano for two hours each day, and was living offcampus so she could continue to care for her brother and all the other domestic responsibilities at home.

My mother graduated with honors from the University of Utah when she was nineteen. My parents were married in the Salt Lake Temple the day after her graduation, and they packed up their belongings in a Model T Ford and moved across the country to Washington DC. My father had started an A&W root beer stand just two weeks prior to their marriage in June of 1927.

Mother had no intentions of being involved in my father's entrepreneurial venture, but she was drawn into the business through taking care of the finances. She had no experience as a bookkeeper, but she learned quickly and did very well.

Their first summer was a success, but they had to find a way to stay in business when cold weather came. They decided to convert their root beer stand into a small coffee shop and feature Mexican food. My mother was called on to be the cook but had no experience cooking Mexican food. She walked over to the Mexican embassy and asked

BUSINESS

ALICE SHEETS MARRIOTT
is the mother of

BILL MARRIOTT

J. W. "Bill" Marriott is the son of Alice Marriott and J. Willard Marriott, the founder of Marriott International. He attended St. Albans School in Washington DC and earned a BS degree in finance from the University of Utah, where he became a member of Sigma Chi. He served as an officer in the United States Navy. He is also an Eagle Scout and a recipient of the Distinguished Eagle Scout Award.

He joined the Marriott Corporation in 1956, was elected executive vice president and member of the board of directors in January 1964, and was named president of the company in November 1964, chief executive officer in 1972, and chairman of the board in 1985.

Marriott is actively involved in various boards and councils, including the U.S. Travel and Tourism Promotional

Advisory Board, the executive committee of the World Travel & Tourism Council, the National Business Council, the board of trustees of the National Urban League, a director of the National Geographic Society, and a director of the Naval Academy Endowment Trust. He serves as chairman of the President's Export Council, a group that advises the president on matters relating to export trade, and serves as chairman of the Leadership Council of the Laura Bush Foundation for America's Libraries.

He was featured in an episode of *60 Minutes*, which aired on April 7, 1996, where Mike Wallace interviewed him regarding his faith, alongside football star Steve Young and President Gordon B. Hinckley. In 1997, Marriott was called to be an Area Authority Seventy and member of the Fifth Quorum of the Seventy. This quorum was split in 2004, and Marriott joined the newly created Sixth Quorum of the Seventy, where he still serves.

On May 4, 2006, Marriott received an honorary doctorate of humanities from Weber State University during the university's 127th commencement. He also delivered the commencement address during these proceedings.

He is married to the former Donna Garff. They have four children, fourteen grandchildren, and three great-grandchildren.

their embassy chef for recipes. Her command of the Spanish language must have fascinated him, and he coached her until she perfected her hot tamale and chili recipes.

When they opened the restaurant that first day, her food was an instant hit, and the restaurant thrived for years to come. Ultimately, more than one hundred Hot Shoppe restaurants were opened, which later lead to government catering contracts, airport and inflight catering, Bob's Big Boy and Roy Rogers Restaurants, Great American theme parks, and, of course, the Marriott global lodging business of hotels and resorts.

When I was born in 1932, my mom's role in the day-to-day business became quite limited, but she continued to be a leveling force for my father and was the much-needed impetus behind helping my father make major decisions, which were often laborious and time consuming.

It is well known that my father was often challenging to deal with, but my mother was able to "tame" this Utah farm boy and help him learn to be a good dad. Her patience, common sense, and wisdom gave her the ability to see beyond the moment, and my father came to rely heavily on her judgment throughout his life. Although she had a tremendous capacity to accomplish almost anything she wished, she was willing to remain behind the scenes throughout the growth and expansion of

She was the *quiet hero* behind the Marriott family's success.

Above: Alice Marriott.

the family business. In the truest sense of the phrase, she was the quiet hero behind the Marriott family's success.

My mother taught me about service by her willingness to spend her time and efforts

and otherwise introduce them to some new friends. She was also heavily involved in Republican politics on a local, state, and national level. She was the first woman to hold the position of treasurer for the National Republican Convention, a role she filled during the presidential election cycles in 1964, 1968, and 1972.

But her volunteer efforts were never more important than her family. Her level-headed influence tempered each of us in the family, setting an example of the importance of our eternal family and of the necessity of always making time to serve others.

In April of 2000, she died at the age of ninety-two, nearly fifteen years after my father passed away. To this day, I miss talking to her, especially when I'm discouraged or am facing seemingly insurmountable challenges. She was always encouraging, reminding me that "this, too, shall pass," and helping me remain determined to do my best, to do what's right, and serve God.

My mother's lifetime of quiet and devoted service was matched only by her compassion, humility, and uncanny common sense. I am blessed to have her voice of wisdom still ringing in my ears.

on behalf of others. She became heavily involved in civic affairs, Church callings, and politics after my brother and I left the nest.

Seeing a need to help the wives of foreign diplomats, ambassadors, members of Congress, and other women who had moved to this strange and intriguing city of Washington, she and a friend organized the "Welcome to Washington" hospitality program. They regularly invited newly arrived women to visit, offer advice, help them adjust to their new environment,

> But her volunteer efforts were *never* more important than her family.

Above: Bill, Dick, and Alice Marriott.

prayers directed me to serve the Lord first and to let other life decisions follow.

Following my mission to Germany, my mother's diligent prayers and her Job-like patience bore fruit, and she again walked arm in arm with my father back to the temple. Thereafter, he rejoined my mother in a rich and fulfilling life of active Church service, temple attendance, and fatherly gospel leadership that continued for the remaining eighteen years of his life.

Mistakenly, I had assumed for years that it was solely my father who had taught me what it means to be a man. He clearly taught me what it meant to be a man of integrity and how to provide for a family. I will always hold a special place in my heart for him—he was a man who was willing to give his life for his country and his family and taught all of his children to respect and revere our mother.

However, it was my mother, my grandmother, and my great-grandmother who showed me that a real man stands tallest when he leads his family in diligent service to the Lord. These women taught me one of this life's greatest lessons—what it means to be a man of faith.

I am eternally grateful and humbled by the spiritual giants comprising three generations of devoted mothers and those who have come after them. Continuing this legacy is my wife, Kelli's, extraordinary devotion to our children and her abiding faith. As I went about my business career, she was too often alone in raising our children. Because of her strong conviction, our children, now young men and women, have served missions and are living lives devoted to the gospel.

My mother continues to teach me enduring gospel principles by her daily example. The past ten years, she has been without my father by her side. Yet, as has always been the case, she stands tall. As time has passed, her walk has become increasingly more uncertain and her health increasingly challenged. But I never fail to see the strong light of the gospel and the eternal love that lives behind her beautiful brown eyes. My mother is a woman who knows her Savior. I am forever indebted, as are generations yet to come, to that little baby girl from Cache Valley who fought to live and won.

"Be thou strong therefore, and shew thyself a man; And keep the charge of the Lord thy God, to walk in his ways." —1 Kings 2:2

> These women taught me one of this life's greatest lessons.

"Angel Mother"

by Mark Allred

Sometimes we Mormons love eulogy better than life itself. This is particularly so around Mother's Day. We picture a strange, angelic caricature . . . a soft, spiritual blossom who floats through her world insulated in an aura of the divine. She may shed a sweet tear at the pain and faltering of her fellow beings. She may even encounter what for others might be terrible adversity. But she herself never stumbles. Anger and depression are as foreign to her as the urge to speak a harsh word. Always her home has the hush and serenity of a temple. Always the gentle harmonies of lovely children at play. "Sweeter sings the brooklet by. . . ."

Let me not disparage reverence, spiritual peace, and other great virtues that can flow from a Christlike life. Only a word of caution. Often the effect of our eulogies is not what we desire. My wife, Darlene, is representative of many women I know. She is a valiant daughter of God and an exceptional mother. Yet, the day of the year she dreads most of all is Mother's Day because more than any other day, on that day, the angelic caricature is placed before her. She knows she is not that perfect creature—which means she must, therefore, be a failure. Hers is a life of struggles that often seem overwhelming. She is fighting life's undertows with every fiber and sometimes fears she might be drowning. She feels riddled with shortcomings. And Mother's Day eulogies bring only despair and the conviction of inadequacy.

This brings me to reflect on my own mother, Sharon. This mother of *eleven* has always been as the woman of old, "full of good works and almsdeeds" (Acts 9:36). Many times people have told me my mother is a "saint" or an "angel." Here, however, I have had to pause, not knowing whether to agree without further explanation. If you think she's the "divine blossom," you've failed to understand my mother's substance. My mother is a woman of character. (And she is a character!) Yet, much of her nobility lies in the war she wages

Much of her *nobility* lies in the war she wages with her own shortcomings.

with her own shortcomings. Tenacity. Guts. And bloody knuckles. Tears sneaking out through clenched eyelids. Not a perfect person but a very righteous one. A person who's trying, who's progressing. One, by the way, whom I respect infinitely more than the caricature.

Sharon can, for example, be highly volatile.

When I was young, I watched an episode of *Gunsmoke or Bonanza*, in which bad guys were handling nitroglycerine for some appallingly evil purpose. The substance, as portrayed in the show, was unpredictable. Nitroglycerine could be carried over mountains by wagon, bouncing and rattling for days, and nothing would happen. Then, suddenly, a seemingly minor jiggle, and KABOOM! A horrific explosion. Bodies and debris flying everywhere. I couldn't say whether that was the way nitroglycerine really worked. But it certainly was how Mom seemed to work. This quality, inherited from my equally wonderful and fiery grandpa, was known among us as the "Wallace temper."

Though maybe Mom was not all that unpredictable. It's possible we children were just too dull to recognize the obvious signs of imminent detonation. She would be in the kitchen, for example. It would be a dangerous part of the month. And I am *not* talking about PMS, the biological cycles of women, or other such hormonal matters of which we children had no awareness. I'm talking about the checkbook. Balancing it was an activity that had to be done and one that invariably caused her misery.

Oh, Mom would approach the moment in good spirits. Hadn't she done everything humanly possible to be frugal? Weren't we still

driving that same battered station wagon to its dying gasp? She may have bought Tony a pair of cheap Grand Central sneakers this

**SHARON RICHARDS
WALLACE ALLRED**

is the mother of

MARK ALLRED

Mark Allred was born in Ogden, Utah, and graduated from Ogden High School. He went on to serve a mission to Germany. In 1981, he graduated from Weber State University with a bachelor of arts degree. That same year, he enlisted in the United States Army National Guard as a German linguist. He was a member of the National Guard until 1984, during which time he spent sixteen months on active army duty, completed the Russian Basic Course at the Defense Language Institute, and was promoted to the rank of warrant officer. He attended law school at the University of Utah in Salt Lake City, and he received his commission through the Air Force Graduate Law Program and the Air Force Reserve Officer Training Corps in 1986.

In 2004, he was promoted to the rank of colonel. Currently, he is the chief trial judge of the United States Air Force. Colonel Allred is a member of the Bar of the United States Supreme Court and the Utah State Bar, and he is licensed to practice before the United States Supreme Court, the Court of Appeals for the Armed Forces, the United States Air Force Court of Criminal Appeals, the United States District Court for the District of Utah, and the Utah Supreme Court.

Mark and his wife, Darlene, have six children and four grandchildren. He is a member of the Dale City ward in Dale City, Virginia, and serves on the high council of the Woodbridge Virginia stake.

past month after the soles had torn right off the canvas of his last ones, but there hadn't been a stitch of anything for anyone else, had there? Certainly not for herself. And everyone knew how Mom scrimped on food: the powdered milk, the hamburgers made mostly of bread and soybean, the virtual elimination of desserts and anything sweet. We had a lot to be thankful for. We were healthy and had enough to eat, while people in China or some such place were no doubt starving. But still, at least to us kids, it often seemed we were gnawing on bark.

Mom had clutched her pennies until she had little images of Lincoln imbedded in her palms—figuratively at least. And she'd tried so hard to live the gospel in every possible

Right: Mark Allred's mother, Sharon Richards Allred.

way. Paid a full tithing. Lived a righteous life. So now, this month, everything should balance out, right? Maybe even a chance to buy one or two things on her "desperate needs" list, right?

No. Wrong. Once again, wrong. Mom would be sitting there at the kitchen table with her ledger, the checkbook, the stack of processed checks, and the pile of bills. She'd be making notes and adding columns of numbers up and down the backs of old envelopes. And that pile of paperwork would gradually become a minefield. She'd wander through it, and there'd be bursts and explosions of bad news. Dental bills. New starter motor for the car. Her financial reckoning ordeal might last most of a morning—starting with optimism, going to bad, and ending worse. Checking and rechecking figures that continually bore the same depressing message.

Sadly, while Mom was caught up in her fiscal woes, she would be little able to focus on anything else. And the rest of her household would spin its way into chaos. Outwardly, she would take no notice. But an inside part of her, just under the edge of consciousness, would register the uproar. Each bit of noise, bickering, and discord coming from her increasingly riotous and anarchist brood would add up. Pressure would build beneath the surface. An observant bystander would no doubt see it all happening. Rational young people would recognize the signs of impending disaster and tread softly. But we didn't. We were simply idiots.

Here's the scene. The TV is blaring in the front room. Above its noise, Mom can hear us quarreling over which program to watch. A young voice whines over and over again, "I was here first." Eventually an older one, filled with disdain, orders the younger voice to "shut up!" Name-calling, a physical clash, someone begins to bawl. Tattling and more tattling to Mom—who is trying not to listen.

Mom yells out a time or two, "Stop it. Would you please stop it, just till I can get through in here?"

Neighbor kids run through the house, shouting. A child wanders about, blubbering—the insincere bawling of one who hasn't gotten his or her way and wants others to pay for it.

"Mark, will you please see what Robby wants?" Mom calls.

But her pleas lack the intensity to make us behave. The situation becomes flammable to the point you can almost smell the fumes.

"I mean it. Settle down!" she calls.

Yet we children carry on, recklessly throwing off sparks.

Then it happens. One last tiny spark of contention. Ignition! And boom!

There's a thunderous roar from Mother as she comes after us!

Artists of the Western world have tried to portray the Apocalypse, to capture that moment when the God of vengeance swoops from the skies to bring swift destruction upon the wicked. The unrighteous wear looks of horror. Their faces show the anguished realization that it is now everlastingly too late to avoid that awful justice they so plainly deserve. The scale may be smaller, but there is certainly an apocalyptic quality to the moment when Mom finally erupts.

The screams, "Darn you brats!" (And, to be honest, worse things.) She goes wild! Sweeps through us in a rampage. Swinging and slapping at anyone within reach. (Many people describe their maternal parent as an "angel mother." My own mother was at

Left: Sharon reading to the kids. _Middle_: Mark, Aaron, and Chris on top. _Right_: Doll, Mark, and Sharon.

times a "*destroying* angel.") Fortunately, we'd learned to scatter and dive for cover.

Actually, I don't think Mom was ever so indiscriminate as to cause bleeding, a bruise, or severe pain. And she was also careful to spare the neighbor kids—though they often deserved punishment as much as we did, none of them was ever touched. "Two shall be grinding at the mill, one shall be taken, and the other one left," as the scripture says.

Now the destroying angel is roaring off, sobbing wildly, to her bedroom, where the door slams and rattles the windows. There then follows a period of stunned and almost absolute silence. We knew Mom had been on the brink—or should have known. Any one of us could have been just a little bit helpful or shown the slightest kindness to someone else, instead of adding to the pressure that pushed her over the edge.

We children remain in our quiet, penitent state for quite some time. The neighbors have departed. Eventually, one of our smaller kids goes and taps softly on Mom's door. Even opens the door slowly and cautiously wanders in. Mom is on her knees at the side of her bed. She has been praying—mostly for forgiveness. And for strength to do better. The small one approaches Mom carefully and gives her an uncertain hug. Mom stirs and hugs back, tentatively at first and then very tightly. Giving a long, drained sigh, Mom then emerges from her bedroom, weary eyes moist and drying. There are more hugs, strong ones, between Mom and kids, and in some cases even between kids and each other.

Forget the money! She runs a brush through her hair, puts on some lipstick, and we all pile in the station wagon and head to Skaggs Drug Store for ice cream cones.

Later that evening, Dad returns from a long teaching day that included night classes. He finds his family gathered in the front room. At least a couple of kids sit beside Mom on the couch; two or three are sprawled on the carpet near her feet, and a baby is breathing warm sighs beneath the blanket at

Her *explosions* would never happen if she had insulated herself in an easier, more selfish life.

her breast. The children are happy to see their father, but Mom's been reading *The Fellowship of the Ring* to them, and they don't want interruptions.

"We're to this super scary part where they're in these places—"

"The mines, they're the Mines of Moria," someone cuts in.

"Yeah, and the orcs are coming! With some giant monster thing—"

"And the drums are going DOOM! DOOM! DOOM!"

"Shut up, you guys! Let Mom read!"

Sharon and Gordon exchange knowing parental smiles, and she returns to the book.

Despite the present tale of monsters and terror, there is serenity in our front room. There is peace and goodness each of us can feel—and love.

And despite my earlier, borderline-sarcastic comments about perfect mothers and "bliss complete," I must now say that there was in our home, on this evening and almost every other evening when our mother read to us, a serenity, not likely found in many other places on Earth.

Later, after the reading, comes the best part of almost any day. There have been "prayers and hugs," our bedtime ritual in which our parents hear our supplications to Heavenly Father, love us, and tuck us in. Now Mom has remained to tickle my back. Her way of making everything right with the world.

I am hugging my pillow, feeling the clean sheets beneath me, while Mom lightly traces the contours of my neck and shoulders with her fingertips. It's a hot summer night. A faint canyon wind is beginning to trickle through the peach leaves outside my open window. Crickets are singing in the blue-white moonlight. And I am thinking about my mom's eruption earlier in the day.

Actually, I am happy and proud of her. I may be too young to articulate them well, but I understand certain things. I know people aren't supposed to curse and lose their tempers. But heaven knows Mom only learned to swear after she began raising her pack of strong-willed children, not before. Her explosions would never happen if she had insulated herself in an easier, more selfish life. But this was a young woman of faith who strode into unconditional, all-out motherhood, not knowing beforehand the things which she should do—only that this was right and was what the Lord wanted of her.

So she discovered some mortal flaws. Wasn't she fighting very hard to overcome each of them? So she was not the great angelic caricature. So what!

After a while, I feel myself slipping from consciousness as if drifting from shore on a small boat. Mom's cool touch is a breeze, gently blowing me in the direction of a peaceful place, where logic and reason are relaxing out of existence. More and more, my thoughts are blending into dreams. But Mom is still there. Her soft gliding strokes are on my back and shoulders. Back on that other shore. Whispers of love.

Ministering of an Angel

by Matthew Dean Barkdull

Not too long ago, the First Presidency powerfully reminded us that motherhood is close to divinity—the highest, holiest service assigned to womankind—and that those who honor its holy calling and service are considered to be next to angels.

As a newly crowned teenager, I didn't appreciate Mom as I should have. Perhaps it was the mixture of immaturity, hormones, and a splash of selfishness. Whatever the reason, I never visualized her as being in the company of angels. It wasn't until I matured a little that the scales of darkness began to fall from my eyes (see 2 Nephi 30:6) and that I finally understood that an angel had been in my midst all along.

Mom is the younger of two children. A vivacious, dimpled redhead who took after her straight-talking mother and quick-witted father, Mom grew up surrounded by love but also the unknown. Her father was born with hemophilia, a severe, hereditary blood clotting disorder. Grandpa was racked with sudden bleeding attacks throughout his life, and each attack resulted in a lengthy hospital stay as doctors tried anything to stop the bleeding, including administering snake venom and distilled tar.

This was Mom's reality. She became accustomed to waking up to her mother shaking her and telling her, "We need to take Daddy to the hospital." Along with Mom's older brother, the small family would bundle up and drive to the LDS Hospital in Salt Lake

ELIZABETH "BUFFIE" BARKDULL

is the mother of

MATTHEW DEAN BARKDULL

Matthew Dean Barkdull is a licensed marriage and family therapist and a certified medical family therapist. He works as a health specialist for the Church in the Welfare Department's administrative division. Matt is a nationally published author and contributor to academic journals, inspirational book chapters, and health magazines. Among his many interests, he especially loves public speaking on inspirational and motivational topics, researching and writing family histories, playing the piano, and learning the Hebrew language. He and his wife, Kristin, are the proud parents of three girls and live in Lehi, Utah. He serves as first counselor in the North Lake second ward's bishopric.

Elizabeth "Buffie" Rytting, high school, 1969.

City, their daddy's second home—a place where he spent nearly a third of his life. The family never knew how long he would be away.

When life is uncertain and the blessing of predictability doesn't exist, we can choose a few ways to respond: become frozen with fear or be propelled by perspective. Mom's parents preferred the latter. People who knew Mom's family would often remark, "They take full advantage of each day as though it were their last."

Like my grandfather, I, too, inherited hemophilia and so did my two younger brothers. Often were the times I awakened to a throbbing hemorrhage in a joint. Sometimes hemorrhages were so terrible that emergency room visits were necessary. Writhing back and forth, unable to swallow painkillers because of a dry throat and pain-driven distraction, I sought any healing balm that could quench the fire. The greatest relief I ever found was within the presence and embrace of my mother. Her presence alone, the softness of her hands over mine, and the whispering of courage while we prayed and as Dad pronounced priesthood blessings, preached sermons equal to those uttered by prophets. Never was a boy so immersed in pain but so comforted with love. As I came out of these crucibles, my testimony was continually reaffirmed: with God, nothing is impossible—an eternal truth my mother quietly taught.

As the oldest hemophiliac in my family, I not only benefited from Mother's love and nurturing, but I was also blessed as a witness. There were nights that I awoke to the sound of a pitiful cry from a younger brother. Making my way upstairs to investigate, I would see a lamp on the kitchen table, lying on its side with its shade removed. Mother and Father would be crouched down around the lamp with one of my hemophiliac brothers, trying to see a vein. Having memorized this scene, I knew exactly what was unfolding, for this drama played out more often than I ever wished. My brother was hemorrhaging internally.

In most circumstances, the only way hemophiliacs can clot is to administer an intravenous drug called Factor. Although my parents were carefully trained to administer the IV at home, the veins of my toddler brothers were small. Many attempts to hit a vein failed, causing my brothers to wail. In desperation, my parents would seek any vein possible that looked big enough to set the needle, including the forehead and ankles.

There were times I was asked to help hold down a brother while this drama ensued. I witnessed my mother's tear-stained cheeks as she plead with the Lord that they could be successful in finding a vein so the hemorrhaging could stop. Although there were times when I couldn't stomach the intensity of these episodes, I knew that Mother's prayers would always be answered and success would follow. Mom's example taught me to trust in the Lord and to pray before I ever attempted to infuse. To this day, I never start an IV without first imploring for the blessings of heaven on my behalf—a lesson I learned from my angel mother.

If hemophilia wasn't enough, on April 1, 1990 (the worst April Fool's Day of my life),

Mom's persona took on the true-to-life **identity** of a stalwart *guardian angel.*

I was rushed to the hospital for what was believed to be a bleeding ulcer. In absolute disbelief and horror, my parents were told by doctors that my kidneys had failed—completely. End stage! Only one thought barrages the mind when the words *end stage* are used—death.

Upon hearing the news, Dad excused himself and walked the hospital corridors, trying to compose himself and gain a measure of spiritual insight and comfort. Mom stayed with me. Hazy childhood memories preclude me from remembering specific details about this uncertain time in my life. Nevertheless, I noticed that something amazing happened to Mother that day—a transformation, if you will. Maybe she possessed this trait all of her life; however, I had never seen it. Mom's persona took on the true-to-life identity of a stalwart guardian angel. Gabriel would have been proud!

Mother educated herself about my condition and challenged the doctors' assumptions when she felt the necessity to do so. I always considered Mom an amateur doctor because she became so well versed in medical literature. She could carry on a lengthy dialogue with the best of medical professionals, asking the hard questions and making sure that treatment options always took into account my bleeding disorder. She always stepped

Previous page: Matt and his mother, Buffie, 2008. *Above:* Buffie and her father, Ralph, 1970.

in to intervene if she felt the doctors weren't considering the whole picture. I have little doubt that Mom saved my life on multiple occasions during that torturous kidney disease.

The stories I can share about my ministering, guardian mother would fill volumes. I consider the time, amid the skepticism of medical specialists, that she accurately diagnosed me with West Nile virus while I was in an induced coma. Forever will I remember her willingness to donate her kidney on two different occasions. But most precious were the quiet moments when her example alone taught me how to properly live, have faith, reach upward, work hard, have fun, and pivot my testimony around the Master Jesus Christ and His role of Savior and Redeemer.

Returning to the subject of angels, I close with a simple message to my angel mother: I love you! Your teachings and example have taught me the power of faith when all seemed lost; you have taught me to smile when there was nothing to smile about; you have always encouraged and motivated me to spread my wings, to act, to live, and to never be at the mercy of circumstance and adversity.

Yes, there's an angel in my midst, and I have the privilege of calling her *Mother.*

A Mother First

by Josh Romney

I am thankful for a mother who has taught me many important life lessons, but most of all, through her example and faith, she has taught me humility, patience, and the importance of family.

My mother, Ann Davies Romney, attended Kingswood School in Bloomfield Hills, Michigan. It was an all-girls high school, and was sister schools with Cranbrook, the boys school my father attended. They grew up just miles apart, attended the same elementary school, and later became high school sweethearts.

After high school, my mom and dad's relationship blossomed, and they talked of marriage, but they both knew my dad would soon be leaving on a mission. When my dad was called to Paris, France, he encouraged her to wait for him. Although not a member of the Church, my mom attended BYU, and on her own accord, she sought out the missionaries and subsequently joined the Church.

Upon my dad's return from his mission, my mom and dad were riding home from the airport and agreed, right then and there, to get married. Fearing their families' response to a seemingly rash and emotional decision, it took them a while to finally announce their engagement.

Left: Mitt and Ann as a young couple.

I grew up in Belmont, Massachusetts, and am the third of five boys, including my older brothers, Tagg and Matt, and my younger brothers, Ben and Craig. We were much like any other family but did have an abundance of testosterone. My brothers and I were constantly pounding on each other for one reason or another. My mom was incredibly patient with us, despite our frequently testing her nerves with our antics.

She was once asked about raising five boys, and she put it best by saying: "There were times when, seriously, I wanted to pull my hair out because I'd wish they would just be quiet for a minute, or sit, or even bake cookies, or pick up their dishes, or any of that, which never happened spontaneously. But then there were the fun times when, honestly, they were so silly, the five all together, that I laughed a lot because there was just so much exuberance and happiness. I learned a lot from having boys."

My mom is an intelligent, wise, and accomplished woman. She studied a year at the University of Grenoble in France and earned a bachelor's degree at BYU, with a concentration in French language. She could have pursued a career in teaching, business, or science. But she always knew that the profession that would bring her the most happiness and fulfillment was that of a mom.

On one occasion, she was asked to speak at a women's conference where other accomplished women also spoke, many of whom were lawyers, doctors, and business professionals. She initially felt sheepish about being included with such a group of distinguished career women. She questioned how those in the audience would think

that she measured up, since she was "only a housewife." She stood before the audience and reported proudly that as a mother, she practiced psychology, nursing, and business, and had become skilled in a host of other professions, all of which she learned on her own without any formal training.

ANN ROMNEY

is the mother of

JOSH ROMNEY

Joshua Romney is the founder of Romney Ventures, a real estate investment and management company based in Salt Lake City. Romney Ventures pursues distressed real estate and debt opportunities throughout the U.S.

Josh currently serves as a board member for the Deseret International Foundation, which partners with local doctors in an effort to establish permanent and sustainable health care in developing countries.

He worked on his father's presidential campaign from 2006–2008, performing a variety of roles. He helped manage campaign events and strategy for the Intermountain West states and promoted fundraising efforts in those states. He participated in multiple interviews with every network and major cable news channel, as well as multiple print interviews. He spoke as a surrogate for his father at more than fifty events in more than twenty states. He also campaigned in each of the ninety-nine counties in Iowa.

Josh earned an undergraduate degree in English from Brigham Young University in 2000 and a master's degree from Harvard Business School in 2005. He and his wife, Jen, reside in Salt Lake City with their five children, Grace, Wyatt, Owen, Nash, and Sawyer.

Above: The entire Romney family, 2011.

The audience responded enthusiastically with the loudest cheers of the day.

As the boys grew and began leaving home, her life took a dramatic change. Not only had she recently lost her mother to cancer, but in 1998, she noticed numbness in her legs and began suffering from chronic fatigue. After stumbling several times, she called her brother Jim and described her symptoms. He listened carefully, and concerned, he encouraged her to see a neurologist.

My mom was *incredibly patient* with us, despite our frequently testing her nerves with our **antics.**

The neurologist ordered a battery of tests. With my dad by her side, he watched as tests were performed that gave them some insight into the seriousness of her illness. My dad remembered it as the hardest day of his life. They later met with the doctor, and he broke the news that she had multiple sclerosis. After the doctor left the room, they sat quietly and wept together.

My mom has always been athletic. Not only was she an accomplished equestrian, but she also played tennis regularly and led a very active life. Facing an existence confined to a wheelchair was terrifying, and she prayed for guidance.

The Most Important Thing

by Steevun Lemon

Of all the lessons my mother taught me, perhaps the one that has made the biggest difference has been her faith that after we have done all that we can do, God will make up the difference.

She taught me this from a very young age. I remember when I was seven years old, I awoke one night from a bad dream. Like any scared child, I wanted my mother, and I knew just where to find her. I walked down the hall to the old storage room where she painted. When I opened the door, she was there, hunched over her easel. When she saw me, she put down her brush, picked me up, and kissed me. Her voice was all the comfort I needed, and I fell asleep in her arms.

At the time, I didn't think much of my mother's late-night painting. That was just what she did. A couple of years later, I was at my friend's house and got curious. I was opening all the doors in the basement, and when his mother asked me what I was doing, I replied with my own question, "Where's your easel?"

"My what?"

"Your easel."

"I don't have an easel."

I did *my* part, and the *Lord* did His.

STEEVUN LEMON

is the son of

LIZ LEMON SWINDLE

Steevun Lemon was born on March 1, 1973. His father is a chemist, and his mother an artist. This combination of analytical and creative forces has been a shaping influence in Steevun's life. He said, "I meet people who think creativity and analytics are opposing forces, but in my experience, they are wonderfully intertwined." Steevun served a mission in the Midwest for the Church before attending BYU, where he graduated with a bachelor's degree in advertising and a master's degree in business. After graduate school, Steevun worked as a project manager for Ten-Fold, a software company, during the dot-com boom. He then became vice president of sales for Mainstream Data, a leading satellite data network company. In 2001, Steevun returned to the family business as the managing director of Foundation Arts, a Christian Art Publisher. Steevun resides in American Fork, Utah, with his wife, Tami, and their five children.

"Then where do you paint at night?" I asked.

Up until that point, I had assumed that everyone's mother had an easel in the basement and painted at night. Many years later, I was thinking back on those late nights and wondering why my mother had chosen to paint at night instead of during the day when it would have been easier on her. I will never forget her answer.

She said, "I knew that raising a family was the most important thing I would do in this life, and I didn't want the art to interfere with that. I also knew I needed the Lord's help as an artist, and I could only expect Him to do His part if I did mine. So I made a choice when I had children that I would only paint after I put you all in bed. I did my part, and the Lord did His."

I realized in that moment that Mother had spent a lifetime giving so quietly that I had never seen her late-night vigil as a sacrifice.

Truly, those long, lonely hours were her legacy of faith. It is that same faith that runs in and through each one of her children. My mother's trust in the Lord is woven into who we are and how we live.

Today, when my life seems overwhelming and the Lord seems far away, I remember that night thirty years ago when I walked into that old storage room. I remember my mother's sacrifice to "do her part" and her unwavering faith that God would make up the difference. Just the thought gives me a newfound courage to get up and get back to work—the peaceful assurance that God has not forgotten me and the knowledge that after I have done all that I can do, He will make up the difference. I testify that He does.

Raising a family was the **most important** thing I would do in this life, and I didn't want the art to *interfere* with that.

Previous page—left: All the family home for Christmas. *Left*: Mom and the love of her life. *Right*: Mom loves to garden with her favorite "child," Sassy. *Above*: Jesus with His Mother.

An Anchor Against the Storm

by Larry Barkdull

H anging on the wall of my home is a large painting of Christ in Gethsemane rendered on purple velvet. It arrived shortly after my mother died in 1987. Someone had taken it down from the place where it had hung in the Idaho Falls temple for more than twenty years and had stored it in the basement of the temple. Later, my sister requested that it be returned to the family.

My mother had painted it when I was a youth. Previously, she had painted many pictures depicting sacred subjects, most of which ended up in our meetinghouse in the junior Sunday School room or in the foyer outside the chapel. Such practices were common in the 1950s and 60s. Each week when our family went to church, I saw Mom's paintings, which taught me more about gospel truths than any sermon I can remember.

It was during that period in her life that Mom determined that she would attempt to express her testimony through art. It was to become the sum of her spiritual yearnings, the fullest extent of her belief, and the crowning artistic statement of her life. She chose for her subject

the Marriotts in the Baltimore/Washington DC area.

But the fairy tale was over. The same illness that had deferred Dean from the military developed into cancer, and at thirty-nine Dean succumbed, leaving Ruth, age thirty-eight, with a three-year-old and four other children. I was the oldest at fifteen. Mom lived more than fifty years as a widow.

Mom taught us that the earth was both beautiful and abundant.

She babysat other people's children and worked part time at the hospital to make ends meet. Eventually she became the director of volunteers and founded the Pink Lady program, but pay was meager at best and the family lived mostly on the fruit and vegetables Mom canned and on powdered skim milk that she bought in bulk. Friends brought by fish they had caught or deer they had shot, and we pulled up the rhubarb that grew by the canal so she could make her famous pies.

Mom taught us that the earth was both beautiful and abundant—that God made enough and to spare for those who learn to save and who know how to wait and to work for what they want.

Above: Richard Eyre with his mother, Ruth.

The blessing of it all was that we didn't know we were living below the poverty line, and Mom never told us that we were poor. Quite the contrary, she told us we were rich—rich in blessings, rich to have a house to live in, rich to be in Logan with its canyons and mountains and rivers and its safe neighborhoods and tree-climbing, rope-swinging, slingshot-making backyards.

The other economic blessing is that we never knew or even imagined any kind of entitlement. Mom told us that we could have anything we wanted—we just had to work hard enough and save long enough to get it. We delivered newspapers, we mowed lawns, we stacked hay bales on the wagons of local farms, and we collected wire hangers and

pop bottles door-to-door to redeem at the dry cleaners and the grocery store.

We bought our own hamburgers and movie tickets. We saved and bought our own clothes and our own bikes. We took care of them, and we mended them and fixed them when they tore or broke. On the rare occasion when someone gave us a toy, or a pair of shoes, or a bell or a basket for our bike, we were almost overwhelmed with gratitude.

Mom was honest with us. She told us she couldn't afford to buy us much other than our food and the roof over our heads. And she also told us that she was saving part of her tiny income each month "for a rainy day." She told us that everyone should have "something in reserve" and she was never apologetic about asking us to go without something so that she could "save a little."

She told us often how blessed we were to be able to work and earn and save, and she

ARTS & ENTERTAINMENT

Ruth Swenson Eyre
is the mother of

RICHARD EYRE

Richard and Linda Eyre are *New York Times* number-one bestselling authors of numerous books on life-balance, parenting, and family-prioritizing. They write regularly for many publications including *Mormon Times*, *Deseret News*, *Meridian Magazine*, and *Success Magazine*. They travel widely as speakers and family advocates. Their two latest books are *5 Spiritual Solutions for Everyday Parenting Problems* and *The Entitlement Trap*. They have nine children and live in Park City, Utah.

First pay the Lord, *then* pay yourself by saving a little, *and* you can still get what you **really** need with what's left.

taught us that we could have whatever we really wanted and that there was always more than one way to get something. When I wanted name-brand shirts, she got some labels from the best clothing store in town and sewed them into my clearance-sale clothes from Sears or Deseret Industries. She actually taught us to pity those who "had to pay full price." It just wasn't, as she said, "very exciting."

She paid her tithing first, and taught us to do the same. "First pay the Lord, then pay yourself by saving a little, and you can still get what you really need with what's left." Buying anything on credit appalled her. First you earn, then you save, then you buy.

All of her children graduated from college, most with graduate degrees, and all paid every penny of their tuition. All five served LDS missions. All were married in the temple. All bought their own homes early in life. Once they were all grown and out of her house, Mom went on a mission herself.

And somehow, along the way, without ever once earning enough to officially move above the poverty line, Mom managed to save enough to set up an educational trust fund for her grandkids (matching funds of course—with kids "earning their share.")

Just before Linda and I left to preside over the London mission, we had written a book called *Teaching Children Joy*. Mom, whose degree was in early childhood education, took the book while we were gone, and turned it into a preschool curriculum— and Joy Schools were born. More than a half million children throughout the world have now benefited from the "joy lessons" that Mom created, and as you might guess, there is plenty in there on the connections between joy and hard work, earning and saving, and delayed gratification.

Ruth Eyre, along with all the other reasons that I love her, was and is the personification of provident living, and I will never be able to repay her for what she taught me about the joy and the wisdom of living with gratitude and with frugality.

Number-One Fan

by Sharlene W. Hawkes

I knew Mom would be waiting to pick me up right after school, and I could hardly wait to ask her. I had just heard a rumor from a very good source that the most popular boy in school—a senior—was planning on asking me—a sophomore—to the prom. I was only a month away from turning sixteen, and at this ripe age, I had never had such a strong crush on anyone as I did on this teenage heartthrob. I was sure that Mom would see this was simply too important to pass up just because I wasn't *exactly* sixteen yet.

I jumped in the car and immediately started sharing the exciting rumor (which was, of course, considered practically factual in junior high and high school). Mom knew of my crush on this young man, so she was very happy for me and even acted as giddy as I was. Then I had to get to the serious part. I told her that the prom would occur before I turned sixteen. She didn't say no, and she didn't say yes. She

and managing a full household. In a letter to my oldest sister back in the States, Dad wrote, "Mom is busier than I am!"

Her grace under pressure, her amazing ability to listen carefully to anyone talking with her, her careful words of wisdom—and looking glamorous all the while!—gave me the perfect role model as a little girl who wondered what I wanted to be when I grew up.

Throughout the three-year mission, Mom's Spanish became so fluent that she was in demand at all the meetings and conferences. As I grew older and was able to travel with Mom and Dad to many mission conferences when we lived in Chile and Argentina, I was mesmerized by Mom's beautiful and poised presence as she delivered such thoughtful messages in flowing Spanish. Her obvious love for the people absolutely radiated with such sincerity that she commanded rapt attention. I loved how she spoke to

the audience as though she were speaking to just one person, and everyone thought they were that one person. I clearly remember wishing I could have that same gift. Mom radiates beauty, talent, and intelligence, but most of all, a love for the Savior that is so profound that it literally guides just about everything she says and does. She has devoted her life to service at home, in the mission field, in the temple . . . and I would leave a big gap if I didn't add at BYU football and basketball games! Mom's zest for life and her passion for cheering all of us to reach our full potential is what makes me *her* number-one fan.

Previous page—left: Family outing. *Right*: Helen and Robert on the dance floor. *Below*: Sharlene and Helen at the Miss America Pageant.

Above—left: Robert E. and Helen Wells. *Right*: Grandma and Grandpa Wells with Sharlene and her family.

Be Anything

by Lauren Johnson

We were back-to-school shopping when I explained to my mom that I refused to buy a certain brand of jeans because I didn't approve of their advertisements using scantily clad, overly skinny-looking models. Exhausted at the lack of our shopping success, she looked at me—her awkwardly shaped, newly adolescent fifteen-year-old daughter—and said, "Honey, if they fit, we're getting them."

Of course, eight years earlier when I wanted a Barbie, it was my mom who decided she didn't want her daughter playing with one. "Are you sure you want a Barbie, Lauren? Barbie is a pretty doll, but I don't think she went to college. You can be anything you want to be, and I'm not so sure you want to be like Barbie."

I never did get my desired Barbie doll. I had to play with them at my friend's home, which I savored—but even then, my mom's words remained with me. I could be anything I wanted to be. I could be strong and independent, and I could choose my path.

Today I am a television reporter, and it was my mother who told me when I was ten years old, while watching anchor Michelle King, that I could one day be a reporter. Those words resonate still, twenty-one years later. I share that story anytime someone wants to understand when I chose my career path. It was when my mom told me I could—and to know that was exciting!

But my mother's life decisions, and her lessons, strike an even finer chord. I can be

My mom taught me all of this while being a stay-at-home mom. She didn't finish college but, instead, sacrificed her degree to be a full-time mother to two toddlers and move across the country so my dad could attend graduate school. She lived her life as a nurturer, steadfast in the gospel of Jesus Christ and dedicated to her husband and six children. That is what she chose. And she wanted to make sure I knew I could choose too, and that I could make my life all I wanted it to be.

"Stay close to the Lord," she would say. "Listen to the Spirit, pray, follow His will, and go after your dreams."

With those lessons, I continued on with life and pondered my mother's words whenever making my major life decisions. Those words created confidence. I could choose to serve a mission, study abroad, graduate college, and go after the career of my dreams.

And life kept going. . . .

Barbie is a *pretty* doll, but I don't think she went to college. You can be **anything** you want to be, and I'm not so sure you want to be like Barbie.

Danelle and Lauren Johnson, 2011.

anything I want to be. And when the time comes, although long awaited, if I choose, I can leave my career; I can be a wife, a mother, and a caretaker, just like her. Through my mother's powerful example, I have learned that this is my greatest desire— to be a woman like her. She's taught me the

Danelle Johnson
is the mother of

LAUREN JOHNSON

Many Idahoans may recognize Lauren Johnson as a local news reporter and anchor who worked for Eastern Idaho's KPVI Channel 6. Johnson recently moved to Salt Lake City and is currently a cohost of the Mormon radio show "The Cultural Hall Podcast" (recorded weekly at Simmons Media and shared at theculturalhallpodcast.com).

Born in New York City and raised in Salt Lake City, Johnson began her journalism career as a live personality during the 2002 Winter Olympics for Washington DC's NBC affiliate. She took time off to serve a mission in Cleveland,

Ohio; travel the country with the Komen Breast Cancer Foundation; and graduate from the University of Utah.

When she isn't reporting, starting new projects, or analyzing her weekend dates, Lauren is an avid blogger at www.laurenruthie.blogspot.com. What Johnson appreciates most about her faith is the people and the sharing of spiritual wisdom and cultural differences that every member brings to this worldwide Church. "Everyone has a story and a perspective," she says, "and I want to help share those stories with the world."

importance and beauty of motherhood.

When the opportunity comes, I realize and know it will be my most important job—the most important position I will have in this life. And I will pass on my mother's lesson, that my children can be anything they want to be, that their lives can be fulfilling and

> I realize and know it will be my *most* important **job**—the *most* important **position** I will have in this life.

purposeful and powerful—at every moment. How blessed we are in life to have mothers who know the truth! Find strength through the Lord, and your potential is endless.

And one day when my daughters ask for a Barbie, I'll tell them to go ask their grandma.

Above: Danelle and Lauren.

St. Janice As Our Mother

by Steven Kapp Perry

Many Latter-day Saints have a soft spot in their hearts for some of Mom's best-known songs, such as "Love Is Spoken Here," "A Child's Prayer," "As Sisters in Zion," and "I'm Trying to Be Like Jesus," but those of us who grew up in her home also have a special liking for some of the lesser-known, unpublished, dare we say even apocryphal songs from her oeuvre.

The first one of these I remember was sung at a family night right about the time an injury caused her to give up sports for music. We gathered around, and she pulled out her guitar and said she was going to teach us a song she had written with a verse for each of us. As you can imagine, we were quite curious to hear our own personal verses. First, she taught us the generic chorus, which worked for everyone:

> Chorus (substitute any name):
>
> Steve, Steve, we all love Steve,
>
> More than we can say.
>
> We love the good, and we love the bad,
>
> We love him any old way.

So far so good! The individual verses, however, started with Dad and then worked their way through each child, pointing out certain . . . um, idiosyncrasies and some way in which we could improve. My verse contained the rhyme "shower" and "hour," which should help you guess the content. Unfortunately (or fortunately), these verses were never written down and so are lost to time, except for one; the concluding verse she wrote for herself. The rest of us recall this one quite clearly:

> There's a sweet and gentle woman
>
> And her age is thirty-eight.
>
> She's more wonderful and kind
> than any other.

You might even say she's perfect
(And so very humble too).
We are blessed to have St. Janice as
our mother!
Mom, Mom, we all love Mom
More than we can say.
We love the good, and we love the good,
We love her any old way.

I hope you noticed that her chorus manages to say "good" twice, with no mention of "bad." Even though we know it was delivered tongue-in-cheek, we kids have teased her a lot over the years for failing to point out her own faults in that song. But in retrospect, as I consider how she has lived her life as the years have flown by—past forty-eight, fifty-eight, sixty-eight, with seventy-eight coming into view—I've come to think that maybe she honestly just couldn't think of any. I know I couldn't have.

There are lots of us who have called "St. Janice" our mother. Steven, Robert, Lynne, John, and Richard were born to her, though Richard only stayed a day; and after that, beginning with David and Bonnie, she and

Dad managed to give us more than thirteen foster siblings from various situations and even countries. When I asked my sister Lynne what she had learned from Mom, she said, "I've been thinking recently about Mom's ability to love other people's children—to take in foster children with tough backgrounds and to soften them somehow."

When Wayne arrived fresh off the Navajo reservation at age ten and was too shy to speak to her that first day, she quietly began planting flowers by the front step and motioned for him to sink his hands into the dirt and help, which he did. In that way, she wordlessly welcomed him while planting seeds of a new relationship as they worked together.

Another brother arrived as a total surprise when the doorbell rang during family night and there stood the bishop with a very tense-looking sixteen-year-old boy. "Hi," said the bishop, "This is Guy. Can he live with you for a couple of weeks?" Perhaps more than any of the others who lived with us, he benefited from experiencing what a loving, gentle mother was like. Those two weeks turned into a year, and bit by bit, he began to relax, bring down the volume of his words to less than a shout, and stop snapping his pencils with a death grip when he was startled, as he realized the abuse he'd been subjected to up to that point in his life was not the norm.

My brother Robb remembers with the rest of us the sound of an IBM Selectric typewriter clacking away in the background late into the night when we were small—reassuring us that although the lights were out and our bedroom door was closed, our mother was still audibly "there." What we didn't know then was that while Dad was in graduate school, she had chosen to do late-night typing of graduate students' dissertations in place of the drugstore job she had previously arranged to take. She had the job and the babysitter arranged, but when the time came

Women in the Church can do it **all**—they just need to do it in *sequence*; there are seasons for **everything.**

to walk out the door and leave her little ones, she simply couldn't do it. I can't remember ever worrying about whether she would be there for us because she always was. I've often heard her share the Brigham Young

quote that women in the Church can do it all—they just need to do it in sequence; there are seasons for everything.

I know only a little of the pressure-filled deadlines she managed for those sweating grad students who felt their future lives were on the line and thought she should be at their

ARTS & ENTAINMENT

STEVEN KAPP PERRY
is the son of

JANICE KAPP PERRY

Steven Kapp Perry is an award-winning songwriter, playwright, and broadcaster, and the son of Douglas C. and Janice Kapp Perry. After serving in the Belgium Antwerp Mission, he attended BYU and performed worldwide with the Young Ambassadors. He has released fourteen albums of original music, including *From Cumorah's Hill,* and he has cowritten several stage musicals, including *Polly* and *Take the Mountain Down,* which have appeared on BYU–Television.

Steve is the host of "Soft Sunday Sounds" on FM100.3, Utah's most listened-to weekend radio program. He and his wife, Johanne, volunteer for Reach-theChildren.org and host Church history tours in the U.S. and Israel. Find more information online at StevenKappPerry.com. Steve and Johanne love the gospel of Jesus Christ, music, history, each other, cream cheese on bagels, and whichever of their four children has a current scholarship. Steven currently serves as elders quorum president in the Cedar Hills third ward in Cedar Hills, Utah.

beck and call. As a family, we all know much more about the toll those years took on her arms and wrists when, as she approached forty, she began to lose the use of her left hand just at the time she began writing music.

When I think about my mother and her hand, I have sometimes been reminded of President Spencer W. Kimball—called to be the mouthpiece of the Lord just when all but a ragged bit of his own voice had been taken from him. Still, in a quiet, humble way, he spoke the words given to him as best he could.

While she admits to being frustrated and occasionally slamming her hands down on the keys and tearfully asking, "Why?" during those first years of her trial, Mom still found a way to keep writing. When an endless succession of doctors, specialists, and even quacks ruled out many causes but could never give her a solid diagnosis, she still kept trying to create and share something useful and beautiful with the gifts God had given her.

Because my brother John manages the office of our family recording company, he, more than any of us, has seen her at the piano composing for hours, using only the thumb and pinky of her balled-up, painful left hand, teaching us that we can learn to accept difficult things with faith, trust in the wisdom and timing of the Lord, and become willing to learn the lessons our challenges have to teach while still contributing to the kingdom.

And with her characteristic sense of humor, Mom has often remarked that her bad left hand is a blessing in disguise. "People write me all the time telling me thank you for writing pieces with a left hand part easy enough for them to play."

Even when a stroke weakened her right side several years ago, I never heard her complain—only testify that it is a tender mercy of the Lord that while she can't feel much of her arm and leg, her hand still goes to the right keys and her foot can still work the pedal.

Lest this sound like a eulogy for St. Janice, I would like to add on a cheerful note that she is blessedly and approachably human, misplaces things occasionally, and admits to wishing the NBA men's shorts were shorter, like in the old days (a la John Stockton's, but we're not naming names). And once, when Lynne and I made her late (yet again) for a meeting, she was heard to mutter under her breath that she would gladly trade both of us for one more Robb (who was usually on time).

I love the story Dad tells of when they picked up John from his mission in Argentina and made a stop in the mountains of Peru to see

Janice Kapp Perry.

Machu Picchu. They were taking it easy to avoid altitude sickness, but that night Mom couldn't sleep. She fumbled for her glasses and made her way to the bathroom, trying not to wake my father. Once she turned on the lights, the room started to swim and her vision blurred, and everything felt strange and wrong. "Doug!" she called out, "I think I'm having a stroke." My father leapt out of the bed and came stumbling to her aid. Then he started laughing. "I think you'll be fine," he said, "as soon as you take off my glasses and put on yours."

Most people who know my mother know her through her music, so I would like to add that my mother is the single best example I know of being willing to "bloom where you are planted." When she submitted some of her early songs to the Church music committee, she was told that they were nice but that she should "bloom where you are planted and beautify your part of the vineyard. If it needs to be heard in the wider world, it will find its way." She then did what almost nobody who hears that advice ever does: she believed it. She accepted it wholeheartedly. She lived it. For years. Almost every one of the ten songs in the *Children's Songbook* people know her for today was written for a stake primary choir, for a ward Young Women event, or some other Church occasion or event—even just for her children and their friends to sing.

She did the same thing on her mission with Dad to Santiago, Chile, and on their Church service mission for years afterward—teaching people to play the piano and conduct music for their local congregations and organizing beautiful adult and youth choirs with people who had no idea how much they could do with music. This is one of the lessons I most hope has rubbed off on me—that our gifts are to bless, not to impress, and that the numbers blessed are not nearly as important as sharing what we have been given.

If the traditional definition of Saint is someone dedicated to the Lord who works miracles for others, in my mind, she qualifies. In any case, a Latter-day Saint she most definitely is. She is the patron saint of our childhood upbringing and young adulthood, and we all—those born into the family and those gathered in along the way—are proud to sing, "We're so blessed to have St. Janice as our mother!"

> Our gifts are to *bless*, not to impress, and the **numbers** blessed are not nearly as important as *sharing* what we have been given.

Angel, Guardian, Mom

by Julie Bellon

W hen you walk into my mother's house, you'll see statues and pictures of angels throughout. She loves to decorate with angels, and every time I see those figures and images, they remind me of her.

From my very earliest memories, my mother, Renee Campbell, has taught me the value of service—not by anything she said but just by watching her. When my parents divorced, my mother was left with four young children to support. She was a hard worker and went back to school while holding down a job and still taking care of us. We never had fancy meals or a big house, but we always had food on the table and warm beds in which to sleep. She rarely missed tucking us in at night, and she often stroked my hair until I drifted off to sleep. I knew she loved me and would watch over me—my guardian angel.

My mother's life was not easy. She was often tired and had many heavy burdens to bear. Yet, she took her responsibility of motherhood very seriously and gave everything she had in serving her family. She taught me how to be a good person, and she made sure I knew that true happiness could only be found when I looked outside of myself and served others.

One night in particular really brought this principle home to me. My mother came home from work one evening, and I could tell she was exhausted. She was working hard and studying hard, and it was taking its toll. Her shoulders were slumped over as she took her coat off, and when she looked at me, I could see that she had dark circles under her eyes—more than normal—but she smiled anyway as she asked how my day had gone. I told her my youthful worries, and she listened for a moment before squeezing my arm in support and heading into the kitchen

I wondered if she would say anything about our predicament or just say we were so sorry we couldn't help this time, but when I looked up at her, my mother just smiled and without hesitation said, "I'll be right there."

to start dinner. It was a routine we had down pat, but tonight was different somehow. Even though I was young, I knew part of her exhaustion was the mental worry because it was macaroni night and macaroni night meant that it was the end of the month and money was tight for us, despite her best efforts.

As I followed my mother and was passing the phone table in the hall, the phone rang. I answered it and heard the voice of our neighbor asking for my mother. I handed

the phone to her and listened as my mom talked. From what I understood, our neighbor's car had broken down and she was stranded and needed a ride. I knew my mother would probably go, but I also knew that this was the end of the month and she would have carefully budgeted our gas money to last us until the next payday. Our neighbor needed us to go all the way across town, and that would take quite a bit of our precious gas that my mother needed to drive to school and work. I wondered if she would say anything about our predicament or just say we were so sorry we couldn't help this time, but when I looked up at her, my mother just smiled and without hesitation said, "I'll be right there."

Money didn't matter when someone else was in trouble. It was her opportunity to serve. The tiredness in her demeanor melted away as she put her coat back on and went out to help our neighbor, knowing that she'd probably have to walk or take the bus to work herself because she

Renee Campbell and Julie Bellon.

True happiness could only be found when I looked *outside* of myself and **served others.**

went to give our neighbor a ride. Yet, that was my mother—always willing to sacrifice anything to help someone else.

She has continued that service and example throughout my entire life. Even though she

Renee Campbell
is the mother of

JULIE BELLON

Julie is the mother of eight children and the author of five suspense novels and one nonfiction book. Her greatest joy is being a mother, but she also loves being a writer and having the opportunity to share her stories and ideas. She graduated from Brigham Young University with a degree in secondary education with an emphasis in English, and she currently teaches a journalism course for BYU Continuing Edu-

cation. She enjoys traveling, (especially to her home country of Canada), trying new things, reading, writing, and spending time with her family. She has a large collection of books, and when she's not busy being a mom, teaching, or writing, you will more than likely find her browsing through bookstores to add to that collection or reading the treasures she's already found. You can keep up with Julie and all her writing projects at www.juliebellon.com.

lives in Canada, she still seems to instinctively know when I need a listening ear or a surprise package of Canadian chocolate in the mail to get me through a rough time. She is someone I can always count on, and I know she loves me—my angel mother.

My mother has always reached out to her children and those around her in both good and bad times, but as her situation has improved, she has begun to reach out to countless girls as a foster mother. She works hard to help in any way she can, and her heart always seems like it has an endless supply of love to give to anyone in need. Several of her foster daughters still keep in touch with her because of the influence she had on their lives over the years.

My mom's health isn't the best anymore, but her service and commitment is still the same. I can always find her babysitting for a young mother, picking up a treat to let someone know she's thinking of them, or climbing in the car to take a friend to an appointment. She is an angel to everyone who comes in contact with her—the human embodiment of the pictures and statues she has in her home.

I am so grateful she is my mother, and I am glad that I have had such a great example of service in my life. It has taught me that even though I am a busy mother of eight children, there is always time for service. No matter how tired I am or what is going on in my life, when a service opportunity comes, I don't hesitate. I simply say, "I'll be right there."

Things She Never Managed to Do

by Greg Olsen

My mother has been gone for several years now, but her influence on me continues to be extraordinary. I remember her as an absolutely *spectacular* mother! I would probably meet some skepticism, however, if I tried to convince the rest of the world that any of the things she did in her life should be labeled as *spectacular*. Often, it was the things she did *not* do that were so amazing.

One such occasion occurred when I was fifteen years old. I had just received my first paying commission as an aspiring artist—two four-by-eight-foot signs for a local grocery store. I needed a large place to work, so I set up a studio in our garage. Unfortunately, it was wintertime in Idaho, and I soon learned that it was much too cold in the garage for the oil-based, enamel paint to dry properly. My mother reluctantly agreed to let me bring the whole operation inside to my bedroom. It was cramped and full of paint fumes, but it was warm. I rigged a makeshift taboret out of a flimsy TV tray and placed two open paint cans on it, one quart of glossy black and one quart of bright orange. I laid down a drop cloth, propped the first sheet of plywood horizontally on top of it, and went to work.

At some point during the process, I had to reposition the large panel of plywood. I grabbed one end, tipped it out away from the wall it had been resting against, and started to slide the panel just a few feet to one side. As I did, it flexed and began to sway back and forth in a mocking wave. Instantly, I was aware of the disaster that was about to happen. It seemed to unfold in slow motion but not slow enough for me to do anything about it. Before I could get the swaying sheet of plywood under control, it slammed into my feeble TV tray, and the two quarts of black and orange paint went flying into the air. Of course, they came down several feet from my drop cloth. The impact not only sent these Halloween horror colors all over my bedroom carpet but also six feet up the wall on the other side of the room and all over my heirloom dresser and even into my partially open underwear drawer. I let out a pathetic scream, the kind only a terrified boy whose voice is changing can emit. I immediately wished I had been able to stifle my girly, bug-eyed squeal because I could hear my mother racing down the hall to

I let out a **pathetic** scream, the kind only a *terrified* boy whose voice is changing can emit.

come to my rescue—or more likely, once she saw the mess, to kill me.

My bedroom door flung open, and there stood my mother, eyes wide and jaw dropped. Without a word, she ran back down the hall, most likely to grab some horrific weapon of death that she could use to serve justice upon me. I could hear her searching in cupboards and slamming drawers, looking for just the right implement through which she could channel her frustrations. Then I could hear her coming back down the hall. It was like a scary movie. I froze as I waited for the end.

When she reappeared in the doorway, I half expected to see a crazed woman with gnashing teeth and hair on fire. Instead, she calmly slipped in with some old rags, a roll of paper towels, and some paint thinner. She quietly handed me a share of the supplies, and together we went to work cleaning up the mess. It took a good long time to completely remove all the

paint from the wall and dresser, and we never could get it all out of the carpet. I ended up using the money I made from the sign commission to pay for some new carpet in my bedroom. My mother did not yell at me; she didn't even scold me during the

JANEL OLSEN

is the mother of

GREG OLSEN

Greg was born in Idaho Falls, Idaho, and grew up in the nearby farming community of Iona. He is the eldest of five children. Greg was blessed with very supportive parents who always encouraged him and provided opportunities for him to pursue his passion for art.

After high school, Greg attended Utah State University, where he studied art. While attending school, he met his wife, Sydnie Cazier. They have six children and are enjoying their new role as grandparents. Greg likes being close to his family. He paints in his studio, thirty-seven steps from the back door of their home. Greg says, "From an early age, I have always been fascinated by paintings that create mood, emotion, and atmosphere, especially those paintings that lift me and transport me to some far-off place. These are the elements I strive to create in my paintings. They, in many ways, record what is most important to me: my feelings and experiences with family and friends along with the spiritual aspects of my life. My hope is that in these images you will find something familiar, something that will resonate and remind you of what is important in your own life."

inoperable aortic aneurism, I was devastated. How could the heart that had beaten faithfully through all of her own trials and supported her five children, eighteen grandchildren, and two great-grandchildren be failing now?

The doctors weren't sure she would live out the year. What bothered her wasn't the diagnosis though; it was the fact that she couldn't stay out and complete her mission. With tears dripping down her cheeks, she told me how disappointed she was that she couldn't fulfill the promise she'd made to the Lord.

"You've done everything you could," I said, wrapping my arms around her. "Besides, Heavenly Father still has a lot more for you to do at home."

The unspoken question in her eyes was clear as she pulled away to look at me. "How can

I guess I won't know *until* I try.

I do anything when the doctors have no idea how long I have left?" I didn't need to answer. I was sure she could hear the words she'd repeated to me so many times as clearly as I could.

"You'll never know until you try."

It's now been nearly ten years since my mother, Vicki Dee (Martin) Savage, was diagnosed, and she is still here, teaching a whole new generation of children the importance of trying.

Previous page: Jeff as child with his mother. *Above—left*: Jeff receiving his Eagle Scout medal from his mother, 1977. *Above—right*: Vicki holding Jeff, 1965. *Right*: Jeff holding on to his mother's hand, 1965.

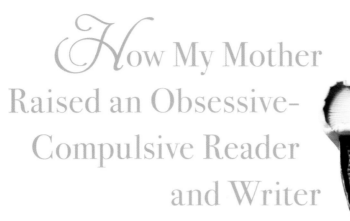

How My Mother Raised an Obsessive-Compulsive Reader and Writer

by Rick Walton

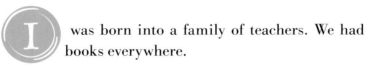

I was born into a family of teachers. We had books everywhere.

With all of those books around, you'd think I would remember my parents reading to me. I don't. I'm sure they did. What I do remember was that they were always reading on their own. I grew up believing that a book was part of the human body. Being surrounded by books felt as natural to me as a fish being surrounded by tartar sauce. I could tell books were important to them. And because of that, books were important to me.

I learned to read when I was four years old. My mother taught me. I'm sure it was because she had plenty of time, having only three children ages four and under in the house. When I was four, my mother started a preschool in our basement. She did it for the money . . . and because she didn't have enough to do. Or so I thought for many years. Eventually, I realized the truth. My mother started a preschool and spent several hours every day at it because she cared about my education.

Because of my parents' example and my mother's devotion, I learned to read early and often. Like my parents, I always had a book in my hands. I read while I ate, while I walked, while I drifted off to sleep. I read a couple of novels a day.

I was addicted to books. But not just to reading them. I was also addicted to owning them! My parents were facilitators who fed my addiction. For birthdays and holidays: books, books, books.

Whenever there was a book order at school, they let me buy every book I wanted on the order. Why not? They had plenty of money to feed their then eight kids *and* my obsession. After all, they were in the lucrative teaching profession!

When I was fourteen, we moved to Provo, about two blocks away from Deseret Industries. It was like an alcoholic moving next door to a bar. Almost every day I was over there, looking for books. I came home one day and told my mom, "There are thirty Hardy Boys books over there! Can I buy them?" Within an hour, I was home with all thirty.

I spent much of my time at Brigham Young University, where my dad worked—usually in the most magical building on campus, the library! It was there that I saw it—a large, leather-bound, four-hundred-year-old volume of *Thomas Aquinas*. In Latin. For sale! I ran home. "Mom! Mom! It's only twenty dollars! Yes, it's in Latin, and I don't read Latin, *but it's 400 years old*!" An hour later. I was back with the book. A book that was printed before the Pilgrims got here. And I owned it!

As I explored music, literature, the arts, math, foreign languages, and the wide, wide world, if it involved education, my parents never said no. I don't remember my mom ever saying "slow down" or "that's impossible" or "we can't afford that."

WILMA NOREEN TOONE WALTON

is the mother of

RICK WALTON

Rick Walton has worked as a cook in a Mexican restaurant, a secretary, a missionary, an arts administrator, a schoolteacher, and a computer software writer and designer. But now he has the best job of all—writing for children. He has published riddle books, picture books, poetry, activity books, minimysteries, and magazine articles.

Rick graduated from Brigham Young University in Spanish, with a Portuguese minor. His wife, Ann, is a computer programmer who  has worked for IBM, Novell, and WordPerfect, and who now works for Rick. They have five children. They live in a hodgepodge house on a secluded lot with a thousand trees in the shadow of the Rocky Mountains.

My love of reading prepared me to follow many different career paths. I started down several—business, law, teaching. All good, solid careers with some job security. Some even promising a life of comfort. My mom supported me as I explored each path.

And then I discovered that I loved to write. I abandoned the goal of becoming an international business lawyer and began my new career, with its promises of rejection, insecurity, and a life of constantly looking for alternative employment to be able to pay the bills.

But my mom was always there beside me, cheering me on. She believed in me. She knew writing made me happy. And that's what she wanted—for me to be happy.

And when I began to publish, she was ecstatic. She loved books, and now she'd had a hand in creating them.

Now, more than eighty published books later, she is my biggest fan.

Being surrounded by books felt as *natural* to me as a fish being surrounded by **tartar sauce.**

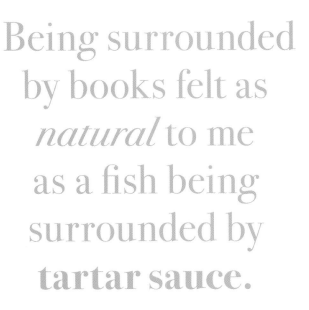

And I hers.

I am who I am today because my mother supported me, taught me, loved me.

Thank you, Mom. I love you.

P.S. My mother's love and support is so pervasive that just a couple of years after I was diagnosed with Parkinson's Disease, she (out of sympathy and solidarity, I'm sure) was similarly diagnosed. Mom, you didn't have to go that far to support me!

Rick as a baby being held by his mother, Wilma.

Service through Music

by Marsha Ward

Marian Virginia Rushworth Davies was born at home in South Salt Lake City to parents who had individually immigrated to the United States from England. Virginia, as she was known throughout her life, was named for her father's favorite mission, the state of West Virginia.

Virginia was a gifted pianist and singer, with a rich alto voice that was suited for choir singing as well as solos. Music was a defining part of her life, and she brought her talents and skills into a new family when she married Orin Granger Williams.

Orin and Virginia met while she was serving a mission at the tender age of eighteen. At that time, the California Mission included a part of southern Arizona, and while Virginia was serving in the Binghampton Branch near Tucson, Arizona, Orin came in contact with her and was smitten. Upon her mission release, he followed her home to Salt Lake City, where he wooed and won her. They married in the Salt Lake Temple, and their family grew to include three sons and four daughters. I was the second girl.

> Momma knew that music could *touch* and *soften* hearts, and her *sensitivity* to the Spirit lent a special touch to her **interpretations** and **direction**.

One of my favorite memories of my mother's musical talents was when she was involved in a Christmas production of the oratorio *The Messiah*, presented by the Phoenix Arizona Stake. It was a huge undertaking because every possible musician in the stake was pressed into service to practice for several weeks and perform the piece on the radio. Momma was the alto soloist. I remember lying on the couch in our darkened living room on Christmas Eve, listening as she sang the solos and duets of that much-loved work in her true, rich voice. Momma was a tremendous example to

me of giving Church service through the use of her musical talents.

Because she had a desire to bind her family together by making use of our inherited musical talents, Momma taught us children to read music and sing in harmony. She also encouraged us to play musical instruments. Momma knew that music could touch and soften hearts, and her sensitivity to the Spirit lent a special touch to her interpretations and direction.

I remember joining the ward choir when I was nine years old because I could read music and sing. Besides, my mother was the choir director, and she encouraged us children to join as soon as we could make a real contribution

Necessary Life Skills

by Tristi Pinkston

My mom is not the most traditional of mothers. She was rarely found in a kitchen—never in an apron—and she practically threw a party to celebrate the day each of her daughters became old enough to take over the cooking. But this is not to say that she didn't teach us valuable skills, things I have used over and over again throughout my life.

Because of my mom, I know the difference between Doris Day and Judy Garland. I know how to make valances to go over my windows. I can anticipate a punch line, give as good as I get, and yell at the Olympic judges through the television screen, even though they'll never hear me. And everything I know about sneaking through the night to toilet paper someone's house, I learned from my mom.

I'm not kidding—she's the master. After hearing one of my friends brag that his house was impossible to toilet paper because of the built-in security system, she called his sister-in-law, found out where the sensors were, drew up a map, and we walked all over his yard without triggering one light. He woke up the next morning to a house absolutely festooned. You just can't wave a temptation like that in front of my mother and expect her not to take the bait.

I've learned other lessons from my mother that don't revolve around defacing private property. As a homeschooled child, I learned how to stand by my convictions, often in the face of well-meaning but misinformed persons who were worried about my welfare but couldn't see that I was not only perfectly all right but also thriving. As the child of entrepreneurs, I was taught to think positively, to push forward, to keep going to reach my dreams even though it might seem that all was

against me. The lessons came in many different forms, from using good posture to dressing modestly, but they all carried the

> You just can't wave a temptation like that in front of my mother and expect her not to take the bait.

same central message: believe in yourself. As a child, this meant something different to me than it does now, but in each stage of my life, it has been equally true, equally needed, and equally emphasized.

As members of The Church of Jesus Christ of Latter-day Saints, we are blessed to have knowledge of the divinity

of Jesus Christ. My mother taught me the truths that shape my life: We know, love, and revere Christ as the Son of God, but we extend this knowledge to another level—that of knowing that He is literally our Elder Brother, that we are all begotten of an Eternal Father, and that our heritage is that of godliness. This belief carries with it a tremendous responsibility on our part to live up to the expectations that are placed on us, to reach ever higher toward the goal of exaltation, and to act and react in ways that are most fitting for a child of God, someone who will someday inherit all that the Father hath. While this is a responsibility, it is also an honor, and we can and should feel confident within ourselves about our priceless inheritance. Because Jesus Christ is our Brother and because God Himself is our Father, we can walk with assurance when we know that we are living in accordance with the things we have been asked to do.

RUTHE CLARK
is the mother of

TRISTI PINKSTON

Tristi Pinkston is a stay-at-home mom, homeschooler, media reviewer, obsessive blogger, editor, author, and headless chicken. She's married to her first and only boyfriend, Matt Pinkston, and together they have four adorable children—Caryn, Ammon, Joseph, and Benjamin.

Tristi is a regularly featured presenter at the annual LDStorymakers Writers Conference and enjoys helping others learn how to fine-tune their writing skills. She also gives presentations

on literacy, the Hole in the Rock pioneers, and the importance of honoring the talents you've been given. Tristi is the author of three historical fiction novels and one contemporary mystery. In addition to the novels she writes, she maintains a blog at TristiPinkston.com, which contains tips for aspiring authors as well as her own personal ramblings. She enjoys reading, watching good movies, and making scrapbooks. She also enjoys cooking and considers it a minor miracle when she can get all four of her children to like the same meal.

Left: Ruthe at 18 months. *Middle*: Ruthe playing guitar, age 19. *Right*: Ruthe Clark, sister missionary.

My mother has never been one to shy away from a challenge. In fact, she's often the one to seek it out, shaking it to death like a pit bull terrier. Because of this example, I know that I don't have to be afraid of life. I know that I can have the courage and the confidence to stand up for myself, especially when armed with the knowledge that I am doing what my Heavenly Father would have me do. When we are given our commission from on high, we never need feel embarrassed about it, and my mother is an example to me of doing what needs to be done.

Challenge . . . she's often the one to *seek* it out, shaking it to death like a pit bull terrier.

We live in a time when it's more crucial than ever that we listen to the Spirit and then do what we're prompted to do. We need to cast aside the fear. We need to stop worrying about what others might think or how they might react when they see us standing up for right. We won't always be popular—followers of Christ rarely are the popular ones. But we will have the quiet assurance that comes through His Spirit that He is proud of us, that we are doing what's right, and that He will walk beside us. Thanks for teaching me to have guts, Mom.

Tristi and Ruthe say farewell at the MTC.

My Mother's Gift to Me

by Janette Rallison

When I was two years old, my mother became ill from what we later learned was cancer. She died when I was six. I have very few memories of her and no memories of her when she wasn't sick. I was the youngest of four children, and I suppose that even before she died, I was half wild. I didn't comb my hair, didn't see the need for more than a periodic bath, and as far as homework went, well, I simply didn't think it applied to me. School was a place to daydream. I also thought that wearing dirty clothes from the bottom of my closet was acceptable fashion. I was grunge before it was cool.

My father was overwhelmed, trying to be the breadwinner, cook, chauffer, handyman, maid, and gardener. Plus, he had to deal with the grief of losing his wife. A lot of things slipped through the cracks during those first few years. While my dad was gone at work and I was home after school, I did things like try to lure stray animals to our home by leaving opened cans of tuna fish in strategic places in our yard. I attempted to dig a hole to China and also made several campfires in an empty field behind our house. As I recall, there was some panicked water dumping on one such fire as it burned uncontrolled toward our home. Another time, I wandered off to see if there really was a pot of gold at the end of a rainbow. I would have found it if the end of the rainbow hadn't kept moving, sliding farther and farther away from my feet.

In my defense, I was destined to become a writer.

My dad started dating Kathryne when I was in fourth grade. My first thought when he introduced her to the family was, *How is it that my father, who is clearly old* (he was, after all, in his early forties) *keeps convincing pretty women to date him?* Kathryne was fun and bubbly and laughed a lot. She told us later that when she first came to our house and saw the painting of our mother that hung on the wall, she felt my mother wrap her arms around her in an embrace and say the word *sister.*

Kathryne didn't know quite what to make of that at the time. She had, after all, just started dating this man. But it wasn't the last time my mother

contacted her. After Kathryne married my father, my mother would occasionally show up in her dreams, and they would converse on how the children should be raised.

Kathryne brought many good things to the family: two young sons, unwavering faith, scented candles, and an awesome chili con queso recipe—but most important, an overabundance of love. This is perhaps even more amazing when one considers her background. Kathryne's early life wasn't easy. She was raised in an abusive family and still carried the scars of that ordeal. Many abuse victims become abusive themselves. Kathryne was just the opposite.

There were no "step" anyones in our family. She loved and worried about each of us with equal enthusiasm. People who met her and knew we had a blended family would sometimes ask her which of the children were hers.

"All of them," she would reply indignantly. She couldn't believe anyone would ever think differently about the matter.

Every day before I went to school, she made sure I was wearing clean, matching clothes, and she brushed and braided my long hair. The difference in my appearance was apparently stunning. I know this because every single teacher I'd had—and some I hadn't—came up to me and congratulated me on having a new mother, then complimented me on

I was grunge *before* it was cool.

the way I looked. It was as if they were breathing a collective sigh of relief that I wouldn't be doomed to live the life of a street urchin.

It wasn't long until I dropped the name Kathryne and started calling her Mom. She nicknamed me Sunshine and put little notes in my lunch to tell me she loved me. She kissed my father in front of my friends, causing them all sorts of embarrassment. (Secretly, I

began to worry for my friends' parents' marriages because they weren't kissing in front of me.) Mom was an example of selflessness that I should have imitated more but didn't nearly often enough. She would tell strangers at the grocery store that they looked nice and offered door-to-door salesmen drinks of water because they seemed hot. She always thought the best of her children whether we deserved it or not.

When I was seventeen, my family moved to Kentucky. One day, some of my friends from school planned a get-together. I was surprised when two of my friends told me in confidence that we couldn't meet at their homes because one of the guys who were coming was black. The girls didn't want their parents to know they were friends with a black guy. They knew their parents wouldn't approve and would worry they'd end up dating him.

Previous page—left: The Johnson family, 1980. *Previous page—right*: Kathryne at an outing. *Above—left*: Johnson girls modeling grandma's wigs, 1988. *Above—middle*: Johnson family, 1976. *Above—right*: Kathryne, 1977.

KATHRYNE JOHNSON
is the mother of

JANETTE RALLISON

Janette Rallison is the award-winning author of seventeen novels that have sold more than a million copies. Her novels have been on many reading and state lists, including IRA Young Adults' Choices List and Utah's Beehive reading list. Her latest book is the story of an incompetent fairy godmother, entitled *My Fair Godmother*. Most of her books are romantic comedies because, hey, there is enough angst in real life, but there's a drastic shortage of both humor and romance. She lives in Chandler, Arizona, with her husband, five kids, and enough cats to classify her as eccentric. You can learn more about her and her books at JanetteRallison.com or janette-rallison.blogspot.com

I had been over at my friends' houses multiple times and considered their parents to be normal, friendly people. I couldn't believe they were so prejudiced. Then, as I thought about it, I wondered if my own parents were prejudiced too. Maybe they had never voiced that opinion because it had never been an issue before.

That day when I went home from school, I told my mother I was considering dating a black guy and asked what she thought. I figured if there was any hidden prejudice lurking in her mind, this statement would ignite it.

My mother said, "Your father and I aren't as concerned about your boyfriend's skin color as much as we're concerned about his values." Then she launched into a lecture on the importance of high moral values, which I only half listened to. I had been curious as to how my parents valued people, and my mother had answered that question even if she didn't know it at the time.

Mom would sometimes forget that she hadn't given birth to *every* one of us.

My friends ended up getting together at my house. I don't remember what we did, but I do remember being glad that my parents weren't prejudiced.

Throughout my life, Mom would sometimes forget that she hadn't given birth to every one of us. I always thought that was funny, but now I find myself doing the same thing. My seventeen-year-old son has the ability to raise one eyebrow when he is giving me a questioning look. I nearly told him that he had inherited the ability from Grandma Johnson—until I thought twice and realized it was a genetic impossibility.

When I became a mother, there was no doubt in my mind that it would be the most vital and important job I would ever have because I knew firsthand what it was like not to have a mother. And I've never forgotten the difference having a mother makes. That has always been my mother's gift to me.

Kathryne and Janette, Mother's Day, 1982.

and investigators. President Ezra Taft Benson, after attending the show one evening, told the folks, "I assume, now, that you're all converted. The Lord bless this project. I highly approve of it."

Mom and Dad were called as missionaries to Nauvoo. They served as guides, but they went further than that, writing and performing short skits that told Nauvoo's story and then full-length missionary plays in the evenings. That tradition still persists, long after they left.

After Nauvoo, in their midseventies, they thought they would retire to Utah and enjoy their grandchildren. But they couldn't handle retirement. Off the stage, they got restless and their health started to fail. That's when they started the Hale Centre Theatres. They even started doing summer plays at the family ranch in Wayne County, Utah, which usually played to packed houses, using as many children and grandchildren as possible in the roles.

In her patriarchal blessing, Mom was told that when she was old and her hair silvered with gray, her family would rally around her and honor her for her example. Certainly that happened. She also received many public awards, culminating in the Presidential Citation at BYU for excellence in the arts.

Elder Merrill was right. It is wonderful to spend your life doing what you love to do. Especially if you put the Lord first.

It is *wonderful* to spend your life doing what you love to do. **Especially** if you put the Lord *first*.

Ruth receiving the BYU Presidential Citation from President Merrill Bateman.

My Mother, the Contradiction

by John Bennion

The east and the west meet in my mother, making her a woman of contrasts. She grew up in Silver Spring, Maryland, but spent most of her married life in Vernon, Utah. She attended the Chevy Chase ward as a teenager, met many people of influence when her father was a tariff expert for Congress, and was a sorority girl in college, but she managed without electricity, telephone, or central heating during the first years of her marriage to my father. Cosetta Castagno, our neighbor when I was growing up, called her the most beautiful woman ever to live in Vernon, but she has none of the self-consciousness or vanity of many lovely or handsome people. She listens to opera solos while playing electronic Scrabble and eating cheap, past-date candy. She is frugal and a bargain hunter but lavishes money on her children and grandchildren on birthdays and at Christmas. She is a contradiction—sophisticated and earthy, soft and hard-edged, selfish and generous, independent and needy.

Growing up, I spent a lot of time with my dad, but my mother was the one who held us all together, made our lives work. She bought our clothing, planned for us at Christmas and birthdays, walked up the road with us to church, took us up to the cemetery on Memorial Day, prepared our picnic for the Fourth of July, came up with ideas for the floats we entered in the parade. She kept the chickens, fed them scraps, reminded me to milk the cow and get something from the garden. I learned to love reading from her because when I was young, we both buried our heads in books all the time. She took me to the bookmobile, which seemed like heaven—walls lined top to bottom with stories.

Many of my best childhood memories are of wonderful Christmases, with quite a few gifts around the tree. Recently, I asked mom how she managed at Christmas without much money, and she said: "I just did the best I could. I had a lot of fun doing it. I tried to make sure everyone had something. I tried to make things, but I wasn't any good at that. I remember one year I made you a stick horse with a Naugahyde head, and you couldn't ride it because the head was so heavy that it just flopped over." She wanted to give us everything.

It's clear that not having enough money worried her, but she also had to adjust to my father, who expected her to live without "amenities" and who was never much of a handyman. Recently, she said, "It was hard learning how to do things without electricity, and I didn't blame Colin for that, but I did blame him for not fixing things. I had this idea that men were supposed to fix things. He didn't have time or know how, so often I had to figure out a way to fix whatever broke." After years of not having enough, she must have been worn down. She described a time when my father hired a man to drill a well on their farm but didn't have money to pay him. Mother said, "They took us to court, and we just settled it outside the door. We had to start paying every month for the well. . . . It was hard because

I'd been to Utah, and it was pretty barren, but it was sort of like an *adventure*, you know. I had a romantic idea of "home on the range," I guess.

there wasn't enough money to go around. It was a funny way of thinking that the family wasn't where your money went. The family was somewhere farther down the list, and it was hard for me to accept that the farm needed money too. . . . I don't know how we managed all those years. So many expenses, so much work, but we just struggled along."

Her battle to give us as much as possible came from her own youth when she felt she didn't have enough. Born in 1932, she grew up during the Depression. Although her family's house in Maryland was quite large, she still thought they were poor. "I know we wore a lot of hand-me-downs, and mother really practiced economy. We had more children than anybody around. . . ." She had the feeling of not having enough money even then. "I didn't get a bicycle until I was nearly too old for one. I longed for one so much, and then they got me an old, beat-up one. It was red and kind of rusty, but it was a bicycle. I loved it."

As a teenager she felt hungry all the time. She often sneaked downstairs to the refrigerator and carefully shaved ice cream off the top of the container. She would take more and more until a noticeable amount was gone, and then she'd get in trouble. During her childhood, she was hungry for confirmation from her father and mother, and for whatever reason, she felt that she didn't get enough of their praise.

When I was a child, I assumed that the sense and direction of my parents' lives was steady and well planned. But I hadn't yet realized that for them, as it was for me, life was composed of hundreds of small decisions. During our interview, I asked her why she wanted to go west with my father. She said, "I'd

SERGENE ELIZABETH BENSON BENNION

is the mother of

JOHN BENNION

John Bennion writes novels, essays, and short fiction about the western Utah desert and the people who inhabit that forbidding country. He has published a collection of short fiction, *Breeding Leah and Other Stories* (Signature Books, 1991) and a novel, *Falling Toward Heaven* (Signature Books, 2000). He has published short work in *Ascent, AWP Chronicle, English Journal, Utah Holiday, Journal of Experiential Education, Sunstone Magazine, Best of the West II, Black American Literature Forum, Journal of Mormon History, The Hardy Society Journal,* and others.

He has written two historical novels (not yet published), *Avenging Saint* and *Ezekiel's Third Wife.* He is currently working on a young adult mystery, *The Hidden Splendor Mine.* An associate professor at Brigham Young University, Bennion teaches creative writing and the British novel. He has made a special study of the late Victorian and modern writer, Thomas Hardy. As a teacher, he specializes in experiential writing and literature programs. His curriculum includes wilderness writing, a class in which students backpack and then write personal narratives about their experiences; and England and literature, a study abroad program during which students study Romantic and Victorian writers and hike through the landscapes where those writers lived. A documentary, *The Christian Eye: An Essay across England,* covers his 2007 tour.

been to Utah, and it was pretty barren, but it was sort of like an adventure, you know. I had a romantic idea of 'home on the range,' I guess." She tried to tell me what it was like to live away from the lush, urban East. "I do remember feeling for a long time that there was something not right because there weren't trees and things growing. But I was happy about my new adventure. It was dusty, dusty, dusty, but on the other hand, the lack of humidity was a great blessing. It was different, but I wasn't unhappy."

She also went because my father was an easy man to love, although I believe he was not an easy man to live with. She met him at Utah State, her father's former school. Initially, she liked him because he was a lot of fun. "He was fourteen years older than me. I didn't know that. I mean, he just seemed like a kid." She didn't know at first that she loved him; it was a gradual discovery. At a sorority meeting once, the women's president announced that Colin Bennion was engaged. "But it wasn't to me. It was to someone else. And I had a really funny sinking feeling. It was strange. Then something said to me, *It will be all right.*" In time, his engagement to the other woman ended, and that February, Colin asked my mother to marry him. "I just suddenly said yes, I'd marry him. . . . He'd been on a little trip, and I'd missed him." I have learned from my mother to follow my heart and my impulses, and to make the best of my fortunate and unfortunate decisions.

When they were first married, they lived with my father's mother, Lucile, on the family ranch in Vernon, and in Delta and Sandy, where he taught school. Early during those first years, she and Dad bought

twenty-five heifers. Mom said, "He did just what his father did: he put them out in the [alfalfa] field and five of them died. . . . It was a hard thing." Talking to her, I had the feeling that she wished my father would not have followed some of his father's traditions. Then their neighbor across the street in Vernon died, and my parents were able to move out of Grandma Lucile's house and buy the neighbor's house. My mom said, "We couldn't borrow the money. They would only lend us part of it. I don't know where we got the rest. We thought we were the richest people around to have a house of our own." While they lived in that house, their last two children were born, Susan and Janet. Red poppies grew in front of the house, and it had a nice lawn and a white picket fence.

I'm not telling the story the way she would. She has been nobody's victim, and my father was a kind and loving man, if flawed. But, then, who is not flawed? My mother has adapted and succeeded. She occasionally substituted for Dad at the elementary school when he was sick or had something he had to do with the cows. There are rules

We thought we were the richest people around to have a house of our own.

now for substituting that would prevent someone from just stepping in for a family member. But she finally got her undergraduate degree, started teaching in Vernon, and kept taking classes for her master of education degree. When she began teaching, she was terrified that she wouldn't do well. But she gradually came to enjoy it. "I liked working with the children. I liked having a check. I liked setting up my own program. Beth [the senior teacher] didn't tell me what to do."

So one of the ways she survived life in the desert was by gradually becoming independent and getting her own money that she could spend on the children, money that wouldn't go to the ranch. With two incomes, my parents made more money than they ever had. "For a while there, we were fantastic, and we were able to send money to Mary Ann and Dell in California." From her, I learned the values of becoming independent and providing for my own.

I think she is a resilient, creative woman. When she was first married, she lived in circumstances like those people dealt with in the nineteenth century. But she figured out how to cook cakes and other food with a wood stove where the temperature is difficult to regulate. She read with the light of a kerosene lamp and got by with cars that broke down often. For many years, she cleaned clothing with a wringer washer and hung them on a line. She bottled fruit and tomatoes, bought food on sale, and managed while the farm sucked money from the family. She wasn't good at chopping wood, but she brought in extra wood whenever there was a storm. While my dad was away at school, she learned how to milk the cow. "It was one of the bravest things I've ever done," she said. "Those animals are huge." She didn't have central heating until she and Dad added to their Vernon house in 1970. She worked hard to give us ambition and the skills to pursue those ambitions. Her children are well educated and financially stable. She sacrificed much for us.

I tease her that she's only happy when she's sitting in a draft, eating the toughest piece of meat. In many situations, it's difficult to find out what she wants; she says herself that this is usually because she doesn't know what she wants beyond "a book and a dish of ice cream." She downplays her many successes and the wonderful way she adapted to a difficult man who loved a difficult environment. She seems to think of her other talents the same way she thinks about her beauty, as if these qualities are just not that significant. My claim is that few women could have adapted with equal facility and grace to the desert and to her new desert family. I will be proud if I can live up to her example of responsibility, independence, flexibility, and devotion to her children.

I tease her that she's only **HAPPY** when she's sitting in a draft, eating the toughest piece of meat.

Obedience = Blessings

by Carol Anne Clayson

othing ever got past my mother.

As a child (and even now sometimes as an adult), this could be quite frustrating. Somehow, some way, she always seemed to know whenever things weren't quite right, and unfortunately for me (her youngest child)—and, well, the rest of my siblings— it made for some interesting experiences growing up. She possesses an unusual gift of discernment, knowing well ahead of time what we should or should not do. To make matters worse, if we didn't follow her advice, we could expect that something bad was going to happen.

For example, when we were living in Anaheim, California, my sister attended a dance class. Many of the other kids often crossed a busy street to buy a soda after class. My mom warned her that even if all the other kids did it, my sister was not to go. One day, since there really was no compelling reason not to cross the street, my sister succumbed to the temptation while she waited for her ride home. Predictably, that was the day a police officer was ticketing jaywalkers at that location.

Years later when I was still a young teenager, I would often catch a flight to visit my sister during the summer months. I was a seasoned traveler, or so I thought. On one occasion, my parents were out of town and my older brother was tasked with driving me to the airport. My mother gave him strict instructions: "Do

EDUCATION

MAXINE HARWOOD CLAYSON
is the mother of

CAROL ANNE CLAYSON

Carol Anne Clayson is currently an associate professor in the Department of Meteorology at Florida State University and the director of the Geophysical Fluids Dynamics Institute. Her research covers the areas of high-resolution air-sea interaction, satellite remote sensing, and ocean modeling, and she has received funding for her research from NASA, NOAA, the Office of Naval Research, and NSF.

She is the recipient of an NSF CAREER award and the Office of Naval Research Young Investigator award. She received a Presidential Early Career Award for Scientists and Engineers from President Bill Clinton. Dr. Clayson is the author or coauthor of more than forty journal articles, two books, two book chapters, and three National Research Council reports; has served on several committees for the American Meteorological Society and the National Research Council; and is currently a member of the AMS Committee on Coastal Environments.

She received her BS degree in physics and astronomy from Brigham Young University, and her MS and PhD degrees in aerospace engineering sciences and the Program in Atmospheric and Oceanic Sciences from the University of Colorado, Boulder. She and her husband, Tristan Johnson, are the parents of three boys. She currently serves as the second counselor in the Primary presidency in her ward.

not just drop your sister off at the curb." Instead, he was to park the car, go inside, and make sure I got on the plane safely. (In those days, you could still see someone off at the gate.)

Nevertheless, as we pulled in to the airport, my brother and I decided that he really didn't need to come inside with me. After all, I had traveled alone several times before, so we unpacked my luggage from the car and off he went. I confidently went inside, lined up at the ticket counter to check my bag, and discovered that the flight had been canceled. The next available flight would not leave until the next day.

I had no way of reaching my brother to have him return to pick me up. I was forced to do something drastic or risk sleeping at the airport. Worst of all, my brother and I would have some serious explaining to do to my mother, and the single thought of facing my mother inspired me to find another solution. Using all the powers of persuasion I could muster, I was able to convince an employee from a competing airline to accept my ticket without any additional fees, since I had no money to speak of. Fortunately,

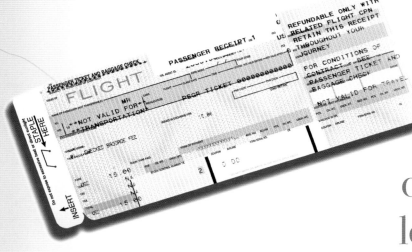

Mom's willingness to listen to inspiration has always been one of the **GREATEST** lessons I've learned from her.

  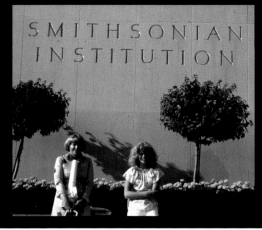

Previous page—*Left:* Maxine with her dog, Brit. *Middle:* Maxine in high school. *Right:* Maxine and Reed on their wedding day, 1953.

Left: Maxine at the piano. *Middle:* Maxine as a student at Utah State University. *Right:* Maxine and Carol Anne at the Smithsonian Institute, 1979.

I was given a seat on another flight, and I arrived safely. My mother never knew what happened. When I finally made it to my sister's house, I told my brother what had happened. He said, "Of course! We should never go against Mother's direct counsel . . . it never turns out well." We waited many years (until we felt she could laugh about it) before telling her what had happened.

Such occurrences are so typical in our family that we now simply roll our eyes, as they happen so often they aren't even worthy of comment.

My mom's willingness to listen to inspiration has always been one of the greatest lessons I've learned from her. She taught me that when we pray, Heavenly Father gives us instruction and we need to follow that counsel to the letter, whether or not we understand it or agree with it. He also gives us guidance and inspiration, and several events of her early life have reinforced this particular lesson.

My mother was born in Smithfield, Utah, and as a sixth grader, she and a friend went on an extended horseback ride up in the mountains for the day. They planned to ride to the other side of Crow Mountain, almost 5,500 feet high, where they knew about a favorite meadow. They had an enjoyable ride and had a lovely time picking flowers. Since it was getting late, they prepared to go home, but their horses had gotten loose. Worse yet, one horse had lost its bridle, and they couldn't find it. After an exhaustive search, my mother and her friend knelt in prayer and asked for guidance and help. Upon opening their eyes, they saw the bridle right in front of them, even though they had searched that location several times before their prayer. They were able to make it home safely and without further incident.

My mother has received answers to her prayers many times that have not only enlightened her and brought her knowledge but have also enlightened her family. I know of many sacred instances where she has

When the Lord commands, do it.

The Clayson family, 2004.

received an answer that prompted her to do something against all her inclinations, and yet she has done it and been blessed for it.

One event had a profound impact while I was an undergraduate student at BYU. My parents were living in Colorado, and one day my mother randomly said to my father that she needed to drive to Provo to be with me that very day. My father pointed out, reasonably so, that it was an eight-hour drive, that she had seen me only a short time before, and that they had plans to drive to Provo in another week's time to bring me home. But my mother persevered, and my father relented, even though he was unable to make the trip with her.

I remember my surprise that night when I learned she was coming. When I awoke the next morning, however, I learned that a dear friend was missing and was presumed to have drowned in a tragic accident. My feelings of grief were intense, but it was an undeniable tender mercy that my mother had arrived at just the right time to console me and give me much-needed comfort and strength. She took me to Temple Square, and there, with my mother, I was able to find peace and be sustained through a very difficult time.

I thought of my mom recently when I read this statement from Joseph Smith: "When the Lord commands, do it."

My mother has not only followed that advice but has lived this rule with exactness. I will always be grateful that she taught her children, by both her word and example, that obedience leads to happiness.

She taught her children, by *both* her word and EXAMPLE.

Mom Lifted Us to See the Wonders of Creation

by H. Wallace Goddard

Mom and Dad started married life with high hopes, lots of love, and no money. In the first years of their marriage, Grandpa gave them a chunk of land in his alfalfa field in Granger, Utah. Mom and Dad bought an old army barracks, moved it onto the property, and began the process of turning it into a home in which they could raise a family.

By the time I landed in mortality, the barracks had become a respectable cottage, and a few scrawny sticks in the yard had started to look like trees.

Perhaps my very first memory of mortal life is the day my mother grabbed me excitedly and said, "I have something to show you, Wally!" She carried me to one of the trees and lifted me up. "Look in the nest."

I gasped. There in the nest were three perfect blue robin eggs. I still think there may be nothing more beautiful on this earth than robin eggs in a nest.

Mom started a process that day of celebrating God's many gifts of life. I cannot count the number of times she has lifted me spiritually to look into the heart of God's creation and rejoice.

Over the years, Mom told stories that inspired awe. She told about a sacred experience when she was a child and saw her departed grandfather. She told about her dear parents and the joy of her childhood.

But Mom didn't just talk about joy; she lived it. I remember times when we traveled places in the family's 1950 Ford. There were times when the brood became restless. Mom, with her inimitable zeal, would say, "Kids, let's sing

> She has lifted me spiritually to look into the *heart* of God's creation and **REJOICE.**

BERNICE WALLACE GODDARD

is the mother of

H. WALLACE GODDARD

H. Wallace Goddard is an extension family life specialist for the University of Arkansas Cooperative Extension Service. He develops programs on parent-

ing, marriage, youth development, and family relations. He is also involved in writing books and web articles, producing television programs, and developing national extension programs.

Goddard grew up in the mountains outside Salt Lake. He had a pet squirrel, a pet skunk, a tree house, a rope swing, and a raft to navigate the local stream.

He earned degrees at Brigham Young University in physics, math, and education before teaching high school. He taught a range of subjects, including general science, filmmaking, folklore, gifted and talented programs, media, and literature. He and his students created a 16mm film that won the Utah student film festival.

After teaching school for twelve years, he returned to college at Utah State University, where he earned his doctorate in family and human development.

Goddard served as an extension specialist at Auburn University in Auburn, Alabama, for six years. He took leave from Auburn University to help Stephen Covey write *The 7 Habits of Highly Effective Families* and to develop application activities for improving family life. He also taught courses for Utah State University.

Goddard has many family experiences on which to draw. He and his wife, Nancy, have three children and three grandchildren. They have cared for twenty foster children; such experiences with mostly troubled teens taught them advanced lessons in humility. His popular wisdom and insights on parenting, marriage, rearing troubled teens, and family relations can be found at www.DrWally.org.

In their spare time, Wally and his wife love to paint their house, build wood projects, work in the yard, volunteer in the community, and write.

Left and far left: Sister Hardy making friends in Nigeria. *Below*: Sister Hardy in Indonesia.

whatever else was needed. As a fairly competent, successful adult myself, I was astonished at what my mother and father were able to accomplish. I don't know that I have what it takes to serve in such challenging circumstances, but there is no longer any doubt in my mind that my mother's courage, perseverance, and faithfulness would have made her a valuable addition to any pioneer company.

There is a Primary song called "To Be a Pioneer" that tries to redefine the meaning of Mormon history for new generations of Latter-day Saints who are far removed in time and geography from nineteenth-century Utah. It talks of not necessarily having to push a handcart to be a pioneer. The song explains that we need only have courage and faith and work for the right cause in order to be a pioneer.

When I sing this song with my children, I think of my mother and how her bravery and devotion have inspired me and shaped my life. I also like to think she has made her Mormon ancestors proud.

My very conservative, somewhat timid, stay-at-home mother was now **LIVING** in *exotic third-world cultures*—not as a tourist but as a deeply involved volunteer who **HELPED** the local people.

Life with Elizabeth

by Patrick Madden

ELIZABETH STONE MADDEN

is the mother of

PATRICK MADDEN

Patrick Madden joined the BYU English Department in 2004, after completing his PhD at Ohio University. He specializes in theory and practice of the personal essay and its sister genres (travel, aphorism, etc.) in literary nonfiction. He is also interested in Latin American literature.

Dr. Madden was raised in Whippany, New Jersey, and Baton Rouge, Louisiana. He received his BS in physics from Notre Dame in 1993, his MA in English from BYU in 1999, and his PhD in English from Ohio University in 2004. He served a mission to Uruguay from 1993–1995 and later returned there as a Fulbright fellow from 2002–2003 to write his dissertation, a collection of travel essays.

His first book, *Quotidiana*, a collection of essays that was runner-up in the 2007 AWP Award Series in Creative Nonfiction, was published in early 2010 by the University of Nebraska Press. He has published individual essays in *The Iowa Review, Fourth Genre, Hotel Amerika, Portland Magazine,* and many other journals; additionally, some of these essays have been anthologized in *The Best American Spiritual Writing 2007* and *The Best Creative Nonfiction vol. 2* or noted in the back of *The Best American Essays.*

He enjoys volleyball, basketball, web design, strategy games, singing, Rush, and Notre Dame football. He and his wife, Karina, have three sons and three daughters.

Late last year I received an unexpected correspondence from a man I'd never met. "I hope you will excuse the intrusion," it began, "however, I just recently came across an essay by a Mr. Patrick Madden about his experiences at Cardinal Spellman's Servicemen's Club while stationed in Fort Monmouth, New Jersey. . . . His recollection of the fine times he spent at the club mirrors my own experiences, and I, too, met a pretty, bubbly, and extremely nice girl named Liz. I believe her full name is Elizabeth Brown. Could she be the same Liz? It would be ever so fantastic if she is."

I wrote back both excited and a little sad. His adjectives seemed to describe my mother, but her maiden name was Stone, not Brown. Certainly she and my father (whose namesake I am and whose essay he had found) had attended events at the club that he would have also attended. He was resigned but undampened in his reply—"It is enough to think that I might have danced with your mother. How cool is that? as the younger generation would say"—and I was grateful for this nudge to think of Elizabeth Stone as she was before she became, simply, "Mom."

Long before I attempted to become a writer, my mother wrote her first book, hand-written and decorated with photographs and crayon drawings, hardbound and sheathed in a red dust jacket. *Life with Elizabeth* adorns its cover in gold capital letters, and a smiling eleven-year-old gazes from within a

"Stone" model television set. Inside, we find an imaginative retelling of her birth in San Francisco, infancy in Manhattan, and childhood in Brooklyn. She recalls deciding to walk on her first birthday ("I could have done it long before, but I was too lazy"), getting lost in the park as a toddler, and donning makeup with a teenage cousin. Black-and-white photographs document her growth and activities, including movies with her father, a surprise tenth birthday party, an overnight Girl Scout campout, and a frightening plane crash in the Atlantic Ocean ("What a time I had to convince myself that it was only a dream" she reveals at the end of the ordeal).

One reviewer, a Mrs. Gerdy, gave the book an A++, calling the work "A lovely book from a lovely girl with a lovely disposition." I concur.

The last chapter looks to the future:

"To be a nurse (in my estimation) is one of the finest professions toward which a girl could aim for. Of course, there's plenty of hard work. Nothing easy!

"Until a year ago I thought I wanted to be an airline stewardess. But soon after reading three Cherry Ames nurse books, I changed my mind. In these books, I learned how she helped people. They made me want to help people also.

"Don't get me wrong I also want to get married and have five children. Two boys and three girls."

I'll go ahead and cut the suspense: Elizabeth Stone never became a nurse, never worked as a stewardess, never attended college, never had the opportunities she dreamed of as a baby-boomer in Brooklyn. It wasn't for reasons of lack of intelligence or lack of trying. When she earned a college scholarship out of high school, her no-nonsense father told her to get a job instead, which she did, utilizing her typing skills as a secretary, like so many women of her generation. She worked in Manhattan, sharing a rented apartment with a friend.

Around this time, she made the most important frivolous decision of my life, by which I mean that she began hanging around the aforementioned Cardinal Spellman's Servicemen's Club on Park Avenue. It was a Catholic organization founded to bring together soldiers and locals for a bit of carefree fun: pool and ping-pong, live music, dances. In February of 1967, shortly after Mom began frequenting the club, she met a tall, shy fellow from Milwaukee who'd been stationed in Fort Monmouth, New Jersey, for electronics repair school. He was on his way to Vietnam. They liked to sit and talk, dance, and play ping-pong, at which she nearly always won.

She did successfully fulfill—for the most part—one of her childhood dreams: she got married and had four children (not quite the five she predicted, and we are three boys and one girl). After Dad returned from the war and my parents wed, Mom spent the next forty-or-so years of her life helping people: fixing dinners and washing laundry, buying shoes and mending clothes, helping with homework and driving to practices, cheering at games and watching kid movies, vacuuming and dusting, and sweeping and picking up after her unruly brood. Her bubbly niceness complements Dad's shy niceness, and they form a fine couple, even after all these years. And she can still beat him at ping-pong.

Elizabeth as a young girl.

My father likes to tell this story: Early in their marriage, perhaps before I was born but certainly before I can remember, my mother woke my father in the middle of the night, complaining. "I'm cold!"

"Why don't you get under the blankets?" he asked.

"Because I'm hot!" came the reply.

As for me, I like this story that my mother told more recently: "For years I've been telling Chris, 'You have to get uninsured and underinsured motorist insurance. Chris, I see people all the time who aren't covered!'" She's worked for most of the past two decades as a legal secretary, pulling in a paycheck to send us children to college, and she often sees scary litigations over automobile accidents. Eventually, Chris capitulated, as my mother says triumphantly: "So finally, she signed up for uninsured and underinsured motorist insurance."

I love this story because you expect right here some ironic plot resolution, the revelation that shortly after Chris made the wise decision to get uninsured and underinsured motorist insurance, she was hit by an uninsured or underinsured motorist. Right? But

Her **BUBBLY** niceness *complements* Dad's shy niceness, and they form a fine couple, even after *all* these years.

the end of the story is just that: Chris finally made the right choice, and life went on as it had before. No accident, no poetic timing. Life doesn't always give you what you expect. Sometimes you're hot; sometimes you're cold. Sometimes you're not so sure. Sometimes what you were hoping for fades, and you find that with a lot of sacrifice and hard work, you get something far better, something you hadn't known to hope for. Sometimes your life becomes meaningful because you give your life in service to others. That's Mom.

A few years ago at Thanksgiving dinner, someone told a joke or recalled a memory from the days when we all lived together in that house on Clemens Terrace that my parents still occupy, and as we laughed aloud, I looked at my youngest brother. His back arched and his head inclined sideways; his lips pulled taut to show his teeth; his eyes shut tight, trailing crow's feet from their outer edges. My mind froze an image of him as I started with the shock that he was the spitting image of Mom.

This was a stark reversal of the assumption that had covered my perception for all of my life. Who knows why—perhaps because I share my father's name; because we are both men; because we enjoy science and math; because we visited his side of the family far more often than Mom's, and they were far more numerous, with far more comments like "you look just like your father"—but I had always believed that in physiology and psychology, my siblings and I took after Dad. I loved my mother and (in my better moments) appreciated her selfless sacrifices for me, but I struggled to find how I was like her. But in that instant during dinner, as

> Sometimes what you were *hoping* for fades, and you find that with a lot of sacrifice and hard work, you get something **FAR BETTER**, something you hadn't *known* to hope for.

my brother laughed, I was shaken out of my erroneous, biased paradigm. And the funny thing is that now, when I look in the mirror, I see her features in me too: her hazel eyes, her sharp nose, her well-defined calves. For most of my life, I've known I was my father's son; I've seen his visage in mine; I've thought thoughts he's thought; I've sought the resonances in my Maddenness. It is only now, as I grow a bit older, perhaps a smidgen wiser, that I find so much of my mother in me. And I'm grateful.

**MYRNA DEE GARDNER
MUHLESTEIN**

is the mother of

KERRY MUHLESTEIN

Dr. Muhlestein received his BS cum laude from BYU in psychology, with a Hebrew minor. His first full-time appointment was a joint position in religion and history at BYU–Hawaii. He was also instrumental in arranging the first-ever Egyptology conference in Hawaii at BYU–Hawaii.

As a rising biblical scholar, Dr. Muhlestein taught in both the Religious Education and History departments of BYU–Hawaii and is now an assistant professor of ancient scripture and ancient Near Eastern studies at Brigham Young University.

His recent publications include "One Continuous Flow: Revelations Surrounding the 'New Translation,'" which analyzes the Joseph Smith Translation of Genesis and its relation to the Doctrine and Covenants.

He focuses mostly on ancient Egypt, the Hebrew Bible, and the Pearl of Great Price, and his research focuses on the texts and iconography of Egyptian religion, international contact between ancient Egypt and her neighbors, the Egyptian juridical process, Egyptian literature, and the overlap of the biblical and Egyptian worlds, including the ancient and modern history of the Pearl of Great Price. He also often travels to Egypt to take part in the BYU Egypt Excavation Project of which he is an integral part.

Dr. Muhlestein is proficient in many languages, both ancient and modern, including Egyptian, Hebrew, Aramaic, Ugaritic, Phoenician, Moabite, Coptic, German, French, Greek, and Akkadian.

He and his wife, Julianne, have six children.

To Love and Learn

by Kerry Muhlestein

The lessons I learned from my mother were not necessarily taught in sudden moments that make good stories but more in the aggregate of a lifetime of little acts, most of which she thought were unseen or unnoticed. Some she did for years, but it only took a glimpse or a moment where I finally saw something through different eyes to sink these lessons deep into my heart, where they came to serve as an anchor for me throughout my life.

One thing I learned was a genuine love for others. I learned early in life that one of the greatest assets I had was how much people liked my mother. It was easier to gain and maintain good friends if I had them come by my house. Meeting both my parents—but especially Mom, since she was home after school when friends came by—always made other kids want to play at our house. She liked all the kids I brought by so much, with such a genuine love, that they wanted to spend time at our house. My friends were happy to come by and say hi to Mom, and before playing, we often hung out in the kitchen for a while, talking with her. She knew all my friends' names and what they liked to do, and she made them feel wanted and welcome. As I grew old enough to date and especially as I was in college, I knew it was to my advantage to have girls I was interested in meet my parents. Mom and Dad both came to like people so quickly and easily that any girls who came by the house immediately felt happy and cared for. All of this came because of a loving

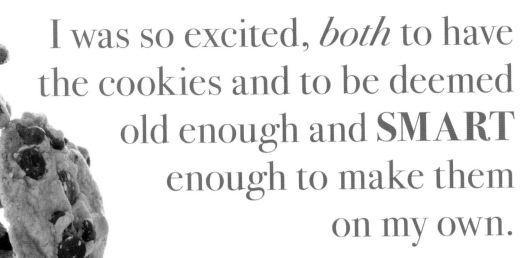

I was so excited, *both* to have the cookies and to be deemed old enough and **SMART** enough to make them on my own.

heart. From Mom, I learned of the powerful effect of genuinely caring.

Many events shaped me, but one I'll share had a lasting influence on me. As a family, we liked to go camping. We loved going to the mountains or boating and waterskiing. We'd purchased a used truck, and my dad had taken it apart and extended the bed so we could load an old camper on it and still have some storage room on the side of the camper and a nice little porch out the back. He'd also built a boat we used when the family was very young, and then we eventually bought a little aluminum boat that seemed to us to be the perfect family skiing toy. Whenever we went camping, Mom prepared as much food ahead of time as she could. She knew that as growing children, we would regularly get hungry between meals, so when we went camping, she always made a lot of snacks to bring along. We loved this because it was one of the few times we would make and eat cookies. I remember one time when we were getting ready for a long trip, she asked me to make a triple batch. I'd helped her bake

cookies before, but this time I was going to make them on my own.

I was so excited, both to have the cookies and to be deemed old enough and smart enough to make them on my own. I thought I'd figured out how to triple the recipe, and I whipped up a huge batch of cookie dough. As the first tray came out of the oven, I could hardly wait to sample them (one of the perks of doing the cooking!). Imagine my disappointment as I tasted one and found it to be horrible! I was so disappointed to have to go tell my mom that I had failed in my cooking assignment. Mom tasted it and told me that she didn't know exactly what I had done wrong, but she could tell that in tripling the recipe, I had somehow not gotten the right ratio of ingredients. She was busy getting ready and had a lot to do, and I could tell that having to help me was causing a problem, but she never acted that way.

I feared that she would tell me I just wasn't ready for this task after all. But she had me work out how to triple it with her there, making sure I now knew what to do. After having me dump the bad dough out in the old irrigation ditch, she had me try again. This time I was sure I would do it right. I worked so hard, excitedly pulled another tray of cookies

out of the oven, and found they tasted worse than the first. I'd found a new way to mess up the recipe. Mom again tasted them, and this time she could detect exactly what mistake I'd made. I'd read "teaspoon" as "tablespoon" when I put the salt in. Tripling that mistake had made for some very salty cookies.

Mom didn't get upset, though I was now taxing her ingredient supply as well as her time. She just explained how to do it right, had me rehearse what I had learned thus far, told me she was sure I would succeed, and set me about my task again. After another trip to the irrigation ditch, I started over.

As I combined the ingredients a third time, I was very careful to make sure I had the right amounts of everything in the recipe. But somehow I grabbed baking soda instead of baking powder. And so a third time, I had to get Mom and have her taste my mistake so she could tell me what I had done wrong. I was sure I would be relieved of duties at this point. Instead, she told me to make sure I didn't clog the ditch with dough, made sure I knew all the things I had learned about following the recipe, and had me try again. On this fourth try, I finally got the recipe right. No cookies ever tasted as good as those did to me.

Though I'd used up lots of time and enough costly ingredients for twelve batches of cookies, Mom didn't get upset or chastise me. Instead, she encouraged me and taught me, giving me chance after chance to succeed. Not only did this instill in me confidence that I could learn and do well, but it also taught me the value of trying again and again rather than giving up after a failure or two. I learned that mistakes weren't tragedies; they were just a chance for us to learn and do better. This lesson has served me well throughout life and, I think, has helped me to better understand our mortal probation and our Heavenly Father's view of our misadventures as we try to learn and grow while here on earth.

As powerful as this experience was, I think the lesson that affected me most was one that came when I saw things she had never planned on me seeing. I remember that Mom was often tired. With six kids close to each other in age, all of whom were more full of energy than wisdom, she had more to do than could be done in a day. Even with all

Previous page—left: The Muhlestein Family, 1991. *Right*: Myrna with Kerry and his family in Waikiki. *Above—left*: Myrna holding Kerry. *Above—middle*: The Muhlestein family, 1984. *Above—right*: The Muhlestein family, 1986.

Mistakes weren't tragedies; they were just a chance for us to **LEARN** and do better.

her Church and household responsibilities, she would find time to give in to my begging as I asked her to read to me at night while I went to sleep. She would tiredly but happily read to me and then stay up late getting things done. With all this, she was also always the first person up. But for years, I didn't know how early she got up.

As I got older and had things to do in the morning that made me get up early, I found her engaging in a consistent morning habit. Just before it was time for her to make breakfast, when I crept into the kitchen before dawn, I would find her at our large table reading her scriptures. All around her were books, like the institute manual, Church manuals for teachers, commentaries, and so on. In the center were the scriptures, and she was reading from them and consulting other materials to try to understand them better. I am not sure she even knew I saw her reading before the day got going in such a way that she would not have time for quiet study and contemplation. But no sermon, talk, or lesson taught me more of the importance of studying the scriptures than when I saw my tired mother up much earlier than she needed to be so she could study the word of God. It gave me a sense of their import in such a manner that everything in my life has been influenced by it.

I would certainly not teach the scriptures for a living; I would definitely not spend time in Jerusalem helping students to better understand the scriptures; I would undoubtedly never write further explanations about the word of God, if I had not seen my mother sacrificing her predawn hours in that way. Whenever I write about the scriptures, the audience I see in my mind is mothers the world over, sitting in their own kitchens, trying to have their moments of study, attunement, and enhancement before they set about the child-raising tasks that will consume their day. I guess that in a way what I am really doing is writing for my mom.

Her Time of Dying

by Gene A. Sessions

Not so long ago, my brothers and I sat somberly at the kitchen table in the house where we had grown up. In our own ways, we all sensed that we were actually at an altar where we had performed the daily rituals of passing from childhood to maturity. Officiating at these rites had been our ever-watchful mother, who was five-foot-three but had the presence of a giant. From dispensing substantial meals and stern counsel to supervising homework, she presided there in that sacred room over her bevy of sons with an all-seeing eye and a clasping hand.

It was a calm afternoon in early August, one of those summer times when Utah's climate can produce the very definition of paradise. We did not notice the gorgeous day, however, as we slumped with our faces in our hands. It had been a tough few weeks during which we had rotated being there alone and sometimes all together. With the help of our wives, children, and cousins, we were maintaining an around-the-clock vigil that now seemed about to end. In a nearby bedroom, on a narrow little bed, lay our virtually unconscious mother, now swollen with a great malignant beast festering in her womb, the womb that had once nurtured each of us from a tiny dot to a healthy baby boy.

My oldest brother had just checked on her and had given her a drop of morphine. Even though she had never complained about pain since we brought her home from the hospital with a death sentence, the hospice workers assured us that she was suffering and needed medication to assuage it. We often discussed the apparent lack of pain and how well she had borne the chemotherapy she had endured a few years before when the beast first attacked her. I remember wondering if the truth was that she had indeed suffered and was suffering terribly but it was not in her nature—ever—to complain about such things, especially to her boys.

Mother certainly had much in her nearly eighty-one years about which to complain. She was born in Moroni, in Sanpete County, of sturdy English and Scandinavian stock. Tough Mormon pioneers, her ancestors had been among the earliest converts to the Restoration. Her heritage included one great-great-grandfather who had founded Spring City, Utah, and a great-grandfather who was a hero of the 1856 handcart rescue, while a grandmother, as a twelve-year-old convert from Sweden, had walked barefoot to the promised land behind one of those handcarts.

Shortly after Mother's birth, her parents moved their little family to eastern Nevada, where Grandpa and his brother tried to make a living running cows in perhaps the most inhospitable place for doing so in the entire American West. They did not remain there long, beneath the bleached rocks of Blue Eagle Mountain. Before Mother was old enough to remember, they relocated to the Uintah Basin where there was a bit more water. There, she and her four brothers grew to adulthood—hard work and tough times as constants, but the hallmarks of the story were not hardships; they were cheerful labor and deep love, not only for one another but also for neighbors and relatives, some of whom always seemed to be staying with them. Grandpa and Grandma had enough to share. When I first heard the innumerable stories of those difficult times, I had no knowledge of the so-called Little Depression of the 1920s that hammered the West long before the Great Depression of the 1930s slammed the rest of the country onto the anvil of economic despair. With that added perspective, I cannot imagine how those hardy people got through it all. My generation does not have even a vague concept of it.

Not long into her adolescence, Mother realized that her gender imposed on her an additional burden due to traditional rural culture. On one occasion, her father collected his children together to discuss dividing his lands among them. When he got to Mother, he said, "Of course, you'll have a husband." Thus, well aware that there might not be much of a future for her in the Basin, she left rural life and her girlhood behind and headed for the Wasatch Front. Joining an exodus of young women who had been fleeing the farms of America for more than a century, she soon found herself in the so-called pink-collar ghetto of typing and stenography. The word that best describes this period of her life is *mystery*. Much happened in those years about which my brothers and I know very little. Photographs of her show a beautiful blonde with an enigmatic smile, but she told us precious little about her life as a young woman in the working world of the 1930s. Unlike today when people seem willing to reveal their whole lives on television or on the Internet, she lived in a time when private things remained hidden, and on this topic even her children could not trespass.

In fact, during that terrible summer, as she grew ever closer to death, we each took opportunities to see if we could pry from her some details of those years, but there were still some things she did not want us to know. One story we did get was that one day at work, an older coworker introduced our mom to

Photographs of her show a *beautiful* blonde with an enigmatic SMILE.

her son, the man who would become our father, a diffident young fellow several years her junior and with considerable burdens of his own, the consequences of bad decisions. We later discovered some of his love letters to her. They revealed a rocky relationship in which she apparently resisted his devotions for some time. He had fallen hard, but she

EDUCATION

LOLA HANNAH ALLRED SESSIONS

is the mother of

GENE A. SESSIONS

Gene A. Sessions was born in Ogden, Utah, and received his PhD from Florida State University in 1974. He is the author and editor of numerous works, including *Mormon Thunder: A Documentary History of Jedediah Morgan Grant* (1982, 2008), *Latter-day Patriots: Nine Mormon Families and Their Revolutionary War Heritage* (1975), *Prophesying upon the Bones: J. Reuben Clark and the Foreign Debt Crisis, 1933–39* (1992),

Camp Floyd and the Mormons: The Utah War (with Donald R. Moorman, 1992), *The Search for Harmony: Essays on Science and Mormonism* (with Craig J. Oberg, 1993), *Utah International: A Biography of a Business* (with Sterling D. Sessions, 2002), and *Mormon Democrat: The Religious and Political Memoirs of James Henry Moyle* (1975, 1998), for which he received the Mormon History Association's annual award for best edited work. Professor Sessions is Presidential Distinguished Professor of History at Weber State University in Ogden. He has also been a consultant on documentaries and committees exploring the Utah War and the Mountain Meadows Massacre and is past president of the Mountain Meadows Association. He and his wife, Shantal, have four children and seven grandsons.

wasn't so sure. She wanted to go to the temple, but his life would not allow that then, so he promised her that if she would marry him, he would take her there eventually. Well, he never did. It was an old and common story in the peculiar annals of Mormon courtship and love.

Dad was in the sheep business as a livestock broker. He bought and sold lambs, and he was very good at it. The enterprise took him all over the West on extended buying excursions. Gone much of the time, he left my mother the job of minding the home and raising the kids pretty much by herself. Even without the traveling, however, he would likely have left that to her anyway because that was his nature. Always kind but never affectionate toward us, Dad provided a comfortable living but did not involve himself much at all in family matters. This made our mother much more than just a full-time homemaker fashioned after the postwar image of Friedan's Feminine Mystique. In some ways, we grew up in a single-parent household.

Because of all this, when Dad died in an accident while on one of his business trips and Mother became a widow at the young age of fifty-three, nothing much seemed to change for her, at least from our shallow perspectives. We were all grown and gone from home, and we could not fathom the loneliness she had endured and would endure, both before and after his death. Her boundless love for us had shielded us from most of it. We saw our mother only in terms of our need for her, always anxious for our welfare and always there to fulfill the role she had accepted and embraced anew upon the birth of each of us.

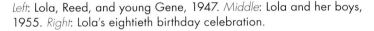
Left: Lola, Reed, and young Gene, 1947. *Middle*: Lola and her boys, 1955. *Right*: Lola's eightieth birthday celebration.

She *doesn't* want to leave you.

As we sat there that dolorous day, my mind flooded with these memories and many more. It was the day before my birthday, and I wondered if God would have it that she would leave the world on the anniversary of the very day she had brought me into it. A couple of days before, her longtime home teacher had come to see her. After holding her nearly lifeless hand for a few minutes and talking softly to her unresponsive face, he emerged with tears in his eyes. My younger brother and I walked him out to the front door. Standing on the porch, he placed his hands on our shoulders. "She doesn't want to leave you," he said. "You boys go in there and release her. Put your hands on her head and let her go." So we got some consecrated oil and did as he had instructed. From that moment, we knew that her departure was imminent.

The visit of that home teacher was emblematic of the whole summer. A vast parade of friends and family members had come to see her, to hold her hand, and to speak to her one last time. Her time of dying had become the perfect reflection of her time of living. The love she had given so effulgently and to so many came washing back upon her like some cresting wave from the past. Dozens of nieces and nephews walked in and out of that little room, all with wet eyes, and all had a story to tell us of Aunt Lola and what an impact she'd had in their lives. Her friends, including a dwindling group of women with whom she had taught Primary for so many years, came to tell tales of their good times together, her jokes and her laughter, and of her steady hand in their lives and in the lives of so many children. She had been their leader, the one who organized little trips to various events, including Weber State basketball games and the Weber Historical Society. Other women came who had spent time with her during the nearly four decades she had volunteered as a "pink lady" at the McKay-Dee Hospital. They remembered how she would always volunteer to work holidays because "she was alone." That broke our hearts. We knew that we had failed her through our inabilities and

Lola Hannah Allred
Sessions.

ignorance, as in the midst of our own lives and endeavors, we had left her to be alone far too much. Our efforts now were small recompense, but we loved her more and more as the last precious moments of her life ticked away on the clock in her kitchen.

Wonderful mothers like mine are among God's greatest gifts to the world. Few of their children appreciate them enough. When we finally walked into her little room that afternoon to find her gone, I collapsed on the floor and wept, not for her but for us because she had flown to the angels, and we were left here with the realization that she had loved us more than we could have hoped to have loved her back. At her funeral some days later, my younger brother told stories of her sacrifices for us and then said, "Isn't that how mothers are?" I don't know about anyone else's, but ours was truly amazing. During that time of her dying, I came to realize that truth more than I ever had. I only regret that I did not comprehend it more fully during the time of her living.

You Might As Well Laugh As Cry

by Douglas Thayer

My mother, Lily Nora Thatcher, or Lil, was strong—uncomplicated, direct, compassionate, but strong. And she passed some of that strength to me; my two brothers, Bob and Rowland; and my sister, Marlene. We learned from her not to complain very much, to laugh rather than cry, accept human weakness, value human decency, deal with physical pain, work hard, and above all, keep going, and endure. Mom divorced my father, Edward Frank Thayer, when I was five. Born in 1865, he was thirty-five years older than she, was blind in one eye, and drank. But Mom never criticized him to us children. She always said, "He did the best he could." I've always been grateful to her for not turning me against my father.

My mother's romantic life was not smooth. Ten years after divorcing my father, she fell in love with a man and dated him for a year, but then he left her a note saying he was going to California to marry another woman. Mom cried for six weeks, but she got over it. We children were often told to get over our disappointments and were expected to. She married another man named Church on the rebound, divorced him after six weeks, and later married Dad Overly, with whom she spent thirty wonderful years and to whom she was sealed.

I never heard Mom say we were poor. I suppose we were, although I never thought so during those Depression years of the 1930s and early '40s. As she said, we had no cause for complaint and should be satisfied: We had a roof over our heads, clothes on our backs, and food on the table, which was all true. What more could we ask for? She received a small state welfare pension and grocery orders at the bishops' storehouse when needed (something that helped convince me that the Church was true), but whatever else we had to live on, she earned as a cleaning lady at a dollar an hour. If she had a bill to pay, she said she would scrub it

As she said, we had *no cause* for complaint and should be SATISFIED.

LILY NORA THATCHER

is the mother of

DOUGLAS THAYER

Douglas H. Thayer is among the foremost contemporary fiction writers dealing with Mormon life. He has been dubbed the "Mormon Hemingway" for his straightforward and powerful writing style. Reared in Provo, Utah, his boyhood was spent in the nearby mountains, hunting, fishing, and hiking. In 1946, he quit high school to join the army, where he served mostly in Germany. He later returned to Germany as a missionary.

He is currently an English professor at BYU, where he has taught for more than fifty years. He is perhaps best known for his coming-of-age stories, and critics call him the "finest chronicler of the Mormon youth in the culture." His first collection of stories, *Under the Cottonwoods and Other Mormon Stories* (1977), is considered a Mormon classic. His other works include a second collection of short stories, *Mr. Wahlquist in Yellowstone* (1989); three novels, *Summer Fire* (1983), *The Conversion of Jeff Williams* (2003), *The Tree House* (2009) and a memoir, *Hooligan: A Mormon Boyhood* (2007).

He has received numerous awards and prizes, including *Dialogue* awards for their short story and essay contests, the P. A. Christensen award, the Association for Mormon Letters Prize in the novel category, the Karl G. Maeser Creative Arts Award, the Utah Institute of Fine Arts Award for short story, and the 2008 Smith-Pettit Foundation Award for Outstanding Contribution to Mormon Letters.

Thayer and his wife, Donlu, have six children, six children-in-law, and fifteen grandchildren and counting.

out—earn the money cleaning other families' houses.

Mom was a great believer in hard work. To be described as not having a lazy bone in your body was a high compliment. She was a firm believer in working your fingers to the bone, giving a good day's work for a good day's pay, keeping your nose to the grindstone, and understanding that work wouldn't kill you. If a job wasn't done right, it had to be done over, and we were told as children to use plenty of elbow grease. Work cured many ills. We learned to forget our aches, pains, and problems and get to work.

As a cleaning lady, Mom had her regular customers and cleaned the same houses for years, becoming friends with some of the housewives, who gave her birthday and Christmas presents. She spent her whole day vacuuming, dusting, washing windows, cleaning bathrooms, and scrubbing and waxing floors on her hands and knees. Later she took on the job of janitor of the Provo sixth ward meetinghouse and, later still, the Clark Clinic on University Avenue—the cleaning job she liked best of all. Mom delighted in people complimenting her on how clean the meetinghouse or the clinic was. We children helped with the cleaning and were certainly taught to do the job right or do it over. We were also expected to get out on our own as soon as possible and earn enough to pay for our own clothes, school expenses, and pleasures. I got my first steady job at age twelve.

Mom was crippled, and she was in pain every waking moment of her life. She had what amounted to clubfeet, and her feet were covered with corns and calluses from her ill-fitting shoes. When she was sitting down, her feet would twitch from the pain.

(As a young woman, she'd had tuberculosis of the spine and was in a full-body cast for a year; she later suffered from high blood pressure, diabetes, and a paralytic stroke, which caused her to lose her voice, from which she recovered completely.) She liked to scrub and wax floors on her hands and knees because she was off her feet. My Aunt Em would come down to trim her corns with a razor blade, sometimes cutting too close and causing a trickle of blood. The sixth ward, through the welfare plan, paid for surgery on both her feet that lessened the pain (another proof to me as a boy that the Church was true). Later in her life, she went to Dr. Bowden, a Provo podiatrist, who cared for her feet and had special shoes made—another blessing.

But Mom never complained, other than to say, "My poor feet, my poor feet." I never heard her refer to herself as a cripple. I never thought of her in that way. She looked forward to the next life when, no longer a cripple, she would be able to dance. She envied people who could dance. Her belief in the next life as taught in the gospel was sure. She often talked about family and friends who had crossed to the other side, what they were doing, how they were getting along with each other, and how a particular member of the family was greeted at death. The dead came to her in dreams. One of her gifts to me was that same assurance of an afterlife.

In spite of her illnesses, the pain, the struggle to make ends meet, and her disappointments, Mom was a cheerful person, happy with her life and often singing gospel hymns as she worked. She laughed a lot. Friends and family often commented on her lovely laugh. It was a high compliment if she said that a person could make a cat laugh; she often remarked that if there weren't any fools, there wouldn't be any fun. People amused her; she liked to hear and tell stories about people. She told stories about the people whose houses she cleaned, stories the wives told her. She wasn't a gossip; she just liked a story, particularly stories about various kinds of disasters. My early interest in people, in writing stories and novels, came from her telling stories at the supper table.

Although Mom was a keen judge of character, she had a wide tolerance for human faults and failings, as she called them; she believed in compassion, generosity, fairness, and laughter. Yet, she could not tolerate a man who was mean to his wife and children. Such a man needed to be horsewhipped, jailed, or, in extreme cases, stood up against a wall and shot. Although she could be very stern, I can't recall being whipped or slapped or even yelled at. When my brothers and I were bad,

> Mom was a *cheerful* person, **HAPPY** with her life and often *singing* gospel hymns as she worked.

Lily, age eighty-six, with her granddaughter Katie.

she threatened to knock our heads together or through the wall, but she never did. She couldn't catch us. But she absolutely would not tolerate sass or backtalk, something we were never guilty of.

Mom had a very keen sense of her own worth. Although she cleaned house for some of the most prominent women in Provo, she never thought them better than she was. She was not impressed by wealth or station. She expected to be picked up by her employers and brought home or provided taxi fare. And before she gave up her English tea, she expected a cup of tea at ten, lunch at twelve,

and tea again at three. If any of the women she worked for ever suggested that they were better than she, she never went back. This sense of equality and our own worth was part of our heritage as children.

Mom was not affectionate with any of us children. I can't ever recall being kissed or hugged or being told she loved me, although I knew she did. Later in life, she said she wished she'd been more loving. She was English, reserved by nature and training. My grandma and grandpa Thatcher were the same way. Converts to the Church, they emigrated from England

Equality and our own worth was part of our heritage as children.

to Provo, Utah, in 1920 with their ten children, and although the whole family often got together for parties, suppers, and reunions—always with much laughter and fun—I never saw them embrace or talk of their love for each other. And those characteristics flowed into my mom's life. Mom made wonderful pies and pudding but never birthday cakes. Yet every year, she would borrow three hundred dollars from Utah Finance to buy Christmas, paying it off twenty-five dollars a month with her hard-earned income. She said we kids deserved a good Christmas. She demonstrated her affections in many more ways than physical show.

Mom died of a perforated bowel, her dying a reflection of her life. I was standing behind her wheelchair in the doctor's office when he told her they could operate. She was eighty-nine and had spent the last four years in a rest home wanting the Lord to take her. She said, "Oh, no thank you. Oh no." She'd had all of this life she desired; she wanted to be with Dad Overly and all the other family and friends she knew were waiting for her. She died ten days later. The day before her death, I asked her how the pain was and if she wanted more medication. She said she was fine. The attendant came in and asked how she was feeling. "Pretty good," she said, "pretty good.

Zella: My Not-So-Perfect, Perfect Mother

by Heather A. Willoughby

ZELLA IRENE SMITH WILLOUGHBY

is the mother of

HEATHER WILLOUGHBY

Heather A. Willoughby lives a full and adventurous life; she attributes her contentment and cheery disposition to a stable, inventive, and humor-filled home life provided by her parents. Creative endeavors have always played a significant role in her life, and she feels privileged to have found a career where she, along with students from throughout the world, can share with others the diversity and wonders of global performing arts and cultures. Including the time spent serving her mission, she has spent nearly a decade living in Seoul, Korea, where she is convinced she has some long-lost ancestry. It is her goal to visit every continent, and, if possible, every country, but she is also fully content when she spends time with family and friends and is surrounded by good food and good music.

She received a BA in music/music education from Brigham Young University in 1991 and an MA and PhD in ethnomusicology from Columbia University. Her major field of interest is in traditional Korean music, with a secondary focus on American popular music. Her research was funded by the Korea Foundation and the Mellon Foundation. She is a member of the faculty of Ewha Women's University in Korea. She serves in the Korea Military District, Seoul English Branch as assistant music director and as assistant visiting teaching coordinator.

It may seem presumptuous to speak of the similarities between my mother and me when my purpose is to honor her, but at times, it seems as though we are twins mistakenly born a generation apart. Numerous have been the occasions when we have uttered a thought at the same time with precisely the same words and inflection—to which we always respond, "Get off my wavelength!" I recall looking in the mirror one day in my early twenties and wondering aloud, "When did I become my mother?" At least I have the advantage of knowing what I will look like as I progress in life—and I am happy with the prospects.

As an example of our ineffable connection, in spring 2009, I decided to inform only my sister of my intended visit home and otherwise surprise the family with an unexpected arrival. This would not be so unusual except that I live some 5,000 miles away from my family, I had not been home for nearly a year, and it was in the middle of my semester of teaching. As I stepped into the house, I took one look at my mother and found her dressed in exactly the same outfit as me (picture included as proof)! But our semblance goes beyond word usage or fashion choices; it is my hope that I have inherited many of the traits I so admire in my spunky mother, who is as unique and splendid as her name, Zella.

When I was a teenager, I was asked to give a talk on Mother's Day. Unlike the majority of other women who are extolled on this special holiday, my mother is not perfect, and I decided to take the opportunity to speak honestly about my mother's real attributes. Of course, it helped that my parents were traveling that particular Sunday and, thus, were not in the congregation to hear my exposé. As I ponder now what to write about my mother, many of the same thoughts come to my mind, and so it is that I want to discuss my not-so-perfect mother.

With this introduction, you may be thinking that I want to air long-held grievances or that I am being disrespectful in an essay that is intended to honor mothers. But let me assure you from the onset that it is my mother's very humanity, and what some may deem as not-so-complimentary traits, that have equipped me and many others with the skills needed to cope with the imperfections and trials of this world.

My mother might be considered a diminutive woman, standing a mere five foot, one inches and weighing in at less than ninety pounds,

I have *learned* much from the quiet, inner STRENGTH displayed by my mother.

but I know she is formidable, indeed. I recall that she once came into our den and kindly asked me and a Finnish exchange student living with us to turn off the television and come do our predinner chores. I moved slowly and reluctantly, but Mikko continued his TV viewing. Mother returned again about ten minutes later with the same request, and since there was no immediate stirring, she turned the television off and started to leave the room. Mikko stood, but rather than follow her to the kitchen as she intended, he headed toward the television and turned it on again. I was stunned—to my knowledge, no one had ever dared disregard Zella in such a blatant manner. My mother returned and stood directly in front of this brawny, towering young man and said nothing at all—no yelling, no fit of anger, no malice, no guile, no harsh or derisive words, just a look; there is no explaining this look, but it has inspired many who have crossed my mother's path to quickly rethink their course of action and choose a better way. I have learned much from the quiet, inner strength displayed by my mother on that and many other occasions and have tried to utilize that same noble power in my life. (For the record, Mikko was normally a pleasant and gentle teenager. His actions that day were certainly inexplicable, but in the end provided a rare learning opportunity for us all.)

Many years ago, a woman who was visiting our congregation responded to something my mother had said or done by saying, "Oh, you're so sweet!" That common representation of women does not seem particularly apt for my mother. In fact, several of us actually laughed out loud when we heard it; one

Heather and her students in Seoul, Korea.

dear friend claimed that my mother would be the only Relief Society president in the history of the Church to be impeached. Gratefully, that never happened, but my mother certainly is not one to coo over every newborn baby, coddle young children, or speak in an affected manner to a morose teenager. However, that does not mean that she fails to value and succor those with whom she interacts.

My parents have literally opened their home to the world; some visitors have stayed a few hours, some a few days, and some several years, but irrespective of circumstance or length of sojourn, any and all are welcomed at our table. Among the most memorable to me were a Hmong refugee who found solace with our family when his own was so far away; the more than twenty exchange students who have brought their cultures into our home, many of whom were displaced from other host families but who

found open arms at our door; and most significantly, a distant cousin who is now considered my sister and forever a part of our family gatherings. So perhaps my mother is not "sweet" in what is oftentimes deemed a conventional or desirable matronly manner, but I have never seen her shun a soul in need, no matter their race, creed, or predicament.

My mother can be seen as stubborn and opinionated—and that is probably because she is! But I do not consider this a fault; rather, I believe she is a determined woman who is tenacious and idealistic and who has made educated, prayerful decisions about what is right and good in the world. While assuredly knowing her own mind, I believe she is also willing to accept others for who they are and their own life choices. The three women my mother reared and nurtured are remarkably diverse, as if we had been born scattered throughout the world and ages, but each of us is revered and loved as herself by my mother. She has nurtured her own five children in a safe, loving, gospel-centered home; many youth and disadvantaged individuals at a Buddhist meditation center; and dozens of students from every continent who enter her college classroom each semester.

Many women today seem to be emotionally and spiritually crippled by the expectation that they need to be perfect; I know of women who dread Mother's Day because they can only see their own limitations and feel the pressure of living up to an unrealistic ideal. My mother is flawed; she is imperfect, as we all are. But my mother is real, and I have learned much goodness from every aspect of her being, even some supposedly negative traits. But most important, my mother has not become disillusioned by the quest to be a perfect woman; rather, she has mastered the art of being perfectly herself. And I love her for that.

Many women today seem to be *emotionally and spiritually* crippled by the expectation that they **NEED** to be perfect.

My mother has not become disillusioned by the *quest* to be a perfect woman; rather, she has **MASTERED** the art of being perfectly *herself.*

Her Touch

by Twila Wood

They call it the "death rattle" when a dying breath weakens. We circle around her bedside for one last "I love you" in a dimmed yellow room in the Beehive House, a rest home. We hope to be heard or to hear; we hope for absolution, resolution, or understanding. Her tired body lies motionless, seems to surrender to the night, yet lingers and clings to one more dawn. Where are you now, Mamma? Come back to this solemn room, back to your family, and the seriousness of dying.

We blur into one, sisters and brother—her blood; we swallow the pain and say good-bye, release her life that pulses through us, and wait. Dad sobs, holds her hand, and pleads his final passioned, "I've loved you so much." His words end the silence, and we are comforted by their love, but there is no reply in this reverent room, where only hearts are heard and only those left behind speak, where only memories remain of Mamma. Her last breath taken, the rattle stops.

The waiting ends, the hesitation stops, bedsores pain her no more; her mind is unburdened, and I am free to touch her. I kiss her cheek, comb her white hair with my fingertips, curl it around her ears, gently straighten her collar, rub her shoulders, and smooth down her arms. I caress her hands, and each lovely finger responds to my direction with no moans, no rules, no reservation.

I can touch her soft skin again, return to my mother, and remember the feel of her, absorb her into me through hungry fingers, longing for one last reunion to heal the painful scars of dementia, the absence of touch. I remember you, Mamma, the kisses good night, the morning back rubs, my head in your lap as your fingers stroked through my hair—your comforting hands.

Do you remember me now?

Do you like me to touch you now?

EDUCATION

NELLIE LEISHMAN

is the mother of

TWILA LEISHMAN WOOD

Twila Leishman Wood grew up on a dairy farm in Wellsville, Utah, where she wrote poetry and dreamed of becoming a movie star, a concert pianist, or a foreign correspondent for *Time*. She married the man of her dreams, graduated from USU, and settled for bigger dreams—raising six children, teaching piano, and a career as an English and drama teacher at North Cache 8/9 Center. She believes life has a way of fulfilling your dreams if you never lose your passions.

The morticians come, and I must get back to business—notices, obituaries, flowers, and a funeral—still no time to find my real mother as I labor over tributes and funeral music. I wrench my soul to describe her with the elegance and honor she deserves and write the most meaningful words I can remember. But when the pen is down, I don't cry. Her scowl still stings in my heart, and I think of the five years of weekly visits to care for her, bring her and Daddy dinner, and endure her changing moods of dementia. On her nice days, I cried on the drive home because I was so happy; but more often I cried on the way home from her rejection, harshness, emptiness.

* * *

My family decides to take dinners to Mom and Dad daily. Thursday is my day, and as always, before dinner we visit. Forgetting irritates her, so she hides it like a thief burying a jewel in her pocket; she smiles, changes subjects, tries to be poised in her new role. I remember her brilliance, talent, wit; I know who she is but see only glimmers of that past.

As she prays for over the food, I remember how her voice commanded attention with expression, clarity, confidence, and warmth, and I reunite with my real mother. She communes with Him, transcending frail bones and shaky memory. I cherish each word of worship as she speaks to her Father. With sincerity, she shares her intimacy with God. Humbled, blessed, I say amen, and return to this country kitchen, heart renewed, time held within the folded arms of prayer.

* * *

Years pass, the dementia progresses, and now my day is Wednesday to take them dinner. She sits at the kitchen table, head bowed, dressed in a clean printed housedress. She puts her fingertips to her temples and slowly slides them back through her hair, massaging her scalp, relieving her stress, until she reaches the back of her head. I ask if I can brush her hair. She says, "Oh, oh, I have a pain in my head."

"Mamma, can you take a pain pill?"

"They don't help."

"Well, I'll hurry and fix dinner."

"You have to fix it? You couldn't just bring it? I'm too hungry. How long will it take you?"

"I've been teaching all day, Mamma. I'm doing the best I can." The kitchen falls silent as she closes her eyes and bows and shakes her head in disappointment.

Finally, we sit down together, Dad trying to smooth over the insult with his charm. We bow our heads. Dad, doing most of the praying now, softens my heart with his thankfulness and meekness; but as I listen to him talk to God, I hear Mom already sneaking the fork and eating the salad. Who are you? Where is my mother?

Above: Frank and Nellie Leishman, 1978.

She begins spooning the broth from the soup, noisy like a child, till there is only meat and vegetables left in the bowl. "Is there more juice?" she asks.

"No, Mom," I say as she again bows her head and shakes it in disappointment. I pause in disgust and whisper, "Can't you just be nice?"

She flails her arms. "Just go. Go on home."

"She's having a bad day," Dad says as he walks me to the door. "Don't take it personally."

"How do you stand it? I worry about you. I can go home. You have to stay here with her every day. How do you stand it?"

"Tomorrow will be a better day."

I drive home, thinking. Yes, there are better days, but only today pounds in my heart. Her body answers, "It's me," with the same hair, same face, and I believe because I do remember her strictness, her impatience; I've met them before on occasions in childhood, as a teenager, with my children. Her expressions of expectance and disturbance cut me to the blood of who she is, who I am, a part of her. So I cry when my husband says, "You are like your mother. You have no patience."

Who is my mother? Where is she? Who am I? How do I accept this reality as anger consumes her in its mindless temper of dementia and her cruelty is now diagnosed? Am I to blame her mean words on a condition of old age? But what about when I was ten, twenty, or thirty-two? What is real, and which is my mother—the authoritarian, the patient, the nurturer?

The word *nurturer* stops my rambling mind. The nurturer is the one I have forgotten. Has she been gone so long I have lost her? I think and remember . . . one evening long ago as a young child, when Mamma asked to rock me. Feeling too big for her lap and too old for a lullaby, I pleased her reluctantly—lay stiff in her arms, wiggling like a kitten determined to escape. I gained my freedom but sacrificed that moment, her rich contralto voice—and now I am left empty-armed to watch this swing in time, yearning to remember that Irish lullaby, to listen from beginning to end.

I remember practicing for her every morning. Before dawn Mother lingered in her bed while I, like young Mozart, poured my love like rich honey onto the keys to sweeten her awakening. Each time I practiced a piece, I listened for her comments. Stirring from sleep in the adjoining room, she would say, "That sounds perfect. Will you play 'Autumn Leaves' for me before you stop?"

Up and dressed, she thanked me with her embrace and rubbed my posture-weary back, her fingers massaging my spine, releasing the ache, our gifts exchanged.

These memories bring her back to me . . . her stories giving us "good cries" as she called them, Sunday dinners, Saturday morning talks. But

Left: Frank and Nellie's sixty-fifth wedding anniversary, 1986. *Below*: Nellie, fifteen-years-old, 1926.

Tomorrow will be a **BETTER** day.

can I even face that gentle part of Mom? It's been so long since I've seen beauty in her. What is beautiful in me that she gave me, traits I cherish in her that are in me? Am I blessed to remember or cursed, enabled, or denied?

* * *

Years pass. Our family begins falling apart. My sister next door to Mom has a nervous breakdown, another sister's back goes out on her, Daddy's hands are operated on for Carpal Tunnel Syndrome, and I still teach school. In August, I move her to the Beehive House in west Logan, a small, personal care facility for the aging. She is ninety-five. The dementia worsens, and many days she just sleeps, does not want to respond to anyone. The doctor says that is common in dementia. I visit her three times a week; she is usually irritable, but one day she comes back to me,

my real mother. On this afternoon, I sit in her yellow room, watching the red bush rustling outside her window, eat her Halloween candy, try to be cheerful, and do most of the talking while she stares through me. "Mamma, the people are really nice here. They really like you."

She closes her eyes and bows her head slowly as she sighs and then shakes her head back and forth with each word. "Why am I here? Why can't I go home?" I repeat the family excuses and then stop. Usually I lie and tell her that as soon as Daddy's hands heal, she can come home, but today I tell the truth.

"Mom, nobody can take care of you at home anymore. But we come to see you here every day."

"No, you don't. Nobody comes to see me." She pauses. "Last night I dreamed that Daddy came

to get me. I just want to be with Daddy." Her voice is tender, lonely, childlike. In one month, she and Dad will celebrate seventy-three years of marriage. This is the first time they have ever been apart. I know her mind is only on him. She asks in a daze, "Doesn't he want me to come home?"

I kneel down in front of her, helpless, crying, "I'm so sorry, Mamma. I wish you could go home too. I'm sorry. I don't want you to be here." I lay my head down on her lap, still sobbing, and for the first time in years, she strokes my hair for a long time with her soothing, magical fingers.

"It's okay, it's okay; don't cry," she says. That is the last time she reaches out to me. In November, she falls and becomes totally bedridden. Her mind is always restless now, and her body in pain; she sleeps most of the time. I visit her, but she doesn't know; I talk to her, but she doesn't hear me. When she is awake, the pain from the fall, the growing bedsores, and the atrophy distress her all the time. I try to soothe her, try to stroke her hair, but she screams out, "Oh, oh, don't touch me." I stop touching her.

* * *

Growing up, I felt very secure within Mom and Dad's circle. They had a passionate love for one another from the moment they met and through seventy-three years of marriage. They were both strong personalities, one

I lay my head down on her lap, still sobbing, and for the first time in *years*, she strokes my hair for a long time with her *soothing*, magical fingers.

* * *

Dutch and one Scotch, but their infatuation for each other never dimmed. Together they worked hard, played hard, teased each other, laughed often, traveled the world, made many friends, served their neighbors, and, most of all, loved life.

It was at the Beehive House that I witnessed the tender love they felt for one another. They often affectionately kissed each other, held hands, and said such romantic things to each other; it touched my heart. Daddy would say, "You are as beautiful as the first time I met you." Or, "You have always been so contented with our life." Mama would reply, "All I ever wanted was you, Daddy"—that's what she called him. One time, she was having a bad day, and I said, "Mamma, soon you will be in heaven with your mom and dad, and you will be able to sing and teach, and you won't hurt anymore."

There was silence for a moment, and then she asked simply, "Will Daddy be there?" That is all she cared about. Their love affair was made in heaven and will last forever.

Hospice helps us through her dying moments, and by the first of January, she passes away. The funeral is over, all the right sentiments spoken, the ceremonies finished, and relatives returned home. The next day, I finally relax in my bedroom and crawl under the quilt, although it is only noon; I feel tired but can't sleep yet. My family visits in the kitchen, but I need to think of Mamma now. I bring a CD out of my drawer, a CD of her singing lullabies, religious songs, love songs, Irish songs. I put it in, listen and remember, reach out for my mother, and she is there.

I am playing for her once again as she sings to many people—but mainly to me. She holds a white laced handkerchief, smiles as she breathes deeply, elegantly raises her head, and sings to me from beginning to end. Tears come, hard burning tears with no reservations, no questions. I feel her love. I finally mourn, consuming myself in a "good cry." I weep all afternoon in reunion as Mamma's healing arms reach out to me, wrap around me. She whispers,

Do you remember me now?

Do you feel me now?

Reflections on My Mother of Faith

Place
photo
here

RICHARD G. HINCKLEY • JANA PETERSON STAPLES • VIVIAN MCCONKIE ADAMS
ARCUS H. MARTINS • NEYLAN MCBAINE • ROBERT L. MCKAY • MIKE WINDER
D • JASON CHAFFETZ • MATTHEW GODFREY • MARK R. VAN WAGONER • DOU
N ROSEMARIE SLOVER MAZZEO • BOB EVANS • SHAWNI EYRE POTHIER • KRISTIN
E PROCTOR • TIFFANY GEE LEWIS • GLENN RAWSON • TRENT TOONE • BRYA
J. W. "BILL" MARRIOTT JR. • ROBERT P. DOTSON • MARK ALLRED • MATTHEW DEA
BARKDULL • RICHARD EYRE • SHARLENE W. HAWKES • LAUREN JOHNSON • ST
SHA WARD • KATHI ORAM PETERSON • TRISTI PINKSTON • JANETTE RALLISON
GRANT HARDY • PATRICK MADDEN • KERRY MUHLESTEIN • GENE A. SESSIO
ERILYN BECK MERRILL, • SILVIA H. ALLRED • ROSEMARY M. WIXOM • RICHARD
BUSHMAN • SUSAN EASTON BLACK • CAMILLE FRONK OLSON • MARCUS
T • MIKE LEE • CHAD B. MCKAY • RONALD C. PACKARD • HARRY REID • JASO
A STALLINGS JENKINS • NATALIE CLEMENS • MARK EUBANK • MAREN ROSEM
CKSON • JORDAN MARIE GREEN • WENDY HALE MCKAY • MAURINE PROCT
DETTE • PETER VIDMAR • KYLE WHITTINGHAM • STEVE YOUNG • J. W. "BI
OMNEY • CLAYTON M. CHRISTENSEN • STEEVUN LEMON • LARRY BARKDU
E BELLON • GREG OLSEN • JEFF SAVAGE • RICK WALTON • MARSHA WA
JOHN BENNION • CAROL ANNE CLAYSON • H. WALLACE GODDARD • GRA
THAYER • HEATHER A. WILLOUGHBY • TWILA WOOD • JULIE B. BECK • GERIL
JANA PETERSON STAPLES • VIVIAN MCCONKIE ADAMS • RICHARD LYMAN BUS
EYLAN MCBAINE • ROBERT L. MCKAY • MIKE WINDER • GARY R. HERBERT • M
ATTHEW GODFREY • MARK R. VAN WAGONER • DOUG WRIGHT • SANDRA STA
AZZEO • BOB EVANS • SHAWNI EYRE POTHIER • KRISTINE WARDLE FREDERICKSO
E LEWIS • GLENN RAWSON • TRENT TOONE • BRYAN MILLER • JIMMER FREDE
ROBERT P. DOTSON • MARK ALLRED • MATTHEW DEAN BARKDULL • JOSH RO
EYRE • SHARLENE W. HAWKES • LAUREN JOHNSON • STEVEN KAPP PERRY • JU
AM PETERSON • TRISTI PINKSTON • JANETTE RALLISON • PHILIP N. HALE • JO
RICK MADDEN • KERRY MUHLESTEIN • GENE A. SESSIONS • DOUGLAS THAYE
SILVIA H. ALLRED • ROSEMARY M. WIXOM • RICHARD G. HINCKLEY • JANA
N EASTON BLACK • CAMILLE FRONK OLSON • MARCUS H. MARTINS • NEYL
B. MCKAY • RONALD C. PACKARD • HARRY REID • JASON CHAFFETZ • MATTH
S • NATALIE CLEMENS • MARK EUBANK • MAREN ROSEMARIE SLOVER MAZZEO
MARIE GREEN • WENDY HALE MCKAY • MAURINE PROCTOR • TIFFANY GEE LEV
MAR • KYLE WHITTINGHAM • STEVE YOUNG • J. W. "BILL" MARRIOTT JR. • ROB
ON M. CHRISTENSEN • STEEVUN LEMON • LARRY BARKDULL • RICHARD EYR
GREG OLSEN • JEFF SAVAGE • RICK WALTON • MARSHA WARD • KATHI OR
N CAROL ANNE CLAYSON • H. WALLACE GODDARD • GRANT HARDY • PATR
A. WILLOUGHBY • TWILA WOOD • JULIE B. BECK • GERILYN BECK MERRILL, • SIL
ES • VIVIAN MCCONKIE ADAMS • RICHARD LYMAN BUSHMAN • SUSAN EAST
RT L. MCKAY • MIKE WINDER • GARY R. HERBERT • MIKE LEE • CHAD B. MCKA
RK R. VAN WAGONER • DOUG WRIGHT • SANDRA STALLINGS JENKINS • NATA
AWNI EYRE POTHIER • KRISTINE WARDLE FREDERICKSON • JORDAN MARIE GR
N TRENT TOONE • BRYAN MILLER • JIMMER FREDETTE • PETER VIDMAR
RK ALLRED • MATTHEW DEAN BARKDULL • JOSH ROMNEY • CLAYTON M. CH

LIE B. BECK • GERILYN BECK MERRILL, • SILVIA H. ALLRED • ROSEMARY M. WIXO
CHARD LYMAN BUSHMAN • SUSAN EASTON BLACK • CAMILLE FRONK OLSON
ARY R. HERBERT • MIKE LEE • CHAD B. MCKAY • RONALD C. PACKARD • HARRY
RIGHT • SANDRA STALLINGS JENKINS • NATALIE CLEMENS • MARK EUBANK • MA
ARDLE FREDERICKSON • JORDAN MARIE GREEN • WENDY HALE MCKAY • MA
LLER • JIMMER FREDETTE • PETER VIDMAR • KYLE WHITTINGHAM • STEVE YOUN
ARKDULL • JOSH ROMNEY • CLAYTON M. CHRISTENSEN • STEEVUN LEMON • LA
N KAPP PERRY • JULIE BELLON • GREG OLSEN • JEFF SAVAGE • RICK WALTON
ILIP N. HALE • JOHN BENNION • CAROL ANNE CLAYSON • H. WALLACE GODD
DOUGLAS THAYER • HEATHER A. WILLOUGHBY • TWILA WOOD • JULIE B. BEC
NCKLEY • JANA PETERSON STAPLES • VIVIAN MCCONKIE ADAMS • RICHARD
ARTINS • NEYLAN MCBAINE • ROBERT L. MCKAY • MIKE WINDER • GARY R. H
HAFFETZ • MATTHEW GODFREY • MARK R. VAN WAGONER • DOUG WRIGHT • S
E SLOVER MAZZEO • BOB EVANS • SHAWNI EYRE POTHIER • KRISTINE WARDLE F
TIFFANY GEE LEWIS • GLENN RAWSON • TRENT TOONE • BRYAN MILLER • JIM
ARRIOTT JR. • ROBERT P. DOTSON • MARK ALLRED • MATTHEW DEAN BARKDULL
RICHARD EYRE • SHARLENE W. HAWKES • LAUREN JOHNSON • STEVEN KAPP P
KATHI ORAM PETERSON • TRISTI PINKSTON • JANETTE RALLISON • PHILIP N. H
ARDY • PATRICK MADDEN • KERRY MUHLESTEIN • GENE A. SESSIONS • DOUG
CK MERRILL,• SILVIA H. ALLRED • ROSEMARY M. WIXOM • RICHARD G. HINCKLI
AN • SUSAN EASTON BLACK • CAMILLE FRONK OLSON • MARCUS H. MARTINS
E • CHAD B. MCKAY • RONALD C. PACKARD • HARRY REID • JASON CHAFFETZ
GS JENKINS • NATALIE CLEMENS • MARK EUBANK • MAREN ROSEMARIE SLOVE
JORDAN MARIE GREEN • WENDY HALE MCKAY • MAURINE PROCTOR • TIFFANY
PETER VIDMAR • KYLE WHITTINGHAM • STEVE YOUNG • J. W. "BILL" MARRIOTT
EY • CLAYTON M. CHRISTENSEN • STEEVUN LEMON • LARRY BARKDULL • RICHA
LLON • GREG OLSEN • JEFF SAVAGE • RICK WALTON • MARSHA WARD • KATH
NNION • CAROL ANNE CLAYSON • H. WALLACE GODDARD • GRANT HARDY
EATHER A. WILLOUGHBY • TWILA WOOD • JULIE B. BECK • GERILYN BECK MER
RSON STAPLES • VIVIAN MCCONKIE ADAMS • RICHARD LYMAN BUSHMAN • S
CBAINE • ROBERT L. MCKAY • MIKE WINDER • GARY R. HERBERT • MIKE LEE
ODFREY • MARK R. VAN WAGONER • DOUG WRIGHT • SANDRA STALLINGS JEN
OB EVANS • SHAWNI EYRE POTHIER • KRISTINE WARDLE FREDERICKSON • JORD
GLENN RAWSON • TRENT TOONE • BRYAN MILLER • JIMMER FREDETTE • PETER
DOTSON • MARK ALLRED • MATTHEW DEAN BARKDULL • JOSH ROMNEY • C
ARLENE W. HAWKES • LAUREN JOHNSON • STEVEN KAPP PERRY • JULIE BELLO
TERSON • TRISTI PINKSTON • JANETTE RALLISON • PHILIP N. HALE • JOHN BEN
ADDEN • KERRY MUHLESTEIN • GENE A. SESSIONS • DOUGLAS THAYER • HEATH
ALLRED • ROSEMARY M. WIXOM • RICHARD G. HINCKLEY • JANA PETERSON S
ACK • CAMILLE FRONK OLSON • MARCUS H. MARTINS • NEYLAN MCBAINE
ONALD C. PACKARD • HARRY REID • JASON CHAFFETZ • MATTHEW GODFREY
EMENS • MARK EUBANK • MAREN ROSEMARIE SLOVER MAZZEO • BOB EVANS
WENDY HALE MCKAY • MAURINE PROCTOR • TIFFANY GEE LEWIS • GLENN RA
HITTINGHAM • STEVE YOUNG • J. W. "BILL" MARRIOTT JR. • ROBERT P. DOTSON